11th Meeting of the ACL Special Interest Group on Computational Morphology and Phonology 2010

(SIGMORPHON 2010)

Held at ACL 2010

Uppsala, Sweden
15 July 2010

ISBN: 978-1-61738-820-0

Printed from e-media with permission by:

Curran Associates, Inc.
57 Morehouse Lane
Red Hook, NY 12571

Some format issues inherent in the e-media version may also appear in this print version.

Printed by Curran Associates, Inc. (2010)

For permission requests, please contact the Association for Computational Linguistics at the address below.

Association for Computational Linguistics
209 N. Eighth Street
Stroudsburg, Pennsylvania 18360

Phone: 1-570-476-8006
Fax: 1-570-476-0860

acl@aclweb.org

Additional copies of this publication are available from:

Curran Associates, Inc.
57 Morehouse Lane
Red Hook, NY 12571 USA
Phone: 845-758-0400
Fax: 845-758-2634
Email: curran@proceedings.com
Web: www.proceedings.com

Introduction

We are delighted to present the Proceedings of the Eleventh Meeting of the ACL Special Interest Group on Computational Morphology and Phonology (SIGMORPHON), to be held on July 15, 2010 at Uppsala University, Uppsala, Sweden.

The purpose of SIGMORPHON is to foster computational research on the phonological, morphological, and phonetic properties of human language. All three of these sub-areas deal largely with the local structure of words and so share many technical methods. Furthermore, computational work that models empirical data must often draw on at least two of these areas, with explicit consideration of the morphology-phonology or phonology-phonetics interface.

We received a large number of submissions, on the full range of sub-areas, and accepted around forty percent. This has enabled us to provide what we hope you will agree is a high quality program.

We are grateful to the program committee for their careful and thoughtful reviews and discussions of the papers submitted this year. We are especially grateful to those reviewers who stepped in at the last minute when the number of submissions became clear.

We hope that you enjoy the workshop and these proceedings.

Jeffrey Heinz
Lynne Cahill
Richard Wicentowski

Organizers:

Jeffrey Heinz, University of Delaware
Lynne Cahill, University of Brighton
Richard Wicentowski, Swarthmore College

Program Committee Members:

Adam Albright, Massachusetts Institute of Technology
Jason Eisner, Johns Hopkins University
Mark Ellison, University of Western Australia
Sharon Goldwater, University of Edinburgh
Grzegorz Kondrak, University of Alberta
Kimmo Koskenniemi, University of Helsinki
Karen Livescu, Toyota Technological Institute at Chicago/University of Chicago
Mike Maxwell, University of Maryland
Jason Riggle, University of Chicago
Shuly Wintner, University of Haifa

External Reviewers:

Timothy Bunnell, A.I. DuPont Hospital/University of Delaware
Roger Evans, University of Brighton
Dafydd Gibbon, University of Bielefeld
Jon Herring, British Library
William Idsardi, University of Marlyand
Greg Kobele, University of Chicago
Katya Pertsova, University of North Carolina

Table of Contents

Conference Program

Thursday, 15 July 2010

9:00–9:30 *Instance-Based Acquisition of Vowel Harmony*
Fred Mailhot

9:30–10:00 *Verifying Vowel Harmony Typologies*
Sara Finley

10:00–10:30 *Complexity of the Acquisition of Phonotactics in Optimality Theory*
Giorgio Magri

10:30-11:00 Morning Break

11:00–11:30 *Maximum Likelihood Estimation of Feature-Based Distributions*
Jeffrey Heinz and Cesar Koirala

11:30–12:00 *A Method for Compiling Two-Level Rules with Multiple Contexts*
Kimmo Koskenniemi and Miikka Silfverberg

12:00–12:30 *Exploring Dialect Phonetic Variation Using PARAFAC*
Jelena Prokic and Tim Van de Cruys

12:30–14:00 Lunch

14:00–14:30 *Quantitative Evaluation of Competing Syllable Parses*
Jason A. Shaw and Adamantios I. Gafos

14:30–15:00 *Toward a Totally Unsupervised, Language-Independent Method for the Syllabification of Written Texts*
Thomas Mayer

Comparing Canonicalizations of Historical German Text
Bryan Jurish

15:30-16:00 Afternoon Break

16:00–16:30 *Semi-Supervised Learning of Concatenative Morphology*
Oskar Kohonen, Sami Virpioja and Krista Lagus

16:30–17:00 *Morpho Challenge 2005-2010: Evaluations and Results*
Mikko Kurimo, Sami Virpioja, Ville Turunen and Krista Lagus

Instance-based acquisition of vowel harmony

Frédéric Mailhot
Institute of Cognitive Science
Carleton University
Ottawa, ON, Canada
fmailhot@connect.carleton.ca

Abstract

I present LIBPHON, a nonparametric regression-based model of phonological acquisition that induces a generalised and productive pattern of vowel harmony—including opaque and transparent neutrality—on the basis of simplified formant data. The model quickly learns to generate harmonically correct morphologically complex forms to which it has not been exposed.

1 Explaining phonological patterns

How do infants learn the phonetic categories and phonotactic patterns of their native languages? How strong are the biases that learners bring to the task of phonological acquisition? Phonologists from the rationalist tradition that dominated the past half-century of linguistic research typically posit strong biases in acquisition, with language learners using innately-given, domain-specific representations (Chomsky and Halle, 1968), constraints (Prince and Smolensky, 2004) and learning algorithms (Tesar and Smolensky, 2000; Dresher, 1999) to learn abstract rules or constraint rankings from which they can classify or produce novel instances.

In the last decade, however, there has been a shift toward empiricist approaches to phonological acquisition, use and knowledge. In this literature, *eager* learning algorithms (Aha, 1997), in which training data are used to update intensional representations of functions or categories then discarded, have been the norm.[1] However, research in related fields—particularly speech perception—indicates that speakers' knowledge and use of language, both in production and comprehension, is at least partly episodic, or instance-based (Goldinger, 1996; Johnson, 1997). Additionally, motivation for instance-based models of categorisation has a lengthy history in cognitive psychology (Medin and Schaffer, 1978), and these methods are well-known in the statistical and machine learning literature, having been studied for over half a century (Fix and Hodges, 1951; Cover and Hart, 1967; Hastie et al., 2009). Consequently, it seems a worthy endeavour applying an instance-based method to a problem that is of interest to traditional phonologists, the acquisition and use of vowel harmony, while simultaneously effecting a *rapprochement* with adjacent disicplines in the cognitive sciences. In sections 2 and 3 I give some brief background on vowel harmony and instance-based models, respectively. Section 4 introduces my model, LIBPHON, and section 5 the languages it learns. I discuss some simulations and results in section 6, and conclude in section 7.

2 Vowel harmony

Vowel harmony is a phonological phenomenon in which there are co-occurrence constraints on vowels within words.[2] The vowels in a language with vowel harmony can be classified into disjoint sets, such that words contain vowels from only one of the sets. The Finnish system of vowel harmony exemplified by the forms in Table 1 provides a standard example from the literature (van der Hulst and van de Weijer, 1995).

	surface form	*gloss*
a.	tuhmasta	'naughty' (elative)
b.	tühmästä	'stupid' (elative)

Table 1: Finnish backness harmony

Crucially, the elative case marker alternates systematically between front and back vowel

[1] Daelemans et al. (1994) is a notable exception.

[2] "Word" is used pre-theoretically here; harmony can occur over both supra- and sublexical domains.

Proceedings of the 11th Meeting of the ACL-SIGMORPHON, ACL 2010, pages 1–8,
Uppsala, Sweden, 15 July 2010.

variants—as *-stä* or *-sta*—depending on whether the stem has front $\{ü, ä\}$ or back $\{u, a\}$ vowels.

2.1 Neutral vowels

In most languages with vowel harmony, there are one or more vowels that systematically fail to alternate. These are called *neutral vowels*, and are typically further subclassified according to whether or not they induce further harmonic alternations in other vowels.

3 Instance-based models

Instance-based approaches to cognitive processing, also called memory-based, case-based, and exemplar-based models, have their modern origins in psychological theories and models of perceptual categorisation and episodic memory (Medin and Schaffer, 1978; Nosofsky, 1986), although the earliest explicit discussion seems to be (Semon, 1921); a theory of memory that anticipates many features of contemporary models. The core features of these models are: (i) explicit storage/memorisation (*viz.* extensional representation) of training data, (ii) classification/processing of novel data via similarity-based computation, and (iii) *lazy evaluation* (Aha, 1997), whereby all computations are deferred until the model is queried with data.[3]

Instance-based models were introduced to linguistics via research in speech perception suggesting that at least some aspects of linguistic performance rely on remembered experiential episodes (Johnson and Mullenix, 1997). The models implemented to date in phonetics and phonology have largely focused on perception (*e.g.* speaker normalisation in Johnson (1997)), or on diachronic processes (*e.g.* lenition in Pierrehumbert (2001), chain shifts in Ettlinger (2007)), leaving the types of phenomena that typically interest "traditional" phonologists, *viz.* productive, generalised patterns, comparatively neglected.[4]

4 LIBPHON

LIBPHON, the **L**azy **I**nstance-**b**ased **Phon**ologist, is a lazy learning algorithm whose purpose (in the context of the simulations described here) is to model an instance-based approach to the core aspects of the acquisition and subsequent productive usage of vowel harmony.

4.1 Decisions & mechanisms

As discussed in (Johnson, 2007), there are some decisions that need to be made in implementing an instance-based model of phonological knowledge involving the basic units of analysis (*e.g.* their size), the relevant type of these units (*e.g.* discrete or continuous), and the mechanisms for similarity-matching and activation spread in the lexicon.

Units The arguments given by Johnson (2007) and Välimaa-Blum (2009) for the "word-sized" (rather than *e.g.* segmental) experience of language, suggest that "words" are the correct basic unit of analysis in instance-based langugage models (*a fortiori* in LIBPHON). Stronger evidence comes from the wealth of psycholinguistic data (reviewed in (Lodge, 2009)) showing that illiterates and literates of non-alphabetic writing systems have poor phonemic (or at least segmental) awareness, both in monitoring and manipulation. On this basis, I take *meaning-bearing unanalysed acoustic chunks* to be the relevant units of representation for LIBPHON.[5]

Feature type Having determined the size of LIBPHON's basic unit, I move now to its embedding space, where distinctive features present themselves as obvious candidate dimensions. Since the middle of the 20th century (*ca.* Chomsky and Halle (1968)), phonological theories have nearly all supposed that lexical representations are stored in terms of articulatory features (*cf.* (Halle, 1997) for explicit discussion of this viewpoint). Coleman (1998), citing evidence from the neuroscientific and psycholinguistic literatures on lexical representation, claims that evidence for this position (*e.g.* from speech perception and phoneme monitoring experiments) is weak at best, and that lexical representations are more likely to be acoustic than articulatory. In addition, Phillips et al. (2000) review neurolinguistic evidence for the role of acoustic cortex in phonetics and phonology, and

[3]Compare *eager* learners, *e.g.* connectionist systems, which build a global intensional representation of the function being learned on the basis of training data which are subsequently discarded.

[4]Kirchner and Moore (2009) give a model of a synchronic lenition process, and Daelemans and colleagues give memory-based analyses of several linguistic phenomena (Daelemans and van den Bosch, 2005).

[5]The assumption that word-level segmentation of the speech signal is available to the language learner prior to acquisition of phonological phenomena is relatively uncontroversial, although there is evidence for the development of at least some phonotactic knowledge prior to the emergence of a productive lexicon (Jusczyk, 1999).

Mielke (2008) discusses several aspects of the induction of distinctive phonological features from acoustic representations. Recognising that the issue is far from resolved, for the purposes of the simulations run here, I take LIBPHON's instance space to be acoustically-based, and use formant values as the embedding dimension. Vowels are specified by their midpoint formant values,[6] and consonants are specified by so-called "locus" values, which can be identified by inspecting the trajectories of consonant-vowel transitions in speech (Sussman et al., 1998). Since I am modelling palatal harmony in particular, and $F2$ magnitude is the primary acoustic correlate of vowel palatality, I omit $F3$ and $F4$, restricting LIBPHON's acoustic representations to sequences of $(F1, F2)$ values, henceforth *trajectories*.

Similarity Given that LIBPHON's instance-space is continuous, and has a fairly intuitive metric, I take simple Euclidean distance to be LIBPHON's similarity (or rather, dissimilarity) function.[7]

Fixed-rate representations For the simulations described here, I use fixed-rate trajectories, in which consonants and vowels are represented in a temporally coarse-grained manner with single $(F1; F2)$ tuples. Evidently, consonants and vowels in actual human speech unfold in time, but modelling segments at this level introduces the problem of temporal variability; repeated tokens of a given word—both within and across speakers—vary widely in duration. This variability is one of the main obstacles in the development of instance-based models of speech production, due to the difficulty of aligning variable-length forms. Although algorithms exist for aligning variable-length sequences, these require cognitively implausible dynamic programming algorithms, *e.g.* dynamic time warping (DTW) and hidden Markov models (Rabiner and Juang, 1993). Even as proofs of concept, these may be empirically inadequate; Kirchner and Moore (2009) use DTW to good effect in an instance-based production model of spirantisation using real, temporally variable, speech signals. However, their inputs were all the same length in terms of segmental content, and the model was only required to generalise within a word type. I am currently investigating whether DTW can function as a proof of concept in a problem domain like that addressed here, which involves learning about variably-sized "pieces" of morphology across class labels.

4.2 Perception/categorisation

LIBPHON's method of perception/categorisation of inputs is a relatively standard nearest-neighbour-based classification algorithm. See Algorithm 1 for a description in pseudocode.

Algorithm 1 PERCEIVE(*input*, k)

Require: *input* as (LABEL $\in$ [LEX](PL)[NOM | ACC], `instance` $\in \mathbb{Z}_{2x\{8,10,12\}}$), $k \in \mathbb{Z}$

```
if LABEL is not empty then
    if LABEL ∉ lexicon then
        Create LABEL in lexicon
    end if
    Associate(instance, LABEL)
else
    neighbours ← k-nearest neighbours of instance
    LABEL ← majority class label of neighbours
    Associate(instance,LABEL)
end if
```

If LABEL is not empty, LIBPHON checks its lexicon to see whether it knows the word being presented to it, *i.e.* whether it exists as a class label. If so, it simply appends the input acoustic form to the set of forms associated with the input meaning/label. If it has no corresponding entry, a new lexical entry is created for the input meaning, and the input trajectory is added as its sole associated acoustic form.

If LABEL is empty, LIBPHON assigns `instance` to the majority class of its k nearest neighbours in acoustic space.

[6] A reviewer asks about the psychological plausibility of Hz-based formant represetations and the choice of point values for vowel and consonant representations, *e.g.* rather than formant values at 20% and 80% of the vowel. These are purely in the interests of simplicity for the work reported here. As discussed below, future work with real speech exemplars in psychophysically-motivated representational formats, *e.g.* perceptual linear predictive coding (Hermansky, 1990), will render this issue moot.

[7] Often the measure of similarity in an instance-based model is an exponential function of distance, $d(x_i, x_j)$ of the form $exp(-cd(x_i, x_j))$, so that increasing distance yields decreasing similarity (Nosofsky, 1986). The Euclidean measure here is sufficient for the purpose at hand, although the shape of the similarity measure is ultimately an empirical question.

4.3 Production

In production, LIBPHON is provided with a LABEL and has to generate a suitable `instance` for it. LABELs are decomposable, signalling an arbitrary "lexical" meaning, an optional plural morpheme, PL, and an obligatory case marker from {NOM, ACC}. Thus, there are several different possibilities to consider in generating output for some queried meaning.

In the two simplest cases, either the full queried meaning (*viz.* lexical label with all inflections) is already in the lexicon, or else there are no class LABELs with the same lexical meaning (*i.e.* LIBPHON is being asked to produce a word that it doesn't know). In the former case, a stored trajectory is uniform[8] randomly selected from the list of acoustic forms associated with the queried label as a seed token, the entire set of associated acoustic forms is used as the analogical set, and an output is generated by taking a distance-weighted mean over the seed's k nearest neighbours.[9] In the case where the lexical meaning of the queried LABEL is unknown, the query is ignored.

In the more interesting cases, LIBPHON has a LABEL in its lexicon with the same lexical meaning, but with differing inflectional specification. Consider the case in which LIBPHON knows only the singular NOM form of a query label that is specified as PL ACC. A seed `instance` is (uniform) randomly selected from the set of trajectories associated to the NOM entry in the agent's lexicon, as this is the only entry with the corresponding lexical meaning, and it is a variant of this meaning that LIBPHON must produce. In this case the analogical set, the set of instances from which the final output is computed, is composed of the seed's nearest neighbours in the set of all trajectories associated with LABELs of the form [LEX PL ACC]. Once again, the output produced is a distance-weighted mean of the analogical set.

This general procedure (*viz.* seed from a known item with same lexical meaning, analogical set from all items with desired inflection) is carried out in parallel cases with all other possible LABEL mismatches, *e.g.* a singular LABEL queried, but only a plural LABEL in the lexicon, a NOM query with only an ACC form in the lexicon, *etc.* In the cases where the lexicon contains multiple entries with the same lexical meaning, but not the query, the seed is selected from the LABEL with the closest "semantic" match. Algorithm 2 gives pseudocode for LIBPHON's production algorithm.

[8] Exemplar models often bias the selection of seed tokens with degrees of "activation" that take into account recency and frequency. Although the results discussed below show that this is not necessary for ultimate attainment, it is likely that this kind of bias will need to be incorporated into LIBPHON to accurately model more nuanced aspects of the acquisition path.

[9] $k = 5$ for all results reported here.

Algorithm 2 PRODUCE(LABEL, k)

Require: LABEL $\in$ [LEX](PL)[NOM | ACC], $k \in \mathbb{Z}$

```
if LABEL ∈ lexicon then
    seed ← uniform random selection from instances associated to LABEL
    cloud ← all instances associated to LABEL
else if ∃ LABEL′ ∈ lexicon s.t. lex(LABEL′) = lex(LABEL) then
    seed ← uniform random selection from instances associated to LABEL′)
    cloud ← all instances associated to plural(LABEL) ∪ case(LABEL)
else
    pass
end if
neighbours ← k-nearest neighbours of seed in cloud
return distance-weighted mean of neighbours
```

4.4 Production as regression

The final steps in LIBPHON's production algorithm, finding the analogical set and computing the output as a weighted average, together constitute a technique known in the statistical learning literature as *kernel-smoothed nearest-neighbour regression*, and in particular are closely related to the well-known Nadaraya-Watson estimator (Hastie et al., 2009):

$$\hat{f}(x) = \frac{\sum_{i=1}^{N} K_\lambda(x, x_i) y_i}{\sum_{i=1}^{N} K_\lambda(x, x_i)}$$

with inverse-distance as the kernel smoother, K, and the bandwidth function, $h_\lambda(x)$ determined by the number k of nearest neighbours. This link to the statistical learning literature puts LIBPHON on sound theoretical footing and opens the door to a variety of future research paths, *e.g.* experimenting with different kernel shapes, or formal analysis of LIBPHON's expected error bounds.

5 The languages

On the view taken here, phonological knowledge is taken to emerge from generalisation over lexical items, and so the key to acquiring some phonological pattern lies in learning a lexicon (Jusczyk, 2000). Consequently, the languages learned in LIBPHON abstract away from sentence-level phenomena, and the training data are simply labelled formant trajectories, (LABEL, `instance`).

In order to get at the essence of the problem (*viz.* the acquisition of vowel harmony as characterised by morphophonological alternations), and in the interests of computational tractability/efficiency, the artificial languages learned by LIBPHON are highly simplified, displaying only enough structure to capture the phenomena of interest.

5.1 Phonological inventory

The phonological inventory consists of three consonants, {b, d, g}, and four vowels—two with high $F2$ and two with low $F2$—which I label {i, e, u, o}, for convenience.[10] The formant values used were generated from formant synthesis equations in (de Boer, 2000), and from the locus equations for CV-transitions in (Sussman et al., 1998).

5.2 Lexical items

LIBPHON's lexicon is populated with `instance` trajectories consisting of four-syllable[11] "roots" with zero, one or two one-syllable "affixes". These trajectories have associated class labels, which from a formal point of view are contentless indices. Rather than employing *e.g.* natural numbers as labels, I use character strings which correspond more or less to the English pronounciations of their associated trajectories. LABELs function, metaphorically-speaking, as "meanings". These are compositional, comprising a "lexical meaning" (arbitrary CVCVCVCV string from the phoneme set listed above), one of two obligatorily present "case markers" (NOM|ACC), and an optionally present "plural marker" (PL). Hence, word categories in the artificial languages come in four forms, NOM-SG, NOM-PL, ACC-SG, and ACC-PL.

[10]Because LIBPHON's representations lack $F3$, the primary acoustic correlate of rounding, the back vowels would be more standardly represented as /ɤ, ɯ/, but these are comparatively uncommon IPA symbols, so we will use the symbols for the rounded variants. Nothing in the results or discussion hinges on this.

[11]All syllables are CV-shaped.

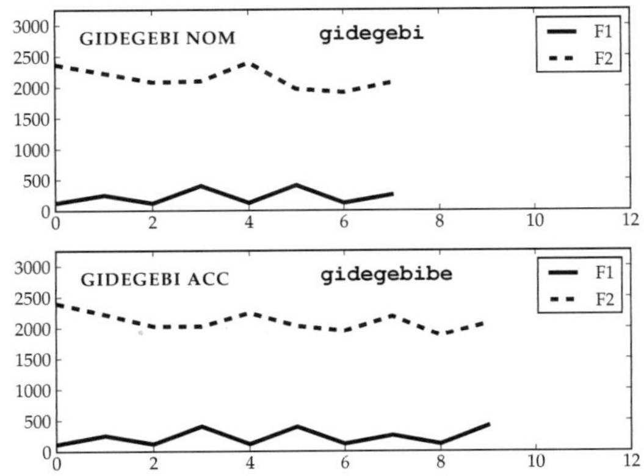

Figure 1: Graphical representation of singular forms of GIDEGEBI, as produced by teacher agent

Figure 1 gives examples of the singular NOM and ACC forms of a high-$F2$ word. The NOM-labelled trajectory has no suffixal morphology, and corresponds to a bare form. The trajectory is eight segments long,[12] and the vowels in this case have all high $F2$ (as in lexical front/back vowel harmony).[13] Note also that ACC is realised with high $F2$, in agreement with the root vowels.

5.3 Neutral vowels

The harmony processes seen thus far are in some sense "local", being describable in terms of vowel adjacency *e.g.* adjacency on a hypothesised autosegmental tier (although the presence of intervening consonants still renders the harmony process "nonlocal" in some more concrete articulatory sense). One of the hallmarks of vowel harmony, as discussed in subsection 2.1, is the phenomenon of *neutral vowels*. These vowels fail to alternate, and may or may not induce harmonic alternations in vowels that precede or follow them. To introduce a neutral vowel, I added a category label, PL, whose realisation corresponds roughly to [gu], and which is treated as being either opaque or transparent in the simulations described below.

Figures 2 and 3 show the "plural inflected" forms of the same root as in 1. We see that the

[12]The even-numbered indices on the x-axis correspond to consonants and the odd-numbered indices, the "pinches" in the graphs, correspond to vowels.

[13]The languages LIBPHON learns have only harmonic singular forms. This is unrealistic, as speakers of vowel harmony languages typically have some exceptional disharmonic forms in their lexicons. The effect of these forms on LIBPHON's performance is currently being investigated.

realisation of PL has fixed, low $F2$, and that the realisation of ACC has alternating $F2$, which realisations corresponding roughly to [be] (high $F2$) and [bo] (low $F2$).

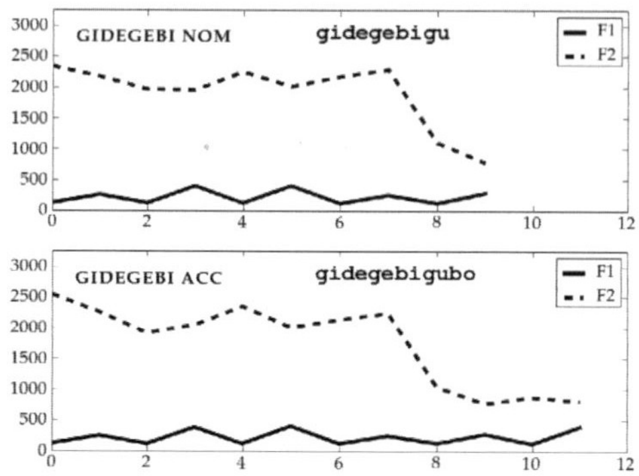

Figure 2: Graphical representation of plural forms of GIDEGEBI, as produced by teacher agent, with opaque PL realisation.

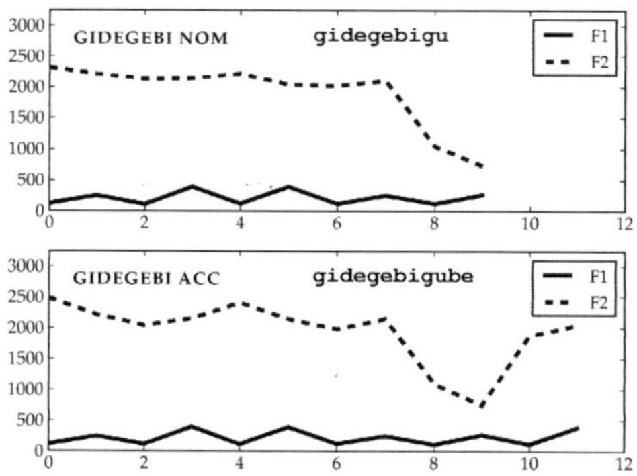

Figure 3: Graphical representation of plural forms of GIDEGEBI, as produced by teacher agent, with transparent PL realisation.

These figures also illustrate the difference between languages with opaque versus transparent PL, as reflected in the realisation of the word-final ACC marker in the two lower graphs, which agrees in $F2$ with the realised form of the PL or root, respectively.

6 The experiments

Assessing successful learning/generalisation in a computational model requires some measurable outcome that can be tracked over time. Because LIBPHON is an output-oriented model, its categorisation of inputs is a poor indicator of the extent to which it has learned a productive "rule" of vowel harmony. In lieu of this measure, I have opted to pursue two difference courses of evaluation.

For the harmony cases, LIBPHON is queried on a held-out test set of 500 previously unseen LABELs and its output is compared to the mean value of the teacher's stored trajectories for the same LABELs. In particular, given some LABEL which was not in the training data, we can query LIBPHON at various stages of acquisition (*viz.* with lexicons of increasing size) by having it produce an output for that LABEL, and track the change in its performance over time.

The actual measure of error taken is the root-mean-squared deviation between the learner's output, y and the mean, t, of the teacher's stored forms for some label, l, over all of the consonants and vowels within a word, averaged across the remaining unseen items of the test set:

$$RMSE = \frac{1}{N} \sum_{l \in lex} \sqrt{\frac{\sum_i (t_i - y_i)^2}{len(t)}}$$

Figures 4 and 5 show RMSE *vs.* lexicon size for both opaque and transparent neutrality (*cf.* the cases in Figures 2 and 3), for five simulation runs each. We can see clearly that error drops as the lexicon grows, hence that LIBPHON is learning to make its outputs more like those of the teacher, but the informativity of this measure stops there. From a linguistic point of view, we are interested in what LIBPHON's outputs look like, *viz.* has it learned vowel harmony?

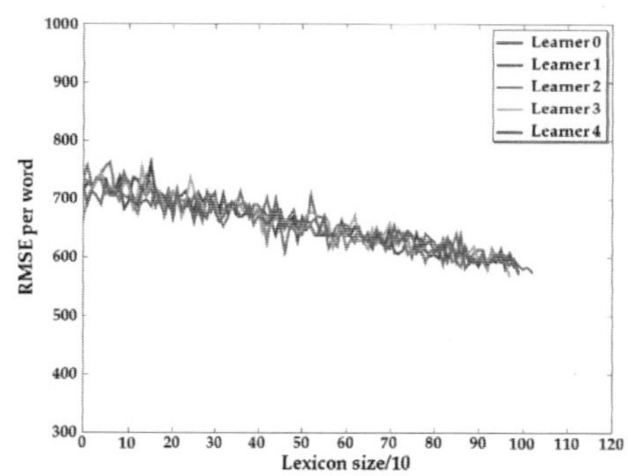

Figure 4: RMSE 1000-word lexicon. Opaque neutrality.

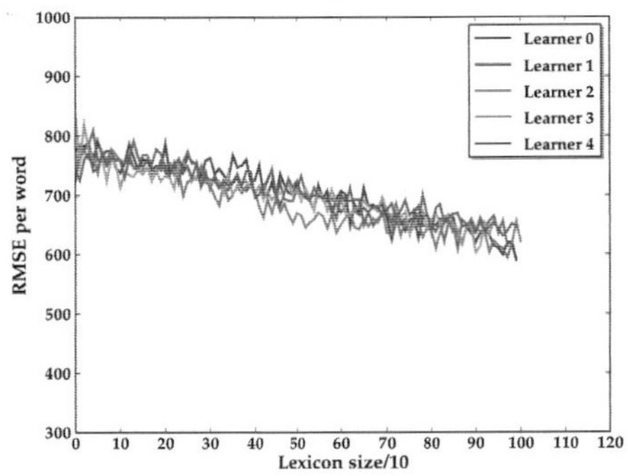

Figure 5: RMSE 1000-word lexicon. Transparent neutrality.

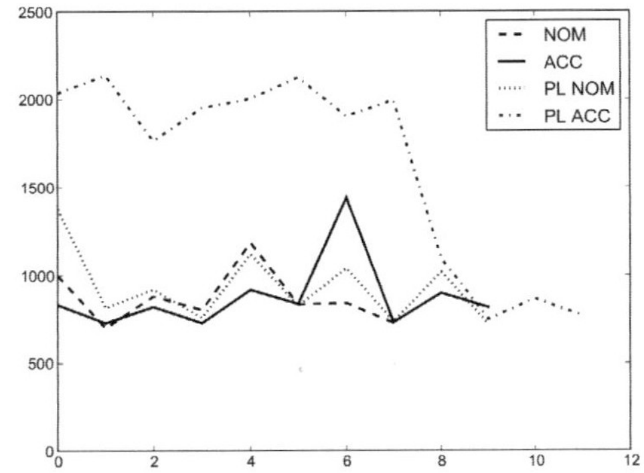

Figure 6: Evolution of `gubogobu` in early acquisition: 10 words

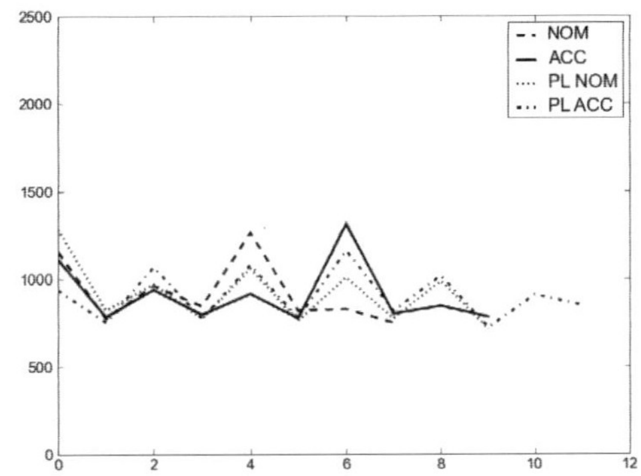

Figure 7: Evolution of `gubogobu` in early acquisition: 30 words

Figures 6 and 7 show that vowel harmony *is* learned, and moreover quite quickly, after going through a brief initial phase of spurious outputs. In these figures, LIBPHON is being asked to produce outputs for all forms of the label GUBOGOBU. For the particular run shown here, at the 10-word stage (*i.e.* when LIBPHON had seen tokens from 10 labels), the only tokens marked PL-ACC were from high $F2$ ("front") trajectories. Hence the nearest neighbour calculation in the production algorithm resulted in a fronted form being output. Although acquisition research in vowel harmony languages is relatively rare, or inaccessible to us due to language barriers, what research there is seems to indicate that harmony is mastered very quickly, with virtually no errors by 2 years of age, hence it is unclear what status to assign to output patterns like the one discussed here. Moreover, given the well-known facts that (i) comprehension precedes production, and (ii) infants avoid saying unfamiliar words, it is unlikely that an infant could be coaxed into producing an output form for such an early-stage class.

7 Discussion and future work

The experiments discussed here show that on the basis of limited input data, LIBPHON, an instance-based learner that produces output via kernel-smoothed nearest-neighbour regression, learns to produce harmonically correct novel outputs. In particular, it is able to generalise and produce correct morphologically complex forms to which it has not been exposed in its training data, *i.e.* a previously unseen case-marked form will be output with harmonically correct $F2$, including neutrality (opaque or transparent). In ongoing research I am (i) evaluating LIBPHON's performance with respect to more traditional measures, in particular F-score, on held-out data as the lexicon grows, and (ii) assessing the viability of DTW-based alignment for preprocessing real speech tokens as inputs to LIBPHON.

Acknowledgments

Many thanks to Ash Asudeh, Lev Blumenfeld, Andrea Gormley, Jeff Mielke, Alan Hogue and Andy Wedel for discussion and comments on this line of research, and to three anonymous referees for feedback that greatly improved this paper. This work carried out with the support of NSERC Discovery Grant 371969 to Dr. Ash Asudeh.

References

David Aha. 1997. Lazy learning. In *Lazy Learning*, pages 7–10. Kluwer Academic Publishers.

Noam Chomsky and Morris Halle. 1968. *The Sound Pattern of English.* Harper and Row.

John Coleman. 1998. Cognitive reality and the phonological lexicon: A review. *Journal of Neurolinguistics*, 11(3):295—-320.

Thomas Cover and Peter Hart. 1967. Nearest neighbor pattern classification. *IEEE Transactions on Information Theory*, 13:21–27.

Walter Daelemans and Antal van den Bosch. 2005. *Memory-Based Language Processing*. Studies in Natural Language Processing. Cambridge University Press.

Walter Daelemans, Steven Gillis, and Gert Durieux. 1994. The acquisition of stress: A data-oriented approach. *Computational Linguistics*, 20(3).

Bart de Boer. 2000. Self-organization in vowel systems. *Journal of Phonetics*, 28:441–465.

B. Elan Dresher. 1999. Charing the learning path: Cues to parameter setting. *Linguistic Inquiry*, 30(1):27–67.

Marc Ettlinger. 2007. An exemplar-based model of chain shifts. In *Proceedings of the 16th International Congress of the Phonetic Science*, pages 685–688.

Evelyn Fix and J.L. Hodges. 1951. Discriminatory analysis, nonparametric discrimination: Consistency properties. Technical Report 4, USAF School of Aviation Medicine.

Stephen Goldinger. 1996. Words and voices: Episodic traces in spoken word identification and recognition memory. *Journal of Experimental Psychology: Learning, Memory, and Cognition*, 22:1166–1183.

Morris Halle. 1997. Some consequences of the representation of words in memory. *Lingua*, 100:91–100.

Trevor Hastie, Robert Tibshirani, and Jerome Friedman. 2009. *Elements of Statistical Learning*. Springer Series in Statistics. Springer-Verlag, 2 edition.

Hynek Hermansky. 1990. Perceptual linear predictive (plp) analysis of speech. *Journal of the Acoustical Society of America*, 87(4):1738–1752.

Keith Johnson and John W. Mullenix, editors. 1997. *Talker Variability in Speech Processing*. Academic Press.

Keith Johnson. 1997. Speech perception without speaker normalization: an exemplar model. In *Talker Variability in Speech Processing*, chapter 8, pages 145–166. Academic Press.

Keith Johnson, 2007. *Decision and Mechanisms in Exemplar-based Phonology*, chapter 3, pages 25–40. Oxford University Press.

Peter Jusczyk. 1999. How infants begin to extract words from speech. *Trends in Cognitive Sciences*, 3(9):323–328.

Peter Jusczyk. 2000. *The Discovery of Spoken Language*. MIT Press.

Robert Kirchner and Roger Moore. 2009. Computing phonological generalization over real speech exemplars. ms.

Ken Lodge. 2009. *Fundamental Concepts in Phonology: Sameness and difference*. Edinburgh University Press.

Douglas Medin and Marguerite Schaffer. 1978. Context theory of classification learning. *Psychological Review*, 85(3):207–238.

Jeff Mielke. 2008. *The Emergence of Distinctive Features*. Oxford Studies in Typology and Linguistic Theory. Oxford University Press.

Robert Nosofsky. 1986. Attention, similarity, and the identification-categorization relationship. *Journal of Experimental Psychology: General*, 115(1):39–57.

Colin Phillips, Thomas Pellathy, Alec Marantz, Elron Yellin, Kenneth Wexler, David Poeppel, Martha McGinnis, and Timothy Roberts. 2000. Auditory cortex accesses phonological categories: An meg mismatch study. *Journal of Cognitive Neuroscience*, 12(6):1038–1055.

Janet Pierrehumbert. 2001. Exemplar dynamics: Word frequency, lenition, and contrast. In *Frequency effects and the emergence of linguistic structure*, pages 137–157. John Benjamins.

Alan Prince and Paul Smolensky. 2004. *Optimality Theory: Constraint interaction in generative grammar*. Blackwell.

Lawrence Rabiner and Biing-Hwang Juang. 1993. *Fundamentals of Speech Recognition*. Prentice Hall.

Richard Semon. 1921. *The Mneme*. George Allen and Unwin.

Harvey Sussman, David Fruchter, Jon Hilbert, and Joseph Sirosh. 1998. Linear correlates in the speech signal: The orderly output constraint. *Behavioral and Brain Sciences*, 21:241–299.

Bruce Tesar and Paul Smolensky. 2000. *Learnability in Optimality Theory*. MIT Press.

Riitta Välimaa-Blum. 2009. The phoneme in cognitive phonology: episodic memories of both meaningful and meaningless units? *Cognitextes*, 2.

Harry van der Hulst and Jeroen van de Weijer. 1995. Vowel harmony. In John Goldsmith, editor, *Handbook of Phonological Theory*. Blackwell.

Verifying Vowel Harmony Typologies

Sara Finley
University of Rochester
Rochester, NY, USA
sfinley@bcs.rochester.edu

Abstract

This paper applies finite state technologies to verify the typological validity of Turbid Spreading, a theory of vowel harmony in Optimality Theory (OT) (Prince & Smolensky, 1993/2004). Previous analyses of vowel harmony in OT have been prone to typological inconsistencies, predicting grammars that do not occur in natural language (Wilson, 2003). However, attempts to eliminate typological pathologies relying on hand-made inputs and candidate sets have been shown to be highly prone to error (Wilson, 2005). Using a modified version of the Contenders Algorithm (Riggle, 2004b), we verify that Turbid Spreading makes typologically valid predictions about the types of harmony processes that may appear in natural language. This modification of the Contenders Algorithm to include complex spreading interactions and intermediate representations demonstrates the utility of computational methods for verifying the typological predictions of complex phonological theories.

1 Introduction

The goal of Optimality Theory (OT) (Prince & Smolensky, 1993/2004) is to understand and explain the mechanisms responsible for linguistic processes. Because it is possible to use constraint rankings to generate a set of possible grammars, OT is fundamentally a theory of cross-linguistic typology.

One of the theoretical assumptions of OT is that it is the job of the grammar to determine which languages are possible and which are not. While the full typology of identifiable languages can never be verified, it is generally agreed that there is a difference between unattested languages that are accidental gaps and unattested languages that are pathological. While both are unattested, accidental gaps are theoretically possible, and might be found given enough time. Pathological languages are languages that are logically possible, but violate general principles of language, and no natural language is expected to contain such pathologies.

Thus, OT assumes that a valid grammar is typologically sound if it does not generate pathologically unattested languages. However, it is extremely difficult to assess the typological validity of phonological analyses because the output of a typological prediction is dependent upon the set of constraints, the output candidates considered, and the underlying forms (inputs) of interest. The theorist must therefore be able to consider all possible inputs, to select an inclusive set of candidates, and to be sure to include the relevant constraints. If any one of these factors is not carefully constructed, the theorist may miss an important typological prediction made by the OT grammar.

These challenges can be significantly diminished through computational tools, such as finite-state techniques. With such tools, it is possible to understand typological predictions that would have likely gone unnoticed without a computational model. This paper presents the results of computational models used to revise and formulate a phonological theory. In this paper, we make use of finite-state methods (specifically Riggle's (2004b) Contenders Algorithm) to understand and verify the typological predictions of a particular theory of vowel harmony, Turbid Spreading (Finley, 2008, in press). Without the computational tools presented in this paper, many unwanted predictions would have been made.

Vowel harmony is a phonological process whereby a particular phonological feature is shared by all vowels in a given lexical domain. For example, in Turkish vowel harmony, if the first vowel of the word is [+Back], all following vowels are [+Back], creating a spreading process whereby [+Back] is spread from the left edge of the word to the right.

Proceedings of the 11th Meeting of the ACL-SIGMORPHON, ACL 2010, pages 9–18,
Uppsala, Sweden, 15 July 2010. ©2010 Association for Computational Linguistics

In simple[1] cases of harmony, all possible vo w-els undergo spreading. However, harmony fails when a vowel is unable to take on the spreading feature (e.g., if the language does not allow [–High] vowels to be [+Back]). In these cases the non-participating vowel can either block harmony and create a new spreading domain (as an opaque vowel; [+ – –]) or allow the spreading domain to skip the nonparticipating vowel (as a transparent vowel; [+ – +]).

There are two reasons that vowel harmony in OT is an ideal candidate for the present case study of the use of finite-state techniques to verify linguistic typologies. First, vowel harmony is cross-linguistically widespread, with a clear typology of patterns that are both frequent as well as those that are unattested. Further, the ways in which vowel harmony interacts with other processes (e.g., epenthesis and deletion) are well understood, such that it is possible to differentiate between accidental gaps and pathological unattested languages. For example, direction of spreading in vowel harmony is determined by the featural, morphological or (left or right) edge status of the potential harmony source trigger vowel. There are no languages that determine the direction of spreading by fewest changes from the input to output (referred to as 'majority rules') (Finley & Badecker, 2008). However, this pattern is easy to produce using Agree constraints which merely require adjacent vowels to agree, and do not specify direction. It is these kinds of unattested interactions that an ideal model of vowel harmony in OT should avoid. This ideal model must also be able to account for the major harmony patterns (transparency, opacity, etc.).

Establishing a theory of vowel harmony in OT with both of these properties has been particularly problematic. In addition to 'majority rules' patterns, interactions between non-participating vowels and directionality of spreading have posed a particular challenge. For example, traditional constraints used for vowel harmony (e.g., Align and Agree) predict harmony interactions that do not exist, such as failure to spread to regularly undergoing vowels in the presence of a non-participating vowel, or deletion of a non-participating vowel in order to preserve agreement of vowel features (Wilson, 2003). These harmony pathologies pose a great challenge for vowel harmony and OT in general. Turbid Spreading is a representational approach to vowel harmony in OT that has been designed with this challenge in mind.

The second reason that vowel harmony is an ideal method for studying the interaction of theoretical and computational methods is that vowel harmony requires rich representations. These rich representations pose a unique opportunity to integrate theoretical and computational methodologies. Specifically, we capture these rich representations through the Contenders Algorithm (Riggle, 2004b).

Further, vowel harmony is an important area of research in computational phonology (Bird & Ellison, 1994; Ellison, 1992; Goldsmith & Xanthos, 2009) because the representation of agreement between vowels across consonants poses unique challenges to the learner. This paper differs from previous computational models of vowel harmony because the present work is an instantiation of a generative OT model. The present work focuses on framing work done in theoretical linguistics in a computational framework.

The paper begins with a brief overview of the Contenders Algorithm (Section 2). This is followed by a description of Turbid Spreading and its formalization in finite-state representations (Section 3). Section 4 presents the results of the typological analysis.

2 The Contenders Algorithm

Riggle's (2004a, 2004b) algorithm uses finite-state techniques to find the set of candidates for a given input that are possible optimal outputs under any possible ranking. In order to compute constraint violations, both GEN and the constraints in CON are represented in terms of a finite state transducer. The use of finite representations of infinite sets of strings has important consequences for Optimality Theory. As long as GEN can be represented in terms of finite-state transducers, it is possible to represent the infinite candidate set in terms of a single computation. When all constraints are combined and a single input is evaluated, there will only be a finite set of contenders[2].

The Contenders Algorithm creates a single finite state transducer via the intersection of finite-state transducers for GEN and CON. This combined transducer is an unranked grammar. Be-

[1] Like most phonological processes, vowel harmony is subject to exceptions (Finley, 2010). Future work will incorporate exceptions into computational methods.

[2] See Riggle (2004b) for proof that the list of contenders will always be a finite set.

cause the goal of the algorithm is to produce a list of candidates that could 'win' under some ranking, the algorithm must entertain all possible rankings.

Violations of constraints are instantiated through costs for specific paths in the transducer (e.g., a path that changes a [+F] vowel to a [–F] vowel may have a cost of 1, incurring a single violation). The combined transducer makes it possible to find the constraint profile for any input-output mappings created by GEN. This is the cost of traversing the transducer from start to finish for a given input-output pair. The Contenders Algorithm compares violation profiles for given constraints and candidates, making it possible to predict which violation profiles (candidates) are able to win under some ranking (i.e., which candidates are contenders).

The Contenders Algorithm uses Ellison's (1994) model of finite-state transducers in OT to find the least costly paths through the finite-state grammar. Because each arc of the transducer corresponds to a segment in the string (along with the input-output mapping for that segment), the costs associated with that segment (i.e. constraint violations) are found in each arc. These costs are stored as n-tuples that can be used to compare the costs associated with different candidates.

Riggle's model is based on Dijktra's (1959) shortest path algorithm. Every time a candidate violates a constraint, it increases the 'distance' through the transducer. According to Dijkstra's model, the shortest path through a transducer is also the shortest path through each intermediate step (as each intermediate step serves as a subset of the shortest path). This means that candidates that incur many violations will have the most costly paths. By comparing each candidate's cost for each constraint, it is possible to find which candidates are harmonically bound (i.e. cannot win under any ranking) and which are not (the contenders).

The Contenders Algorithm selects each node of the intersected finite-state transducer and records the cost of each arc outside that node. The cost of visiting that particular node is recorded if that cost is less than or equal to previously recorded costs. After all nodes have been evaluated, a list of the costs associated with each node is produced. The Contenders Algorithm then generates a list of all candidates whose costs do not exceed that of the least-cost list; these are the contenders for a given input.

The output of the Contenders Algorithm for a large set of inputs can be used to create a typological analysis (Bane & Riggle, in press). This typological analysis provides information about the relationship between the different contenders and the rankings that produce them. The typology is formed by inputing the list of contenders for a range of inputs into an algorithm that computes Elementary Ranking Conditions (ERCs) (Prince, 2002). ERCs produce a set of possible ranking interactions from a set of candidates and their violation profiles.

The present paper modifies Riggle's (2004b) model in several ways. First, Riggle's model is relatively simple in terms of the types of segments used. Riggle is able to model epenthesis and deletion of segments listed as /a/ and /b/. In the present model, we include binary vowel features ([±F]) that are active in vowel harmony (in addition to consonants). Second, the number and complexity of constraints are increased. The present model allows for deletion and insertion, as well as feature agreement and featural markedness. Third, the present model adds an intermediate level of representation between the input and the output, thereby increasing the level of complexity in both the constraints and the evaluation. This demonstrates that Riggle's model is capable of handling rich representations, complex phonological processes and multiple assumptions about the architecture of representations in phonology. Thus, the Contenders Algorithm is important for a wide range of problems in phonological theory, and has the ability to bring computational approaches to problems that affect researchers in phonology beyond the computational linguist.

3 Turbid Spreading

Turbid Spreading is a representational approach to vowel harmony based loosely on Turbidity Theory (Goldrick, 2001), a model for opaque representations in phonology. This model uses hidden representations as a method for accounting for incremental phonological processes in a parallel fashion. Turbid Spreading extends this idea of hidden representations. In Turbid Spreading, featural representations for segments have three levels: the underlying representation (UR), the projection level (PR), and the surface level (SR). Relations between the underlying form and the surface form are achieved at the projection level. All segments have a feature value at the projection level. Because we are concerned with spreading between vowels, we focus solely on the representations for vowels. In the present implementation, there is a single harmonic feature of interest (±F) and a secondary unary feature (B) that is penalized when a segment that possess both B and +F feature values (and can therefore block harmony, such as a [+High] vowel that cannot be [+Back]). All ± notations refer to the feature F. Thus, +B is a [+F, B] vowel and –B is a [–F, B] vowel.

All projection level representations are marked ±U, ±R, ±L, and ±P. The ± refers to the feature value for F (+F/–F), and the letter (U, L, etc.) refers to the source of the projection, described below.

The source of the projected feature value can be the underlying form (a faithful representation, marked as ±U, in which +U refers to a +F vowel projected by its underlying form, and –U refers to a –F vowel projected by its underlying form), a neighboring vowel (via spreading, marked as ±L/±R, in which +L refers to a +F vowel projected by the vowel to its left) or the phonetic representation, via the surface level (marked as ±P, in which +P refers to a +F vowel projected by its surface form). Each vowel has one and only one source for its projection value.

In Turbid Spreading, vowel harmony is achieved when the feature value at the projection level of the triggering vowel spreads to an adjacent vowel. In the example of spreading given in Figure 1, the pictoral representation of spreading is given on the left, with the notational features given on the right. The first vowel spreads [+F] to the second vowel, causing the second vowel to be represented as +L at the projection level (because it receives a [+F] feature from the vowel to the left). The underlying form and the surface form do not change as a result of spreading.

[+F]	[–F]	UR: +F –F
↓		
[+F] →	[+F]	PR: +U +L
[+F]	[+F]	SR: +F +F

Figure 1: Spreading

An important restriction on spreading is that the features at both sides of the 'arrows' must match (e.g., [–F] → [+F] is prohibited[3]). In other words, vowels may only spread the feature value at the projection level. However, this does not preclude feature values from changing at different levels (e.g., from [+F] in the UR to [–F] in the PR). Allowing changes to feature values at different levels captures both direct spreading processes, as well as opaque interactions between spreading and the surface form. For example, a transparent vowel is created when [+F] spreads to a non-participating vowel (giving +L/+R at the PR) but the non-participating vowel pronounces [–F] at the SR. In this case, the feature values at the projection and pronunciation levels will not match. Transparent vowels therefore satisfy spreading constraints, but violate the constraints requiring the feature values of the surface form and the projection level to match.

For the purpose of formalizing Turbid Spreading into regular expressions for the Contenders Algorithm, we treat each level of representation (UR, PR and SR) as an element of a triple. There are four feature values that appear in the UR and the SR: /+F, –F, +B, –B/. The feature B (potential harmony blocker) is a placeholder for a feature that may or may not spread that harmonic feature. This allows us to place restrictions on which vowels can undergo spreading (e.g., a restriction that non-high vowels cannot undergo back harmony). This secondary feature is important for evaluating the typology of interactions between participating and non-participating vowels.

The projection level (PR) representation contains both featural information as well as the source of spreading. The feature values for F are shortened to be simply +/–. For example, a +F vowel projected by U is written as +U rather than +FU. Thus, ±U implies a faithful ±F feature representation of the underlying form (e.g., –U implies a faithful representation of the –F feature value in the underlying form). ±P implies that the phonetics has caused a change in the representation. ±R implies leftward spreading (the vowel to right spread to the current vowel). ±L implies rightward spreading (the vowel to the left spread to the current vowel). The representation for each string of vowels is written as [UR: PR: SR]. The pictorial representation in Figure 1 is therefore [+F –F: +U +L: +F +F].

We implemented Turbid Spreading in the Contenders Algorithm by using finite state implementations of GEN and of the constraints known to interact with spreading[4]. Each arc of the transducer represents a single segment, pre-

[3] The present model does not account for dissimilation, but we assume that will be accounted for by some other mechanism, and is subject to future work.

[4] Text versions of the FSA's can be found at: http://www.cog.jhu.edu/grad-students/finley/fsa.pdf

sented as a tuple. A '.' notation indicated that the position in the tuple could be filled by any feature value. Non-crucial arcs were removed from the diagrams of finite-state transducers (but were included in the formal analysis). These include the potential for vowel epenthesis (notated as [-]) and vowel deletion (notated as an [x]). Note that the symbols 'x' and '-' are used solely for 'bookkeeping' purposes in the FSA's and are not necessarily part of the phonological representation.

We also removed several arcs allowing for the presence of consonants (represented as [C]). Because projection from the surface form (+P/–P) works the same as projection from the UR (in terms of vowel harmony), these are left out of the descriptions (but were included in the formal analysis).

The transducer for Gen is given in Figure 2. This finite state transducer accepts strings of concatenated vowels for all potential inputs. This transducer provides the basis for restrictions on the representations for spreading. One such restriction is that the feature value of the projection must match the source feature value. For example, a vowel with a [+U] projection must have [+F] in the UR (e.g., arc 0 to 1). A second restriction is a practical one; the first vowel in a word cannot be projected by the vowel to its left (because such a vowel does not exist). The third restriction is that vowels have one and only one projection. Gen only produces segments that have a single value at the projection.

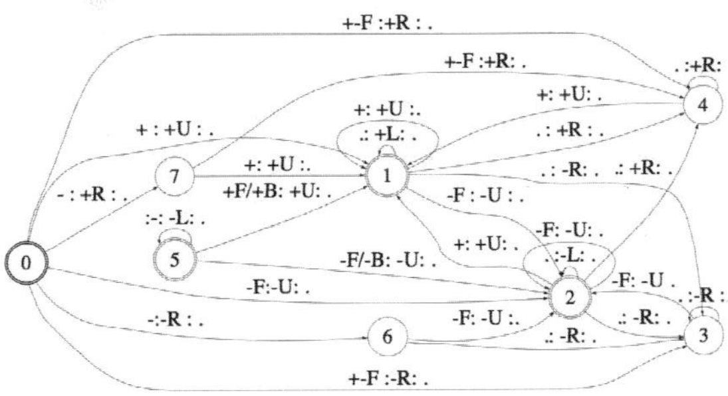

Figure 2: GEN

Spreading is initiated by a vowel whose projection is its underlying form (+U/–U). A vowel may only be projected by +L if it follows a vowel that is projected by +U (and likewise for –L). This ensures that the only initiator for rightwards spreading is a vowel projected by its underlying form.

In Turbid Spreading, deletion of a segment entails deletion of only the surface form; all vowels with a UR have a representation at the PR. Epenthesis can occur at either the PR level (requiring representations at both the PR and SR) or the SR (requiring only a representation at the SR). Epenthetic vowels at the PR level undergo spreading (e.g., arc 0 to 6), whereas epenthetic vowels at the SR only are transparent to spreading. The difference between epenthetic and deleted vowels is based on the fact that epenthetic vowels may interact with spreading (at the projection level) or be transparent (and appear only at the pronunciation level), but deleted vowels may not interact with spreading (and therefore appear only at the pronunciation level).

Rightwards spreading is instantiated in the arcs from state 0 to states 3, 4, 6 and 7. Transitions from 0 to 6 and 0 to 7 involve epenthetic vowels (marked with a /-/ in the UR). Arcs from 0 to 3 and 0 to 6 involve spreading -F to the left (/-R/ at the PR). Arcs from 0 to 7 and 0 to 4 involve spreading +F to the right (/+R/ at the PR). In order for a /+R/-R/ projected vowel to reach a final state, the source of spreading must be +U/-U, which is reflected in the arcs from 3 to 2, and 4 to 1. Spreading from the left to right involves a vowel projected by its underlying form (transitions 0 to 1 and 0 to 2). From there a vowel may be projected as +L (state 1) or as –L (state 2).

Constraints Turbid Spreading is instantiated through several constraints. SPREAD-R and SPREAD-L initiate vowel harmony. ID[F]-UR regulates featural identity between the underlying representation and the projection. ID[F]-SR regulates featural identity between the surface representation and the projection. Constraints that govern epenthesis and deletion are MAX, DEP, and *CC. The finite state transducers of these constraints assign violation marks (e.g., -1) to the output whenever a violation of the constraint is encountered.

ID[F]-UR is violated once for every vowel not projected by its underlying form. Any vowel that has an underlying form (i.e., not an epenthetic vowel), but is not marked with ±U at the PR incurs a violation.

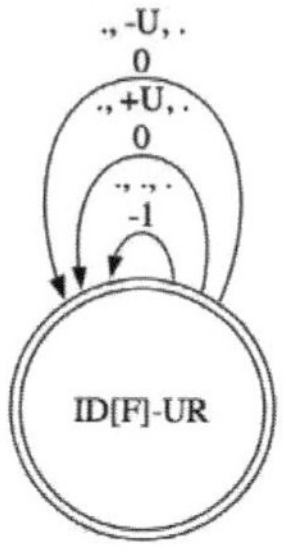

Figure 3: ID[F]-UR

*B is a placeholder for a featural markedness constraint (e.g., *[+Back, –High]). This constraint is violated when a vowel is marked ±B in the input and is +F in the output (e.g., a [–High] vowel becoming [+Back]). All other representations do not receive a violation[5].

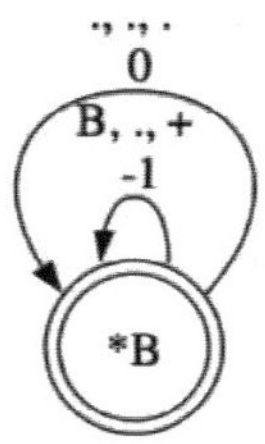

Figure 4: *B

The ID[F]-SR constraint is violated whenever the feature values at the projection and the pronunciation level do not match. For example, if the pronunciation is [+], the projection must be +U, +L, +R or +P.

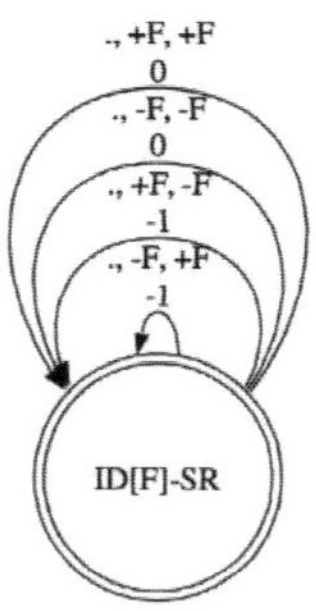

Figure 5: ID[F]-SR

[5] This constraint assumes that no vowels may lose their /B/ specification from the input to the output (e.g., change from [–HIGH] to [+HIGH] in order to allow spreading of [+Back]). This process is called 're-pairing' (Bakovic, 2000), and is subject to future research.

The 'x' symbol is used to denote deleted vowels, which violate MAX, which assigns a violation if 'x' appears in the pronunciation.

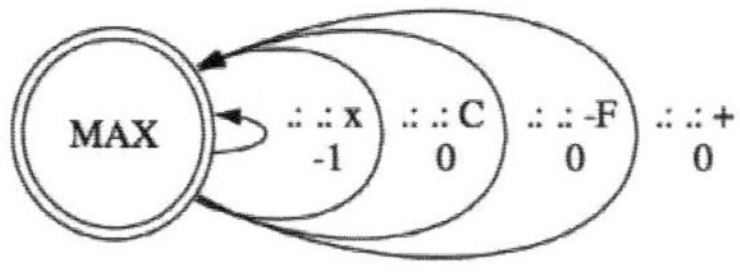

Figure 6: MAX

DEP is the constraint violated by epenthesis, represented by the symbol '-' in the underlying form. DEP searches for any vowel with (-) in the UR and assigns a violation for each feature value that appears on the projection and pronunciation levels. Epenthesis at the pronunciation level incurs two violations of DEP, but epenthesis at the projection level incurs one violation.

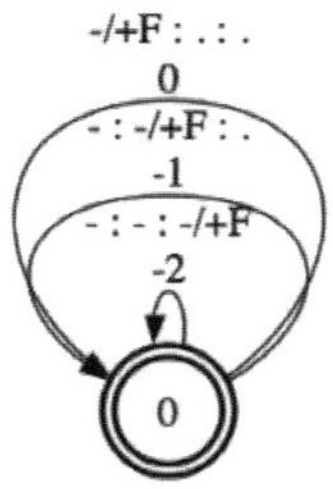

Figure 7: DEP

I assume that epenthesis is driven by the markedness constraint *CC[6]. This constraint scans the pronunciation level for two consonants in a row, and assigns a violation for every pair of consonants. *CC requires two states because *CC is violated only when there are two consecutive consonants, making one state for the first consonant (no violations), and a second state for an adjacent consonant (a violation).

[6] In addition to *CC, other constraints such as *#C or *C# may trigger epenthesis. For simplicity, these additional constraints are not included in the present analysis.

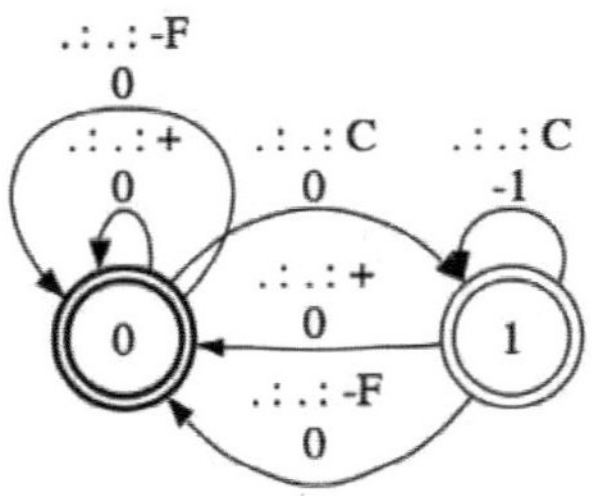

Figure 8: *CC

Violations for both spreading constraints are assigned directionally such that a violation on the first vowel is more severe than violations later in the word (Eisner, 2000), formalized in a simplified version where violations at different parts of the word are greater than other parts of the word. In order to prevent 'gang' effects, violations are assigned exponentially such that for a three-vowel input, violation on the second vowel incurs 100 violations, while a violation on the third vowel incurs only 10 violations. This simplified version of directional evaluation only allows for a finite number of vowels in the input. However, because the theory is tested with inputs of 3 and 4 vowels in length, these simplified transducers capture the data analyzed here. Future work will analyze directional spreading for an unlimited number of vowels in the input.

SPREAD-R is satisfied if a vowel projects an L (+/–L only occurs if a vowel spreads rightwards). Spreading is represented in terms of the target of spreading (e.g., a [+L] vowel is the target of spreading). Because initial vowels cannot be a target of rightward spreading (as there is no vowel to the left), the initial vowel automatically satisfies SPREAD-R.

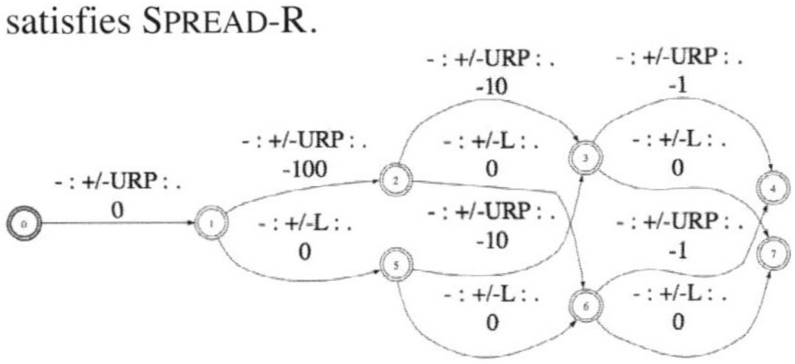

Figure 9: SPREAD-R

From state 1, vowels that project an L satisfy SPREAD and move to state 5. All other vowels move to state 2 and incur 100 violations. From states 2 and 5, if the third vowel satisfies SPREAD, it moves to state 6. If the final vowel satisfies SPREAD, it moves to state 7. If the third vowel fails to satisfy SPREAD, it moves to state 3 (from state 5 or 2) and incurs 10 violations. If the fourth vowel fails to satisfy SPREAD, it moves to state 4 (from states 6 or 3) and incurs 1 violation.

One might assume that SPREAD-L simply is a reversed version of SPREAD-R. However, this simple reversal is not possible because the opposite vowels trigger spreading for each constraint. In SPREAD-R, the initial vowel is the optimal trigger for harmony, but for SPREAD-L the final vowel is the optimal trigger for harmony.

The final vowel always satisfies SPREAD-L because final vowels cannot be targets for leftward spreading. Thus, the final vowel (state 7) never incurs a violation. If the first vowel is projected by +R or -R, then it satisfies SPREAD-L (state 3), otherwise it violates the constraint, and incurs 1 violation (state 4). If the second non-final vowel violates SPREAD-L, it moves to state 2 and incurs 10 violations. If the third non-final vowel violates SPREAD-L, it moves to state 3 and incurs 100 violations.

Violations of harmony from epenthetic vowels are assigned based on the position of the word. If an epenthetic vowel does not get its projected feature from the right, it will incur a violation of SPREAD-L. Epenthesis before the initial vowel incurs 1 violation, epenthesis after the initial vowel incurs 10 violations, etc.

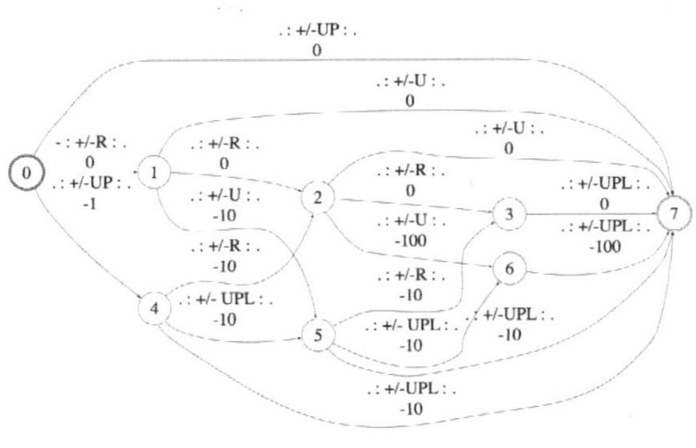

Figure 9: SPREAD-L

4 Results

The finite state transducers implementing GEN and the constraints were fed into the Contenders Algorithm. This was a modified version of Riggle's java script program[7]. This program co m-putes the contenders for a single input over the grammar. While the finite-state transducers represent an infinite candidate set, it would be impossible to compute contenders for every possible input. We limited the input to 4 vowels be-

[7] Thanks to Colin Wilson for these modifications.

cause all previously reported pathologies did not change for words longer than four vowels (3 with epenthesis)[8]. We used Microsoft Excel to co m-pute all possible feature combinations for up to four vowels (+F, –F, +B, –B) without epenthesis. There were 256 combinations with 4 vowels in the input, 64 combinations with 3 vowels, 16 combinations with 2 vowels, and 4 with 1 vowel in the input. The input list with epenthesis used the vowel combinations for up to 3 vowels, and CC clusters were inserted at the left edge, right edge, and medially (when applicable).

The results of the Contenders Algorithm were fed into the Erculator program for computing typologies using Elementary Ranking Conditions (ERCs) (Riggle, 2007). Without epenthesis, there was a typology containing 16 languages: 6 spread right, 6 spread left and 4 with no spreading. For the no spread cases, there was one language that allowed the marked segment ([+B]), and three that did not. In the three that did not allow [+B] in the output, underlyingly /+B/ segments were treated differently. In one language, underlyingly /+B/ segments got their [–F] feature from the vowel to its left, in another language, underlyingly /+B/ segments got their [–F] feature from the vowel to its right, and in the third language, underlyingly /+B/ segments got their [–F] feature from the pronunciation level.

The six spread-right and spread-left languages were identical except for direction of spreading. In one language all vowels participated in harmony. The second language was a case of 'allophonic harmony'. In this case, a [+B] vowel only appears as a result of harmony. That is, harmony creates allophones of a phoneme that would otherwise not appear on the surface. Non-participating vowels were transparent in the third and fourth cases. In the third case, an underlyingly +B vowel was changed via spreading; in the fourth case, an underlyingly +B vowel was changed at the pronunciation level. In the fifth and sixths cases, non-participating vowels were opaque, blocking harmony and starting a new harmonic domain. In the fifth case, underlyingly /+B/ segments changed to [–F] via projection from the surface. In the sixth language, underlyingly /+B/ segments could undergo spreading of [–F] from either the left or the right, if possible.

With epenthesis, the predicted typology contained 68 languages. There were 16 languages with no epenthesis, 16 languages with epenthesis always on the projection level and 16 languages with epenthesis at the pronunciation level (giving 48 languages). Each of these sets of 16 languages corresponded to the 16 languages with no epenthesis above. The final 20 languages were from cases in which epenthesis occurred at the projection level only if spreading were possible from the vowel to the left (10 languages) or the vowel to the right (10 languages). These 20 languages differed depending on how non-derived vowels behaved. There were two sets of 4 no-spread languages, 6 spread-right languages, and 6 spread-left, described above.

Pattern	Examples
1. All vowels participate	Kalenjin (Local & Lodge, 1996) Degema (Elugbe, 1984)
2. Transparent Vowels	Hungarian (Goldsmith, 1985) Finnish (Goldsmith, 1985)
3. Opaque Vowels	Mongolian (Goldsmith, 1985) Turkish (Underhill, 1976)
4. Bi-Directional Harmony	Lango (Woock & Nooonan, 1979) Kalenjin (Local & Lodge, 1996) Turkana (Dimmendaal, 1983)
5. Allophonic Harmony	Pasiego (Penny, 1969) Akan (Clements, 1981) Kinande (Archangeli & Pulleyblank, 2002) Nawuri (Casali, 2003)
Epenthetic Vowels	
6. Transparent	Karchevan (Vaux, 1995) Agulus (Vaux, 1998)
7. Undergo Harmony	Turkish (Clements & Sezer, 1982; Underhill, 1976) Yawelmani (Archangeli, 1988) Yoruba (Archangeli & Pulleyblank, 1989)
8. Directional Harmony	Levantine Arabic (Kenstowicz, 1981) Mohawk (Postal, 1968), Sesotho (Rose & Demuth, 2006)
9. Epenthetic Vowels Only	Ponapean (Kitto & DeLacy, 1999) Barra Gaelic (Sagey, 1987) Marash (Vaux, 1998)

Table 1. Patterns of harmony languages

Importantly, all 68 of these languages represent possible or known languages; none of these langauges share the properties of pathological typological predictions described by Wilson

[8] Pilot tests with longer inputs did not change the results.

(2003). An important result of these computations is that epenthesis is never blocked by a failure to participate in harmony, a prediction that previous analyses of vowel harmony incorrectly predicted to be possible (Wilson, 2003).

Because the resulting languages varied systematically, we were able to divide the 68 languages into nine different patterns. Examples from real languages are presented in Table 1. The first pattern is that all vowels participate in harmony; there are no non-participating vowels. The second and third patterns are vowel harmony languages with nonparticipating vowels, either transparent to harmony (case 2) or opaque to harmony (case 3). Case 4 occurs when spreading applies both from right-to-left as well as left-to-right. Case 5 involves allophonic harmony, discussed above. Cases 6-9 apply to epenthetic vowels. In case 6, harmony skips epenthetic vowels. In case 7, harmony applies to epenthetic vowels as if they were an underlying vowel. In case 8, harmony applies to epenthetic vowels, but directionally (e.g., the epenthetic vowel gets its features from the right or left, or defaults if there is no vowel to spread to the epenthetic vowel). Case 9 occurs when harmony does not apply to underlying vowels in the language, and only epenthetic vowels undergo harmony.

The important result found in these 9 case patterns is that all the major harmony phenomena are predicted (directionality, epenthesis, transparency and opacity), without predicting typologically implausible languages. This is an important result because many previous theories of vowel harmony in OT made pathological predictions when harmony interacted with non-participating vowels, deletion and epenthesis. For example, alignment constraints predict failure to epenthesize a vowel in the presence of a non-participating vowel (Wilson, 2003). Such pathologies are not found in Turbid Spreading.

While there other instances of vowel harmony that are not covered in the present analysis, the present approach provides a mechanism for understanding the typology of vowel harmony processes and the mechanisms that produce the attested and the unattested patterns.

It is important to note that while the present results are successful, the model is a result of revisions based on previous iterations of the Contenders Algorithm. Many of the unwanted predictions in previous models could not have been found without the use of the computational tools used in this paper.

5 Conclusion

Computations over finite-state transducers made it possible to compute a complete typology of vowel harmony interactions, including interactions of vowel harmony and epenthesis. The computational model verified that Turbid Spreading only predicts languages known to be attested in natural language, but does predict the common pathologies known to be problematic for previous vowel harmony analyses in OT.

Because we used all possible vowel combinations for up to four vowels, we can be fairly certain that all relevant inputs were considered. Because the Contenders Algorithm models the infinite candidate set in GEN, we can be certain that the relevant candidates were considered. This paper demonstrates the power of computational tools for measuring and evaluating theories of phonological phenomena.

Acknowledgments

I am indebted to Colin Wilson, who provided crucial guidance and encouragement. I am also grateful to Jason Riggle, who laid the groundwork for this project. In addition, I am extremely grateful to Paul Smolensky for his help implementing the inputs using Excel, and his guidance in forming Turbid Spreading. I am also thankful to Matt Goldrick, Joan Chen-Main, Gaja Jarosz-Snover, Rebecca Morley, and Neil Bardhan for their helpful comments. Funding was provided by: NSF IGERT and NIH Grant DC00167. All errors are my own.

References

Archangeli, D. (1988). *Underspecification in Yawelmani Phonology and Morphology*. New York & London: Garland Publishing, Inc.

Archangeli, D., & Pulleyblank, D. (1989). Yoruba vowel harmony. *LI, 20*, 173-217.

Archangeli, D., & Pulleyblank, D. (2002). Kinande vowel harmony: domains, grounded conditions and one-sided alignment. *Phonology, 19*, 139-188.

Bakovic, E. (2000). *Harmony, dominance and control.* Unpublished doctoral dissertation, Rutgers University.

Bane, M., & Riggle, J. (in press). The typological consequences of weighted constraints. *Proceedings of the 45th Annual Meeting of the Chicago Linguistics Society.*

Bird, S., & Ellison, T. M. (1994). One-level phonology: Autosegmental representations and rules as finite automata. *Computational Linguistics, 20*(1), 55-90.

Casali, R. F. (2003). [ATR] value asymmetries and underlying vowel inventory structure in Niger-Congo and Nilo-Sahaan. *Linguistic Typology, 7*, 307-382.

Clements, G. N. (1981). Akan vowel harmony: A non-linear analysis. *Harvard Studies in Phonology, 2*, 108-177.

Clements, G. N., & Sezer, E. (1982). Vowel and consonant disharmony in Turkish. In v. d. H. a. Smith (Ed.), *The structure of Phonological Representations* (Vol. II, pp. 213-255). Dordrecht: Foris.

Dijkstra, E. (1959). A note on two problems in connexion with graphs. *Numerische Mathematik, 1*, 269-271.

Dimmendaal, G. J. (1983). *The Turkana language*. Dordecht: Foris.

Eisner, J. (2000). Directional constraint evaluation in Optimality Theory. *Proceedings of the 18th International Conference on Computational Linguistics (COLING)*, 257-263.

Ellison, M. T. (1992). *Learning vowel harmony*. Paper presented at the SHOE Workshop, ITK, Tilburg, Netherlands.

Ellison, M. T. (1994). Phonological derivation in Optimality Theory. *Proceedings of the 15th International Conference on Computational Linguistics*, 1007-1013.

Elugbe, B. O. (1984). Morphology of the gerund in Degema and its reconstruction in proto-Edoid. *Studies in African Linguistics, 15*(1), 77-89.

Finley, S. (2008). *Formal and cognitive restrictions on vowel harmony*. Unpublished doctoral dissertation, Johns Hopkins University.

Finley, S. (2010). Exceptions in vowel harmony are local. *Lingua, 120*, 1549-1566.

Finley, S. (in press). The interaction of epenthesis and vowel harmony. *Proceedings of the 44th Annual Meeting of the Chicago Linguistics Society*.

Finley, S., & Badecker, W. (2008). Analytic biases for vowel harmony languages. *WCCFL, 27*, 168-176.

Goldrick, M. (2001). Turbid output representations and the unity of opacity. *NELS, 30*, 231-245.

Goldsmith, J. (1985). Vowel harmony in Khalka Mongolian, Yaka, Finnish and Hungarian. *Phonology Yearbook, 2*, 253-275.

Goldsmith, J., & Xanthos, A. (2009). Learning phonological categories. *Language, 85*(1), 4-38.

Kenstowicz, M. (1981). Vowel harmony in Palesitinian Arabic: A suprasegmental analysis. *Linguistics, 19*, 449-465.

Kitto, C., & DeLacy, P. (1999). Correspondence and epenthetic quality. In C. Kitto & C. Smallwood (Eds.), *Proceedings of AFLA VI*. Holland: Academic Graphics.

Local, J., & Lodge, K. (1996). Another travesty of respresentation: Phonological representation and phonetic interpretation of ATR harmony in Kalenjin. *York Papers in Linguistics, 17*, 77-117.

Penny, R. J. (1969). Vowel harmony in the speech of Montanes de Pas. *ORBIS- Bulletin International de Documentation Linguistique*, 148-166.

Postal, P. M. (1968). Mohawk vowel doubling. *International Journal of American Linguistics, 35*, 291-298.

Prince, A. (2002). Arguing optimality. In A. Coetzee, A. Carpenter & P. De Lacy (Eds.), *Papers in Optimality Theory II*. Amherst, MA: GLSA.

Prince, A., & Smolensky, P. (1993/2004). *Optimality theory: Constraint interaction in generative grammar*. Cambridge: Blackwell.

Riggle, J. (2004a). Contenders and learning. In B. Schmieser, A. K. Chand & A. Rodriquez (Eds.), *WCCFL* (Vol. 23, pp. 101-114). Somerville, MA: Cascadilla Press.

Riggle, J. (2004b). *Generation, recognition and learning in finite-state Optimality Theory*. Unpublished doctoral dissertation, UCLA.

Riggle, J. (2007). Erculator: http://clml.uchicago.edu/?page_id=11.

Rose, Y., & Demuth, K. (2006). Vowel epenthesis in loanword adaptation: Representational and phonetic considerations. *Lingua, 116*, 1112-1139.

Sagey, E. (1987). *Non-constituent spreading in Barra Gaelic*.Unpublished manuscript, UC Irvine.

Underhill, R. (1976). *Turkish grammar*. Cambridge: MIT Press.

Vaux, B. (1995). Vowel harmony in the Armenian dialect of Karchevan. *NSL, 9*(1-9).

Vaux, B. (1998). *The phonology of Armenian*. Oxford: Clovendon Press.

Wilson, C. (2003). *Analyzing unbounded spreading with constraints: marks, targets, and derivations*.Unpublished manuscript, UCLA.

Wilson, C. (2005). *Localizing constraint violation: Theoretical consequences of myopic spreading*.Unpublished manuscript, Paper presented at HOWL3, Johns Hopkins.

Woock, E. B., & Nooonan, M. (1979). Vowel harmony in Lango. *CLS, 15*, 20-29.

Complexity of the Acquisition of Phonotactics in Optimality Theory

Giorgio Magri
Institut Jean Nicod, École Normale Supérieure, Paris
magrigrg@gmail.com

Abstract

The problem of the acquisition of Phonotactics in OT is shown to be not tractable in its *strong* formulation, whereby constraints and generating function vary arbitrarily as inputs of the problem.

Tesar and Smolensky (1998) consider the basic ranking problem in Optimality Theory (OT). According to this problem, the learner needs to find a ranking consistent with a given set of data. They show that this problem is solvable even in its *strong* formulation, namely without any assumptions on the generating function or the constraint set. Yet, this basic ranking problem is too simple to realistically model any actual aspect of language acquisition. To make the problem more realistic, we might want, for instance, to require the learner to find not just *any* ranking consistent with the data, rather one that furthermore generates a *smallest* language (w.r.t. set inclusion). Prince and Tesar (2004) and Hayes (2004) note that this computational problem models the task of the acquisition of phonotactics within OT. This paper shows that, contrary to the basic ranking problem considered by Tesar and Smolensky, this more realistic problem of the acquisition of phonotactics is *not* solvable, at least not in its strong formulation. I conjecture that this complexity result has nothing to do with the choice of the OT framework, namely that an analogous result holds for the corresponding problem within alternative frameworks, such as Harmonic Grammar (Legendre et al., 1990b; Legendre et al., 1990a). Furthermore, I conjecture that the culprit lies with the fact that generating function and constraint set are completely unconstrained. From this perspective, this paper motivates the following research question: to find phonologically plausible assumptions on generating function and constraint set that make the problem of the acquisition of phonotactics tractable.

1 Statement of the main result

Let the *universal specifications* of an OT typology be a 4-tuple $(\mathcal{X}, \mathcal{Y}, Gen, \mathcal{C})$, as illustrated in (1): $\mathcal{X}$ and $\mathcal{Y}$ are the sets of *underlying* and *surface* forms; Gen is the *generating function*; and $\mathcal{C}$ is the *constraint set*.

$$\begin{aligned} \mathcal{X} &= \mathcal{Y} = \{\text{ta, da, rat, rad}\} \\ Gen &= \left[\text{ta, da} \rightarrow \{\text{ta, da}\}\ \text{rat, rad} \rightarrow \{\text{rat, rad}\}\right] \\ \mathcal{C} &= \left\{ \begin{array}{r} F_{\text{pos}} = \text{IDNT[VCE]/ONSET}, \\ F = \text{IDNT[VCE]}, \\ M = {}^*[+\text{VCE}, -\text{SON}] \end{array} \right\} \end{aligned} \quad (1)$$

Let $\gg, \gg', \ldots$ be *rankings* over the constraint set, as illustrated in (2) for the constraint set in (1).

$$F_{\text{pos}} \gg M \gg F \qquad F_{\text{pos}} \gg' F \gg' M \quad (2)$$

Let $\mathsf{OT}_{\gg}$ be the *OT-grammar* corresponding to a ranking $\gg$ (Prince and Smolensky, 2004), as illustrated in (3) for the ranking $\gg$ in (2).

$$\begin{array}{ll} \mathsf{OT}_{\gg}(\text{/ta/}) = [\text{ta}] & \mathsf{OT}_{\gg}(\text{/da/}) = [\text{da}] \\ \mathsf{OT}_{\gg}(\text{/rat/}) = [\text{rat}] & \mathsf{OT}_{\gg}(\text{/rad/}) = [\text{rat}] \end{array} \quad (3)$$

Let $\mathcal{L}(\gg)$ be the *language* corresponding to a ranking $\gg$, illustrated in (4) for the rankings (2).

$$\begin{aligned} \mathcal{L}(\gg) &= \{\text{ta, da, rat}\} \\ \mathcal{L}(\gg') &= \{\text{ta, da, rat, rad}\} \end{aligned} \quad (4)$$

A *data set* $\mathcal{D}$ is a finite set of pairs $(x, \hat{y})$ of an underlying form $x \in \mathcal{X}$ and an intended winner surface form $\hat{y} \in Gen(x) \subseteq \mathcal{Y}$, as illustrated in (5).

$$\mathcal{D} = \{(\text{/da/}, [\text{da}]),\ (\text{/rat/}, [\text{rat}])\} \quad (5)$$

A data set $\mathcal{D}$ is called *OT-compatible with a ranking* $\gg$ iff the corresponding OT-grammar accounts for all the pairs in $\mathcal{D}$, namely $\mathsf{OT}_{\gg}(x) = \hat{y}$ for every pair $(x, \hat{y}) \in \mathcal{D}$. A data set $\mathcal{D}$ is called *OT-compatible* iff it is OT-compatible with at least a ranking. Suppose that the actual universal specifications $(\mathcal{X}, \mathcal{Y}, Gen, \mathcal{C})$ are fixed and known. The

Proceedings of the 11th Meeting of the ACL-SIGMORPHON, ACL 2010, pages 19–27,
Uppsala, Sweden, 15 July 2010.

basic *Ranking problem* (Rpbm) is (6). The learner is provided with a set of data $\mathcal{D}$ corresponding to some target language; and has to come up with a ranking compatible with those data $\mathcal{D}$.

$$\begin{aligned} &\textit{given:} \text{ an OT-comp. data set } \mathcal{D} \subseteq \mathcal{X} \times \mathcal{Y}; \\ &\textit{find:} \text{ a ranking } \gg \text{ over the constraint set } \mathcal{C} \text{ that is OT-compatible with } \mathcal{D}. \end{aligned} \tag{6}$$

At the current stage of the development of the field, we have no firm knowledge of the actual universal specifications. Thus, the Rpbm (6) is of little interest. It is standard practice in the OT computational literature to get around this difficulty by switching to the *strong formulation* (7), whereby the universal specifications vary arbitrarily as an input to the problem (Wareham, 1998; Eisner, 2000; Heinz et al., 2009). Switching from (6) to (7) presupposes that the learner does not rely on peculiar properties of the actual universal specifications.

$$\begin{aligned} &\textit{given:} \text{ univ. specs } (\mathcal{X}, \mathcal{Y}, Gen, \mathcal{C}), \\ &\qquad \text{an OT-comp. data set } \mathcal{D} \subseteq \mathcal{X} \times \mathcal{Y}; \\ &\textit{find:} \text{ a ranking } \gg \text{ over the constraint set } \mathcal{C} \text{ that is OT-compatible with } \mathcal{D}. \end{aligned} \tag{7}$$

To complete the statement of the Rpbm (7), we need to specify the *size* of its instances, that determines the time that a solution algorithm is allowed to take. Let $width(\mathcal{D})$ be the cardinality of the largest candidate set over all underlying forms that appear in $\mathcal{D}$, as stated in (8).

$$width(\mathcal{D}) \stackrel{\text{def}}{=} \max_{(x,\hat{y})\in\mathcal{D}} |Gen(x)| \tag{8}$$

Of course, the size of an instance of the Rpbm (7) depends on the cardinality $|\mathcal{C}|$ of the constraint set and on the cardinality $|\mathcal{D}|$ of the data set. Tesar and Smolensky (1998) (implicitly) assume that it also depends on $width(\mathcal{D})$, as stated in (9). [1]

$$\begin{aligned} &\textit{given:} \text{ univ. specs } (\mathcal{X}, \mathcal{Y}, Gen, \mathcal{C}), \\ &\qquad \text{an OT-comp. data set } \mathcal{D} \subseteq \mathcal{X} \times \mathcal{Y}; \\ &\textit{find:} \text{ a ranking } \gg \text{ of the constraint set } \mathcal{C} \text{ that is OT-compatible with } \mathcal{D}; \\ &\textit{size:} \max\{|\mathcal{C}|,\ |\mathcal{D}|,\ width(\mathcal{D})\}. \end{aligned} \tag{9}$$

[1] A potential difficulty with the latter assumption is as follows: $width(\mathcal{D})$ could be very large, namely superpolynomial in the number of constraints $|\mathcal{C}|$; thus, letting the size of an instance of the Rpbm depend on $width(\mathcal{D})$ might make the problem too easy, by loosening up too much the tight dependence on $|\mathcal{C}|$. Yet, this potential difficulty is harmless in the case of the strong formulation of the Rpbm, since that formulation requires an algorithm to work for *any* universal specifications, and thus also for universal specifications where $|\mathcal{C}|$ is large but $width(\mathcal{D})$ small.

Tesar and Smolensky (1998) prove claim 1. This claim is important because it shows that no harm comes from switching to the strong formulation, at least in the case of the Rpbm.

Claim 1 *The Rpbm (9) is tractable.*

Yet, the Rpbm (9) is way too simple to realistically model any aspect of acquisition. Here is a way to appreciate this point. The two rankings $\gg$ and $\gg'$ in (2) are both solutions of the instance of the Rpbm (9) corresponding to the universal specifications in (1) and to the data set in (5). As noted in (4), the language corresponding to $\gg$ is a proper subset of the language corresponding to $\gg'$. A number of authors have suggested that the ranking $\gg$ that corresponds to the subset language is a "better" solution than the ranking $\gg'$ that corresponds to the superset language (Berwick, 1985; Manzini and Wexler, 1987; Prince and Tesar, 2004; Hayes, 2004). This intuition is captured by problem (10): it asks not just for *any* ranking OT-compatible with the data $\mathcal{D}$; rather, for one such ranking whose corresponding language is as small as possible (w.r.t. set inclusion). The latter condition requires the learner to rule out as *illicit* any form which is not entailed by the data. Problem (10) thus realistically models the task of the acquisition of phonotactics, namely the knowledge of licit vs. illicit forms.

$$\begin{aligned} &\textit{given:} \text{ univ. specs } (\mathcal{X}, \mathcal{Y}, Gen, \mathcal{C}), \\ &\qquad \text{an OT-comp. data set } \mathcal{D} \subseteq \mathcal{X} \times \mathcal{Y}; \\ &\textit{find:} \text{ a ranking } \gg \text{ OT-comp. with } \mathcal{D} \text{ s.t. there is no ranking } \gg' \text{ OT-comp. with } \mathcal{D} \text{ too s.t. } \mathcal{L}(\gg') \subsetneq \mathcal{L}(\gg). \end{aligned} \tag{10}$$

The *Problem of the Acquisition of Phonotactics* (APpbm) in (10) involves the language $\mathcal{L}(\gg)$, which in turn depends on the number of forms in $\mathcal{X}$ and on the cardinality of the candidate set $Gen(x)$ for all underlying forms $x \in \mathcal{X}$. Thus, (11) lets the size of an instance of the APpbm depend generously on $|\mathcal{X}|$ and $width(\mathcal{X})$, rather than on $|\mathcal{D}|$ and $width(\mathcal{D})$ as in the case of the Rpbm (9).[2]

$$\begin{aligned} &\textit{given:} \text{ univ. specs } (\mathcal{X}, \mathcal{Y}, Gen, \mathcal{C}), \\ &\qquad \text{an OT-comp. data set } \mathcal{D} \subseteq \mathcal{X} \times \mathcal{Y}; \\ &\textit{find:} \text{ a ranking } \gg \text{ OT-comp. with } \mathcal{D} \text{ s.t. there is no ranking } \gg' \text{ OT-comp. with } \mathcal{D} \text{ too s.t. } \mathcal{L}(\gg') \subsetneq \mathcal{L}(\gg); \\ &\textit{size:} \max\{|\mathcal{C}|,\ |\mathcal{X}|,\ width(\mathcal{X})\}. \end{aligned} \tag{11}$$

[2] Letting the size of an instance of the APpbm depend on $|\mathcal{C}|$, $|\mathcal{X}|$ and $width(\mathcal{X})$ ensures that the problem is in $\mathcal{NP}$, namely that it admits an efficient verification algorithm.

Prince and Tesar (2004) offer an alternative formulation of the APpbm. They define a *strictness measure* as a function μ that maps a ranking $\gg$ to a number $\mu(\gg)$ that provides a relative measure of the cardinality of the corresponding language $\mathcal{L}(\gg)$, in the sense that any solution of the problem (12) is a solution of the APpbm (10).[3]

given: univ. specs $(\mathcal{X}, \mathcal{Y}, Gen, \mathcal{C})$, an OT-comp. data set $\mathcal{D} \subseteq \mathcal{X} \times \mathcal{Y}$; (12)
find: a ranking with minimal measure μ among those OT-comp. with $\mathcal{D}$.

As usual, assume that the constraint set $Con = \mathcal{F} \cup \mathcal{M}$ is split up into the subset $\mathcal{F}$ of faithfulness constraints and the subset $\mathcal{M}$ of markedness constraints. Consider the function μ_{PT} defined in (13): it pairs a ranking $\gg$ with the number $\mu_{\mathrm{PT}}(\gg)$ of pairs of a faithfulness constraint and a markedness constraint such that the former is $\gg$-ranked above the latter. Prince and Tesar (2004) conjecture that the function μ_{PT} in (13) is a strictness measure. The intuition is that faithfulness (markedness) constraints work toward (against) preserving underlying contrasts and thus a small language is likely to arise by having few pairs of a faithfulness constraint ranked above a markedness constraint.

$$\mu_{\mathrm{PT}}(\gg) \stackrel{\mathrm{def}}{=} |\{(F, M) \in \mathcal{F} \times \mathcal{M} \mid F \gg M\}| \quad (13)$$

Let me dub (12) with the mesure μ_{PT} in (13) *Prince and Tesar's reformulation* of the APpbm (PTAPpbm), as in (14). The core idea of strictness measures is to determine the relative strictness of two rankings without reference to the entire set of forms $\mathcal{X}$. Thus, (14) lets the size of an instance of PTAPpbm depend on $|\mathcal{D}|$ and $width(\mathcal{D})$, rather than on $|\mathcal{X}|$ and $width(\mathcal{X})$ as for the APpbm (11).

given: univ. specs $(\mathcal{X}, \mathcal{Y}, Gen, \mathcal{C})$, an OT-comp. data set $\mathcal{D} \subseteq \mathcal{X} \times \mathcal{Y}$; (14)
find: a ranking with minimal measure μ_{PT} among those OT-comp. with $\mathcal{D}$;
size: $\max\{|\mathcal{C}|, |\mathcal{D}|, width(\mathcal{D})\}$.

The APpbm (11) and the PTAPpbm (14) have figured prominently in the recent computational OT literature. The main result of this paper is claim 2. This claim says that there is no efficient algorithm for the APpbm nor for the PTAPpbm. I conjecture that the culprit lies in the switch to the strong formulation. Comparing with claim 1, I thus conclude that the switch is harmless for the easy Rpbm, but harmful for the more realistic APpbm and PTAPpbm.

Claim 2 *The APpbm (11) and the PTAPpbm (14) are intractable.*

In the next section, I prove NP-completeness of PTAPpbm by showing that the *Cyclic Ordering* problem can be reduced to PTAPpbm. I then prove NP-completeness of APpbm by showing that PTAPpbm can be reduced to it. NP-completeness of APpbm holds despite the generous dependence of its size on $|\mathcal{X}|$ and $width(\mathcal{X})$. Furthermore, the proof actually shows that the PTAPpbm remains NP-complete even when the data have the simplest "disjunctive structure", namely for each underlying/winner/loser form there are at most two winner-preferring constrains.[4] And furthermore even when the data have the property that the faithfulness constraints are never loser-preferring.

2 Proof of the main result

Given a data set $\mathcal{D}$, for every pair $(x, \hat{y}) \in \mathcal{D}$ of an underlying form x and a corresponding winner form $\hat{y}$, for every loser candidate $y \in Gen(x)$ different from $\hat{y}$, construct a row $\mathbf{a}$ with $|\mathcal{C}|$ entries as follows: the kth entry is an L if constraint C_k assigns more violations to the winner pair $(x, \hat{y})$ than to the loser pair (x, y); it is a W if the opposite holds; it is an E if the two numbers of violations coincide. Organize these rows one underneath the other into a tableau $\mathbf{A}(\mathcal{D})$, called the *comparative tableau corresponding to* $\mathcal{D}$. To illustrate, I give in (15) the tableau corresponding to the data set (5).

$$\mathbf{A}(\mathcal{D}) = \begin{array}{c} \begin{matrix} F & F_{\mathrm{pos}} & M \end{matrix} \\ \begin{bmatrix} \mathrm{W} & \mathrm{W} & \mathrm{L} \\ \mathrm{W} & \mathrm{E} & \mathrm{W} \end{bmatrix} \end{array} \quad (15)$$

Generalizing a bit, let $\mathbf{A} \in \{\mathrm{L}, \mathrm{E}, \mathrm{W}\}^{m \times n}$ be a tableau with m rows, n columns, and entries taken from the three symbols L, E or W, called a *comparative tableau*. Let me say that $\mathbf{A}$ is *OT-compatible* with a ranking $\gg$ iff the tableau obtained by reordering the columns of $\mathbf{A}$ from left-to-right in

[3] The Rpbm (7) corresponds to *Empirical Risk Minimization* in the Statistical Learning literature, while problem (12) corresponds to a *regularized* version thereof, with regularization function μ.

[4] Of course, if there were a unique winner-preferring constraint per underlying/winner/loser form triplet, then the data would be OT-compatible with a unique ranking, and thus the PTAPpbm would reduce to the Rpbm.

decreasing order according to $\gg$ has the property that the left-most entry different from E is a W in every row. Tesar and Smolensky (1998) note that a data set $\mathcal{D}$ is OT-compatible with a ranking $\gg$ iff the corresponding comparative tableau $\mathbf{A}(\mathcal{D})$ is OT-compatible with it. Thus, the PTAPpbm (14) is tractable iff the problem (16) is tractable. Note that this equivalence crucially depends on two facts. First, that the size of an instance of the PTAPpbm depends not only on $|\mathcal{C}|$ and $|\mathcal{D}|$, but also on $width(\mathcal{D})$. Second, that we are considering the strong formulation of the PTAPpbm, and thus no assumptions need to be imposed on the given comparative tableau in (16), besides it being OT-compatible. The set $\mathcal{F}$ provided with an instance of (16) says which one of the n columns of the comparative tableau $\mathbf{A}$ correspond to faithfulness constraints. The size of an instance of problem (16) of course depends on the numbers m and n of rows and columns of $\mathbf{A}$.

given: a OT-comp. tabl. $\mathbf{A}\in\{\text{L, E, W}\}^{m\times n}$, (16)
a set $\mathcal{F}\subseteq\{1,\ldots,n\}$;
find: a ranking $\gg$ with minimal measure μ_{PT} among those OT-comp. with $\mathbf{A}$;
size: $\max\{m,\, n\}$.

The decision problem corresponding to (16) is stated in (17). As it is well known, intractability of the decision problem (17) entails intractability of the original problem (16). In fact, if the original problem (16) can be solved in polynomial time, then the corresponding decision problem (17) can be solved in polynomial time too: given an instance of the decision problem (17), find a solution $\gg$ of the corresponding instance of (16) and then just check whether $\mu_{\text{PT}}(\gg)\leq k$. From now on, I will refer to (17) as the PTAPpbm.

given: a OT-comp. tabl. $\mathbf{A}\in\{\text{L, E, W}\}^{m\times n}$, (17)
a set $\mathcal{F}\subseteq\{1,\ldots,n\}$,
an integer k;
output: "yes" iff there is a ranking $\gg$ OT-comp. with $\mathbf{A}$ s.t. $\mu_{\text{PT}}(\gg)\leq k$;
size: $\max\{m,\, n\}$.

Let me now introduce the problem I will reduce to PTAPpbm. Given a finite set $A=\{a,\,b,\,\ldots\}$ with cardinality $|A|$, consider a set $S\subseteq A\times A$ of pairs of elements of A. The set S is called *linearly compatible* iff there exists a one-to-one function $\pi : A\rightarrow\{1,2,\ldots,|A|\}$ such that for every pair $(a,b)\in S$ we have $\pi(a)<\pi(b)$. It is useful to let S be not just a set but a *multiset*, namely to allow S to contain multiple instances of the same pair. The notion of cardinality and the subset relation are trivially extended from sets to multisets. Consider the problem (18), that I will call the *Max-ordering problem* (MOpbm).

given: a finite set A, (18)
a multiset $P\subseteq A\times A$,
an integer $k\leq|P|$;
output: "yes" iff there is a linearly compatible multiset $S\subseteq P$ with $|S|\geq k$;
size: $\max\{|A|,\,|P|\}$.

The PTAPpbm (17) is clearly in $\mathcal{NP}$, namely it admits a verification algorithm. Claim 3 ensures that MOpbm (18) is NP-complete. Claim 4 shows that MOpbm can be reduced to PTAPpbm (17). I can thus conclude that PTAPpbm is NP-complete.

Claim 3 *The MOpbm (18) is NP-complete.*[5]

Proof. The MOpbm is obviously in $\mathcal{NP}$. To show that it is NP-complete, I need to exhibit an NP-complete problem that can be reduced to it. Given a finite set $A=\{a,\,b,\,\ldots\}$ with cardinality $|A|$, consider a set $T\subseteq A\times A\times A$ of triplets of elements of A. The set T is called *linearly cyclically compatible* iff there exists a one-to-one function $\pi : A\rightarrow\{1,2,\ldots,|A|\}$ such that for every triplet $(a,b,c)\in T$ either $\pi(a)<\pi(b)<\pi(c)$ or $\pi(b)<\pi(c)<\pi(a)$ or $\pi(c)<\pi(a)<\pi(b)$. Consider the *Cyclic Ordering* problem (COpbm) in (19).[6] Galil and Megiddo (1977) prove NP-completeness of COpbm by reduction from the *3-Satisfability* problem; the COpbm is problem [MS2] in (Garey and Johnson, 1979, p. 279).

input: a finite set A; (19)
a set $T\subseteq A\times A\times A$;
output: "yes" iff T is linearly cyclically compatible;
size: $|A|$

Given an instance (A,T) of the COpbm (19), consider the corresponding instance (A,P,k) of the MOpbm (18) defined as in (20). For every triplet

[5] A similar claim appears in (Cohen et al., 1999).

[6] It makes sense to let the size of an instance of the COpbm (19) be just the cardinality of the set A. In fact, the cardinality of the set T can be at most $|A|^3$. On the other hand, it makes sense to let the size of an instance of the MOpbm (18) depend also on the cardinality of the multiset P rather than only on the cardinality of the set A, since P is a multiset and thus its cardinality cannot be bound by the cardinality of A.

(a, b, c) in the set T, we put in the multiset P the three pairs (a, b), (b, c) and (c, a). Furthermore, we set the threshold k to twice the number of triplets in the set T. Note that P is a multiset because it might contain two instances of the same pair coming from two different triplets in T.

$$\begin{aligned} P &= \Big\{(a,b),\ (b,c),\ (c,a) \,\Big|\, (a,b,c) \in T\Big\} \\ k &= 2|T| \end{aligned} \tag{20}$$

Assume that the instance (A, T) of the COpbm admits a positive answer. Thus, T is cyclically compatible with a linear order π on A. Thus, for every triplet $(a, b, c) \in T$, there are at least two pairs in P compatible with π. Hence, there is a multiset S of pairs of P with cardinality at least $k = 2|T|$ linearly compatible with π,[7] namely the instance of the MOpbm defined in (20) admits a positive answer. Vice versa, assume that the instance (A, P, k) of the MOpbm in (20) admits a positive answer. Thus, there exists a linear order π on A compatible with $2|T|$ pairs in P. Since the three pairs that come from a given triplet are inconsistent, then each triplet must contribute two pairs to the total of $2|T|$ compatible pairs. Hence, π is cyclically compatible with all triplets in T. ■

Claim 4 *The MOpbm (18) can be reduced to the PTAPpbm (17).*

Proof. Given an instance (A, P, k) of the MOpbm, construct the corresponding instance $(\mathbf{A}, \mathcal{F}, K)$ of the PTAPpbm as follows. Let $n = |A|$, $\ell = |P|$; pick an integer d as in (21).

$$d > (\ell - k)n \tag{21}$$

Let the threshold K and the numbers N and M of columns and rows of the tableau $\mathbf{A}$ be as in (22).

$$\begin{aligned} K &= (\ell - k)(n + d) \\ N &= \ell + n + d \\ M &= \ell + nd \end{aligned} \tag{22}$$

Let the sets $\mathcal{F}$ and $\mathcal{M}$ of faithfulness and markedness constraints be as in (23). There is a faithfulness constraint $F_{(i,j)}$ for every pair (a_i, a_j) in the multiset P in the given instance of the MOpbm. Markedness constraints come in two varieties. There are the markedness constraints $M_1, \ldots, M_n$, one for every element in the set A in the given instance of the MOpbm; and then there are d more markedness constraints $M'_1, \ldots, M'_d$, that I'll call the *ballast* markedness constraints.

$$\begin{aligned} \mathcal{F} &= \{F_{(i,j)} \mid (a_i, a_j) \in P\} \\ \mathcal{M} &= \{M_1, \ldots, M_n\} \cup \{M'_1, \ldots, M'_d\} \end{aligned} \tag{23}$$

The comparative tableau $\mathbf{A}$ is built by assembling one underneath the other various blocks. To start, let $\overline{\mathbf{A}}$ be the block with ℓ rows and $N = \ell + n + d$ columns described in (24). It has a row for every pair $(a_i, a_j) \in P$. This row has all E's but for three entries: the entry corresponding to the faithfulness constraint $F_{(i,j)}$ corresponding to that pair, which is a W; the entry corresponding to the markedness constraint M_i corresponding to the first element a_i in the pair, which is an L; the entry corresponding to the markedness constraint M_j corresponding to the second element a_j in the pair, which is a W.

$$\begin{array}{r} \\ \\ (a_i, a_j) \Rightarrow \\ \\ \end{array} \begin{array}{c} \cdots\ F_{(i,j)}\ \cdots \quad \cdots\ M_i\ \cdots\ M_j\ \cdots\ M'_1\ \cdots\ M'_d \\ \left[\begin{array}{ccc|ccccc|ccc} & \vdots & & & \vdots & & \vdots & & \vdots & & \vdots \\ \ldots & \text{W} & \ldots & \ldots & \text{L} & \ldots & \text{W} & \ldots & \text{E} & \ldots & \text{E} \\ & \vdots & & & \vdots & & \vdots & & \vdots & & \vdots \end{array}\right] \end{array} \tag{24}$$

Next, let $\mathbf{A}_i$ be the block with d rows and $N = \ell + n + d$ columns described in (25), for every $i = 1, \ldots, n$. All entries corresponding to the faithfulness constraints are equal to E. All entries corresponding to the the markedness constraints $M_1, \ldots, M_n$ are equal to E, but for those in the column corresponding to M_i, that are instead equal to W. All entries corresponding to the ballast constraints $M'_1, \ldots, M'_d$ are equal to E, but for the diagonal entries that are instead equal to L.

$$\begin{array}{c} F_1\ \cdots\ F_\ell \quad M_1\ \cdots\ M_i\ \cdots\ M_n \quad M'_1\ \cdots\ M'_d \\ \left[\begin{array}{ccc|c|ccc} \text{E} & \ldots & \text{E} & \text{W} & \text{L} & & \\ \vdots & & \vdots & | & & \diagdown & \\ \text{E} & \ldots & \text{E} & \text{W} & & & \text{L} \end{array}\right] \end{array} \tag{25}$$

Finally, let the comparative tableau $\mathbf{A}$ be obtained by ordering the $n + 1$ blocks $\overline{\mathbf{A}}, \mathbf{A}_1, \ldots, \mathbf{A}_n$ one underneath the other, as in (26). Before I turn to the details, let me present the intuition behind the

[7] Note that, in order for the latter claim to hold, it is crucial that P be a multiset, namely that the same pair might be counted twice. In fact, T might contain two different triplets that share some elements, such as (a, b, c) and (a, b, d).

definitions (21)-(26).

$$
\begin{array}{r}
\\ \\ \\ \mathbf{A}_1 \\ \\ \\ \\ \mathbf{A}_n \\ \\
\end{array}
\begin{array}{c|c|c}
\multicolumn{3}{c}{F_1 \ \dots \ F_\ell \quad M_1 \ \dots \ M_n \quad M'_1 \ \dots \ M'_d} \\
\hline
\multicolumn{3}{c}{\overline{\mathbf{A}}} \\
\hline
\mathrm{E} \dots \mathrm{E} & \mathrm{W} \qquad\quad & \mathrm{L} \qquad\quad \\
\vdots \quad \vdots & \mid \qquad\quad & \qquad \diagdown \\
\mathrm{E} \dots \mathrm{E} & \mathrm{W} \qquad\quad & \qquad\quad \mathrm{L} \\
\hline
\vdots & \vdots & \vdots \\
\hline
\mathrm{E} \dots \mathrm{E} & \qquad\quad \mathrm{W} & \mathrm{L} \qquad\quad \\
\vdots \quad \vdots & \qquad\quad \mid & \qquad \diagdown \\
\mathrm{E} \dots \mathrm{E} & \qquad\quad \mathrm{W} & \qquad\quad \mathrm{L}
\end{array}
\qquad (26)
$$

Since the markedness constraints $M_1, \dots, M_n$ correspond to the elements $a_1, \dots, a_n$ of A, a linear order π over A defines a ranking $\gg$ of the markedness constraint $M_1, \dots, M_n$ as in (27), and viceversa. Thus, π is linearly compatible with a pair $(a_i, a_j) \in P$ iff the row of the block $\overline{\mathbf{A}}$ in (24) corresponding to that pair is accounted for by ranking M_j above M_i, with no need for the corresponding faithfulness constraint $F_{(i,j)}$ to do any work. Suppose instead that M_j is not ranked above M_i, so that the corresponding faithfulness constraint $F_{(i,j)}$ needs to be ranked above M_i in order to protect its L. What consequences does this fact have for the measure μ_{PT} in (13)? Without the ballast constraints $M'_1, \dots, M'_d$, not much: all I could conclude is that the faithfulness constraint $F_{(i,j)}$ has at least the two markedness constraints M_i and M_j ranked below it. The ballast markedness constraints $M'_1, \dots, M'_d$ ensure a more dramatic effect. In fact, the block $\mathbf{A}_i$ forces each of them to be ranked below M_i. Thus, if the faithfulness constraint $F_{(i,j)}$ needs to be ranked above M_i, then it also needs to be ranked above all the ballast markedness constraints $M'_1, \dots, M'_d$. If the number d of these ballast constraints is large enough, as in (21), then the corresponding effect on the measure μ_{PT} in (13) is rather dramatic.

$$M_j \gg M_i \iff \pi(a_j) > \pi(a_i) \qquad (27)$$

Assume that the given instance (A, P, k) of MOpbm admits a positive answer. Thus, there exists a multitset S of k pairs of P that is compatible with a linear order π on A. Consider a ranking $\gg$ over the constraint set (23) that satisfies the conditions in (28): $\gg$ assigns the k faithfulness constraints $F_{(i,j)}$ that correspond to pairs in S to the k bottom strata, in any order; $\gg$ assigns the d ballast markedness constraints $M'_1, \dots, M'_d$ to the next d strata, in any order; $\gg$ assigns the n markedness constraints $M_1, \dots, M_n$ to the next n strata, ordered according to π through (27); finally, $\gg$ assigns the remaining $\ell - k$ faithfulness constraints $F_{(i,j)}$ that correspond to pairs in $P \setminus S$ to the top $\ell - k$ strata, in any order.

$$
\begin{array}{c}
\{F_{(i,j)} \mid (a_i, a_j) \notin S\} \\
\mid \\
M_{\pi^{-1}(n)} \\
\mid \\
\vdots \\
\mid \\
M_{\pi^{-1}(1)} \\
\mid \\
\{M'_1, \dots, M'_d\} \\
\mid \\
\{F_{(i,j)} \mid (a_i, a_j) \in S\}
\end{array}
\qquad (28)
$$

This ranking $\gg$ is OT-compatible with the comparative tableau $\mathbf{A}$ in (26). In fact, it is OT-compatible with the n blocks $\mathbf{A}_1, \dots, \mathbf{A}_n$ in (25), since the markedness constraints $M_1, \dots, M_n$ are $\gg$-ranked above the ballast markedness constraints $M'_1, \dots, M'_d$. It is OT-compatible with each row of the block $\overline{\mathbf{A}}$ in (24) that corresponds to a pair $(a_i, a_j) \notin S$, since the corresponding faithfulness constraint $F_{(i,j)}$ is $\gg$-ranked above the corresponding markedness constraints M_i. Finally, it is OT-compatible with each row of the block $\overline{\mathbf{A}}$ that corresponds to a pair $(a_i, a_j) \in S$, since $\pi(a_j) > \pi(a_i)$ and thus $M_j \gg M_i$ by (27). The measure $\mu_{\text{PT}}(\gg)$ of the ranking $\gg$ is (29): in fact, the faithfulness constraints $F_{(i,j)}$ corresponding to pairs $(a_i, a_j) \in S$ have no markedness constraints $\gg$-ranked below them; and each one of the $\ell - k$ faithfulness constraints $F_{(i,j)}$ corresponding to pairs $(a_i, a_j) \notin S$ has all the $n + d$ markedness constraints $\gg$-ranked below it. In conclusion, the instance $(\mathbf{A}, \mathcal{F}, K)$ of the PTAPpbm constructed in (21)-(26) admits a positive answer.

$$\mu_{\text{PT}}(\gg) = (\ell - k)(n + d) = K \qquad (29)$$

Vice versa, assume that the instance $(\mathbf{A}, \mathcal{F}, K)$ of the PTAPpbm constructed in (21)-(26) admits a positive answer. Thus, there exists a ranking $\gg$ over the constraint set (23) OT-compatible with the tableau $\mathbf{A}$ in (26) such that $\mu_{\text{PT}}(\gg) \leq K$. Consider the multiset $S \subseteq P$ defined in (30). Clearly, S is compatible with the linear order π univocally defined on $A = \{a_1, \dots, a_n\}$ through (27).

$$S = \Big\{(a_i, a_j) \in P \,\Big|\, M_j \gg M_i\Big\} \qquad (30)$$

To prove that the given instance (A, P, k) of the MOpbm has a positive answer, I thus only need to show that $|S| \geq k$. Assume by contradiction that $|S| < k$. I can then compute as in (31). In step (31a), I have used the definition (22) of the threshold K. In step (31b), I have used the hypothesis that the ranking $\gg$ is a solution of the instance $(\mathbf{A}, \mathcal{F}, K)$ of the PTAPpbm and thus its mesure μ_{PT} does not exceed K. By (13), $\mu_{\text{PT}}(\gg)$ is the total number of pairs of a faithfulness constraint and a markedness constraint such that the former is $\gg$-ranked above the latter. In step (31c), I have thus lower bounded $\mu_{\text{PT}}(\gg)$ by only considering those faithfulness constraints $F_{(i,j)}$ corresponding to pairs (a_i, a_j) not in S. For each such constraint $F_{(i,j)}$, we have $M_i \gg M_j$, by the definition (30) of S. Thus, $F_{(i,j)}$ needs to be $\gg$-ranked above M_i in order to ensure OT-compatibility with the corresponding row of the block $\overline{\mathbf{A}}$ in (24). Since M_i needs to be $\gg$-ranked above the d ballast constraints $M'_1, \ldots, M'_d$ in order to ensure OT-compatibility with the block $\mathbf{A}_i$ in (25), then $F_{(i,j)}$ needs to be $\gg$-ranked above those d ballast markedness constraints too. In conclusion, each faithfulness constraint $F_{(i,j)}$ corresponding to a pair (a_i, a_j) not in S needs to be $\gg$-ranked at least above d markedness constraints. Since there are $\ell - |S|$ such faithfulness constraint $F_{(i,j)}$ corresponding to a pair $(a_i, a_j) \notin S$, then we get the inequality in (31d). In step (31e), I have used the absurd hypothesis that $|S| < k$ or equivalently that $|S| \leq k - 1$. The chain of inequalities in (31) entails that $d \leq (\ell - k)n$, which contradicts the choice (21) of the number d of ballast constraints.

$$\begin{aligned}
&(\ell - k)d + (\ell - k)n \\
&\overset{(a)}{=} K \\
&\overset{(b)}{\geq} \mu_{\text{PT}}(\gg) \overset{(13)}{=} |\{(F_{(i,j)}, M) \mid F_{(i,j)} \gg M\}| \\
&\overset{(c)}{\geq} |\{(F_{(i,j)}, M) \mid F_{(i,j)} \gg M,\ (a_i, a_j) \notin S\}| \\
&\overset{(d)}{=} (\ell - |S|)d \\
&\overset{(e)}{\geq} (\ell - (k-1))d \\
&= (\ell - k)d + d
\end{aligned} \tag{31}$$

The preceding considerations show that given an arbitrary instance (A, P, k) of the MOpbm (18), the corresponding instance $(\mathbf{A}, \mathcal{F}, K)$ of the PTAPpbm (17) defined in (21)-(26) admits a positive solution iff the original instance (A, P, k) of the MOpbm does. I conclude that the MOpbm can be reduced to the PTAPpbm. ■

Let me now turn to the APpbm (11). Once again, in order to show that it is intractable, it is sufficient to show that the corresponding decision problem (32) is intractable. In fact, if problem (11) can be solved, then (32) can be solved too: given an instance of the latter, find a solution $\gg$ of the corresponding instance of the problem (11) and then just check whether $|\mathcal{L}(\gg)| \leq k$.[8] From now on, I will refer to (32) as the APpbm.

(32)

given: univ. specs $(\mathcal{X}, \mathcal{Y}, Gen, \mathcal{C})$,
an OT-comp. data set $\mathcal{D} \subseteq \mathcal{X} \times \mathcal{Y}$,
an integer k;

output: "yes" iff there is a ranking $\gg$ OT-comp. with $\mathcal{D}$ s.t. the corresponding language $\mathcal{L}(\gg)$ has cardinality at most k;

size: $\max\{|\mathcal{C}|, |\mathcal{X}|, \mathit{width}(\mathcal{X})\}$.

The APpbm (32) is clearly in $\mathcal{NP}$, namely it admits a verification algorithm. The following claim 5 together with the NP-completeness of PTAPpbm, entails that the APpbm is NP-complete too, thus completing the proof of claim 2.

Claim 5 *The PTAPpbm (17) can be reduced to the APpbm (32).*

Proof. Given an instance $(\mathbf{A}, \mathcal{F}, k)$ of the PTAPpbm (17), construct the corresponding instance $((\mathcal{X}, \mathcal{Y}, Gen, \mathcal{C}), \mathcal{D}, K)$ of the APpbm (32) as follows. Let m and n be the number of rows and of columns of the comparative tableau $\mathbf{A}$; let ℓ be the cardinality of the set $\mathcal{F}$; let $d = \ell(n - \ell)$. Define the threshold K as in (33).

$$K = m + k + d \tag{33}$$

Define the sets $\mathcal{X}$ and $\mathcal{Y}$ of underlying and surface forms as in (34).

$$\mathcal{X} = \underbrace{\{x_1, \ldots, x_m\}}_{\mathcal{X}_1} \cup \underbrace{\{x'_1, \ldots, x'_d\}}_{\mathcal{X}_2} \cup \underbrace{\{x''_1, \ldots, x''_d\}}_{\mathcal{X}_3}$$

$$\mathcal{Y} = \underbrace{\begin{Bmatrix} y_1, \ldots, y_m \\ z_1, \ldots, z_m \end{Bmatrix}}_{\mathcal{Y}_1} \cup \underbrace{\begin{Bmatrix} u_1, \ldots, u_d \\ v_1, \ldots, v_d \end{Bmatrix}}_{\mathcal{Y}_2} \cup \underbrace{\begin{Bmatrix} u_1, \ldots, u_d \\ w_1, \ldots, w_d \end{Bmatrix}}_{\mathcal{Y}_3} \tag{34}$$

[8] The generous dependence of the size of the APpbm (11) on $|\mathcal{X}|$ and $\mathit{width}(\mathcal{X})$ provides us with sufficient time to trivially compute the language $\mathcal{L}(\gg)$.

Define the generating function Gen as in (35).

$$\begin{aligned} Gen(x_i) &= \{y_i, z_i\} \subseteq \mathcal{Y}_1 && \text{for } x_i \in \mathcal{X}_1 \\ Gen(x_i') &= \{u_i, v_i\} \subseteq \mathcal{Y}_2 && \text{for } x_i' \in \mathcal{X}_2 \\ Gen(x_i'') &= \{u_i, w_i\} \subseteq \mathcal{Y}_3 && \text{for } x_i'' \in \mathcal{X}_3 \end{aligned} \tag{35}$$

Define the data set $\mathcal{D}$ as in (36).

$$\mathcal{D} = \{(x_1, y_1), \ldots, (x_m, y_m)\} \tag{36}$$

Let the constraint set $\mathcal{C}$ contain a total of n constraints $C_1, \ldots, C_n$; let C_h be a faithfulness constraint iff $h \in \mathcal{F}$, and a markedness constraint otherwise. Since, $Gen(\mathcal{X}_i) \subseteq \mathcal{Y}_i$, constraints need only be defined on $\mathcal{X}_i \times \mathcal{Y}_j$ with $i = j$. The set $\mathcal{X}_1$ contains m underlying forms $x_1, \ldots x_m$, one for every row of the given comparative tableau $\mathbf{A}$. Each of these underlying forms x_i comes with the two candidates y_i and z_i. The data set $\mathcal{D}$ in (36) is a subset of $\mathcal{X}_1 \times \mathcal{Y}_1$. Define the constraints $C_1, \ldots, C_n$ over $\mathcal{X}_1 \times \mathcal{Y}_1$ as in (37). This definition ensures that $\mathbf{A}$ is the comparative tableau corresponding to $\mathcal{D}$, so that (40) holds for any ranking.

$$\gg \text{ is OT-comp. with } \mathbf{A} \text{ iff } \gg \text{ is OT-comp. with } \mathcal{D} \tag{40}$$

The set $\mathcal{X}_2$ contains a total of $d = \ell(n - \ell)$ underlying forms $x_1', \ldots, x_2'$, one for every pair of a faithfulness constraint and a markedness constraint. Pair up (in some arbitrary but fixed way) each of these underlying forms with a unique pair of a faithfulness constraint and a markedness constraint. Thus, I can speak of "the" markedness constraint and "the" faithfulness constraint "corresponding" to a given underlying form $x_i' \in \mathcal{X}_2$. Each of these underlying forms x_i' comes with two candidates u_i and v_i. Define the constraints $C_1, \ldots, C_n$ over $\mathcal{X}_2 \times \mathcal{Y}_2$ as in (38). This definition ensures that the grammar $\mathsf{OT}_{\gg}$ corresponding to an arbitrary ranking $\gg$ maps x_i' to v_i rather than to u_i iff the faithfulness constraint corresponding to the underlying form x_i' is $\gg$-ranked above the markedness constraint corresponding to x_i'. Since $\mu_{\mathrm{PT}}(\gg)$ is defined in (13) as the total number of pairs of a faithfulness and a markedness constraint such that the former is ranked above the latter, then condition (41) holds for any ranking.

$$\mu_{\mathrm{PT}}(\gg) = |\{x_i' \in \mathcal{X}_2 \mid \mathsf{OT}_{\gg}(x_i') = v_i\}| \tag{41}$$

Finally, define the constraints $C_1, \ldots, C_n$ over $\mathcal{X}_3 \times \mathcal{Y}_3$ as in (38). This definition ensures that the forms $u_1, \ldots, u_d$ are *unmarked* — as the forms [ta] and [rat] in the typology in (1). Thus, they belong to the language corresponding to any ranking $\gg$, as stated in (42).

$$\{u_1, \ldots, u_d\} \subseteq \mathcal{L}(\gg) \tag{42}$$

Assume that the instance $(\mathbf{A}, \mathcal{F}, k)$ of the PTAPpbm admits a positive answer. Thus, there exists a ranking $\gg$ OT-compatible with the comparative tableau $\mathbf{A}$ such that $\mu_{\mathrm{PT}}(\gg) \leq k$. Since $\gg$ is OT-compatible with $\mathbf{A}$, then $\gg$ is OT-compatible with $\mathcal{D}$, by (40). Furthermore, the language $\mathcal{L}(\gg)$ corresponding to the ranking $\gg$ contains at most $K = m + k + d$ surface forms, namely: the m surface forms $y_1, \ldots, y_m \in \mathcal{Y}_1$, because $\gg$ is OT-compatible with $\mathcal{D}$; the d surface forms $u_1, \ldots, u_d$, by (42); and at most k of the surface forms $v_1, \ldots, v_d$, by (41) and the hypothesis that $\mu_{\mathrm{PT}}(\gg) \leq k$. Thus, $\gg$ is a solution of the instance $((\mathcal{X}, \mathcal{Y}, Gen, \mathcal{C}), \mathcal{D}, K)$ of the APpbm (32) constructed in (33)-(39). The same reasoning shows that the vice versa holds too. ■

Acknowledgments

I wish to thank A. Albright for endless (and ongoing) discussion on the problem of the acquisition of phonotactics. This work was supported in part by a 'Euryi' grant from the European Science Foundation to P. Schlenker.

$$\begin{aligned} C_h(x_i, y_i) < C_h(x_i, z_i) &\iff \text{the } k\text{th entry in the } i\text{th row of } \mathbf{A} \text{ is a W} \\ C_h(x_i, y_i) = C_h(x_i, z_i) &\iff \text{the } k\text{th entry in the } i\text{th row of } \mathbf{A} \text{ is a E} \\ C_h(x_i, y_i) > C_h(x_i, z_i) &\iff \text{the } k\text{th entry in the } i\text{th row of } \mathbf{A} \text{ is a L} \end{aligned} \tag{37}$$

$$\begin{aligned} C_h(x_i', v_i) &< C_h(x_i', u_i) && \text{if } C_h \text{ is the faithfulness constraint corresponding to } x_i' \\ C_h(x_i', v_i) &> C_h(x_i', u_i) && \text{if } C_h \text{ is the markedness constraint corresponding to } x_i' \\ C_h(x_i', v_i) &= C_h(x_i', u_i) && \text{otherwise} \end{aligned} \tag{38}$$

$$C_h(x_i', u_i) \leq C_h(x_i', w_i) \quad \text{for every constraint } C_h \tag{39}$$

References

Robert Berwick. 1985. *The acquisition of syntactic knowledge*. MIT Press, Cambridge, MA.

W. Cohen, William, Robert E. Schapire, and Yoram Singer. 1999. Learning to order things. *Journal of Artificial Intelligence Research*, 10:243–270.

Jason Eisner. 2000. "Easy and Hard Constraint Ranking in Optimality Theory". In J. Eisner, L. Karttunen, and A. Thériault, editors, *Finite-State Phonology: Proceedings of the Fifth Workshop of the ACL Special Interest Group in Computational Phonology (SIGPHON)*, pages 22–33, Luxembourg.

Zvi Galil and Nimrod Megiddo. 1977. "Cyclic Ordering is NP-complete". *Theoretical Computer Science*, 5:179–182.

Michael R. Garey and David S. Johnson. 1979. *Computers and Intractability. A Guide to the Theory of NP-Completeness*. W. H. Freeman and Company, New York.

Bruce Hayes. 2004. "Phonological Acquisition in Optimality Theory: The Early Stages". In R. Kager, J. Pater, and W. Zonneveld, editors, *Constraints in Phonological Acquisition*, pages 158–203. Cambridge University Press.

Jeffrey Heinz, Gregory M. Kobele, and Jason Riggle. 2009. "Evaluating the Complexity of Optimality Theory". *Linguistic Inquiry*, 40:277–288.

Géraldine Legendre, Yoshiro Miyata, and Paul Smolensky. 1990a. "Harmonic Grammar: A formal multi-level connectionist theory of linguistic well-formedness: An application". In *Proceedings of the twelfth annual conference of the Cognitive Science Society*, pages 884–891, Cambridge, MA. Lawrence Erlbaum.

Géraldine Legendre, Yoshiro Miyata, and Paul Smolensky. 1990b. "Harmonic Grammar: A formal multi-level connectionist theory of linguistic well-formedness: Theoretical foundations". In *Proceedings of the twelfth annual conference of the Cognitive Science Society*, pages 388–395, Cambridge, MA. Lawrence Erlbaum.

M. Rita Manzini and Ken Wexler. 1987. "Parameters, Binding Theory, and Learnability". *Linguistic Inquiry*, 18.3:413–444.

Alan Prince and Paul Smolensky. 2004. *Optimality Theory: Constraint Interaction in Generative Grammar*. Blackwell. As Technical Report CU-CS-696-93, Department of Computer Science, University of Colorado at Boulder, and Technical Report TR-2, Rutgers Center for Cognitive Science, Rutgers University, New Brunswick, NJ, April 1993. Rutgers Optimality Archive 537 version, 2002.

Alan Prince and Bruce Tesar. 2004. "Learning Phonotactic Distributions". In R. Kager, J. Pater, and W. Zonneveld, editors, *Constraints in Phonological Acquisition*, pages 245–291. Cambridge University Press.

Bruce Tesar and Paul Smolensky. 1998. "Learnability in Optimality Theory". *Linguistic Inquiry*, 29:229–268.

Harold Todd Wareham. 1998. *Systematic Parameterized Complexity Analysis in Computational Phonology*. Ph.D. thesis, University of Victoria, Dept. of Computer Science.

Maximum Likelihood Estimation of Feature-based Distributions

Jeffrey Heinz and Cesar Koirala
University of Delaware
Newark, Delaware, USA
{heinz,koirala}@udel.edu

Abstract

Motivated by recent work in phonotactic learning (Hayes and Wilson 2008, Albright 2009), this paper shows how to define feature-based probability distributions whose parameters can be provably efficiently estimated. The main idea is that these distributions are defined as a product of simpler distributions (cf. Ghahramani and Jordan 1997). One advantage of this framework is it draws attention to what is minimally necessary to describe and learn phonological feature interactions in phonotactic patterns. The "bottom-up" approach adopted here is contrasted with the "top-down" approach in Hayes and Wilson (2008), and it is argued that the bottom-up approach is more analytically transparent.

1 Introduction

The hypothesis that the atomic units of phonology are phonological features, and not segments, is one of the tenets of modern phonology (Jakobson et al., 1952; Chomsky and Halle, 1968). According to this hypothesis, segments are essentially epiphenomenal and exist only by virtue of being a shorthand description of a collection of more primitive units—the features. Incorporating this hypothesis into phonological learning models has been the focus of much influential work (Gildea and Jurafsky, 1996; Wilson, 2006; Hayes and Wilson, 2008; Moreton, 2008; Albright, 2009).

This paper makes three contributions. The first contribution is a framework within which:

1. researchers can choose which statistical independence assumptions to make regarding phonological features;
2. feature systems can be fully integrated into strictly local (McNaughton and Papert, 1971) (i.e. n-gram models (Jurafsky and Martin, 2008)) and strictly piecewise models (Rogers et al., 2009; Heinz and Rogers, 2010) in order to define families of provably well-formed, feature-based probability distributions that are provably efficiently estimable.

The main idea is to define a family of distributions as the normalized product of simpler distributions. Each simpler distribution can be represented by a Probabilistic Deterministic Finite Acceptor (PDFA), and the product of these PDFAs defines the actual distribution. When a family of distributions $\mathcal{F}$ is defined in this way, $\mathcal{F}$ may have many fewer parameters than if $\mathcal{F}$ is defined over the product PDFA directly. This is because the parameters of the distributions are defined in terms of the factors which combine in predictable ways via the product. Fewer parameters means accurate estimation occurs with less data and, relatedly, the family contains fewer distributions.

This idea is not new. It is explicit in Factorial Hidden Markov Models (FHMMs) (Ghahramani and Jordan, 1997; Saul and Jordan, 1999), and more recently underlies approaches to describing and inferring regular string transductions (Dreyer et al., 2008; Dreyer and Eisner, 2009). Although HMMs and probabilistic finite-state automata describe the same class of distributions (Vidal et al., 2005a; Vidal et al., 2005b), this paper presents these ideas in formal language-theoretic and automata-theoretic terms because (1) there are no hidden states and is thus simpler than FHMMs, (2) determinstic automata have several desirable properties crucially used here, and (3) PDFAs add probabilities to structure whereas HMMs add structure to probabilities and the authors are more comfortable with the former perspective (for further discussion, see Vidal et al. (2005a,b)).

The second contribution illustrates the main idea with a feature-based bigram model with a

Proceedings of the 11th Meeting of the ACL-SIGMORPHON, ACL 2010, pages 28–37,
Uppsala, Sweden, 15 July 2010.

strong statistical independence assumption: no two features interact. This is shown to capture exactly the intuition that sounds with like features have like distributions. Also, the assumption of non-interacting features is shown to be too strong because like sounds do not have like distributions in actual phonotactic patterns. Four kinds of featural interactions are identified and possible solutions are discussed.

Finally, we compare this proposal with Hayes and Wilson (2008). Essentially, the model here represents a "bottom-up" approach whereas theirs is "top-down." "Top-down" models, which consider every set of features as potentially interacting in every allowable context, face the difficult problem of searching a vast space and often resort to heuristic-based methods, which are difficult to analyze. To illustrate, we suggest that the role played by phonological features in the phonotactic learner in Hayes and Wilson (2008) is not well-understood. We demonstrate that classes of all segments but one (i.e. the complement classes of single segments) play a significant role, which diminishes the contribution provided by natural classes themselves (i.e. ones made by phonological features). In contrast, the proposed model here is analytically transparent.

This paper is organized as follows. §2 reviews some background. §3 discusses bigram models and §4 defines feature systems and feature-based distributions. §5 develops a model with a strong independence assumption and §6 discusses featural interaction. §7 dicusses Hayes and Wilson (2008) and §8 concludes.

2 Preliminaries

We start with mostly standard notation. $\mathcal{P}(A)$ is the powerset of A. Σ denotes a finite set of symbols and a string over Σ is a finite sequence of these symbols. Σ^+ and Σ^* denote all strings over this alphabet of nonzero but finite length, and of any finite length, respectively. A function f with domain A and codomain B is written $f : A \rightarrow B$. When discussing partial functions, the notation $\uparrow$ and $\downarrow$ indicate for particular arguments whether the function is undefined and defined, respectively.

A *language* L is a subset of Σ^*. A *stochastic language* $\mathcal{D}$ is a probability distribution over Σ^*. The probability p of word w with respect to $\mathcal{D}$ is written $Pr_{\mathcal{D}}(w) = p$. Recall that all distributions $\mathcal{D}$ must satisfy $\sum_{w \in \Sigma^*} Pr_{\mathcal{D}}(w) = 1$. If L is language then $Pr_{\mathcal{D}}(L) = \sum_{w \in L} Pr_{\mathcal{D}}(w)$. Since all distributions in this paper are stochastic languages, we use the two terms interchangeably.

A *Probabilistic Deterministic Finite-state Automaton* (PDFA) is a tuple $\mathcal{M} = \langle Q, \Sigma, q_0, \delta, F, T \rangle$ where Q is the state set, Σ is the alphabet, q_0 is the start state, δ is a deterministic transition function, F and T are the final-state and transition probabilities. In particular, $T : Q \times \Sigma \rightarrow \mathbb{R}^+$ and $F : Q \rightarrow \mathbb{R}^+$ such that

$$\text{for all } q \in Q,\ F(q) + \sum_{\sigma \in \Sigma} T(q, \sigma) = 1. \quad (1)$$

PDFAs are typically represented as labeled directed graphs (e.g. $\mathcal{M}'$ in Figure 1).

A PDFA $\mathcal{M}$ generates a stochastic language $\mathcal{D}_{\mathcal{M}}$. If it exists, the (unique) *path* for a word $w = a_0 \ldots a_k$ belonging to Σ^* through a PDFA is a sequence $\langle (q_0, a_0), (q_1, a_1), \ldots, (q_k, a_k) \rangle$, where $q_{i+1} = \delta(q_i, a_i)$. The probability a PDFA assigns to w is obtained by multiplying the transition probabilities with the final probability along w's path if it exists, and zero otherwise.

$$Pr_{\mathcal{D}_{\mathcal{M}}}(w) = \left(\prod_{i=0}^{k} T(q_i, a_i) \right) \cdot F(q_{k+1}) \quad (2)$$

$$\text{if } \hat{d}(q_0, w)\downarrow \text{ and } 0 \text{ otherwise}$$

A stochastic language is *regular deterministic* iff there is a PDFA which generates it.

The *structural components* of a PDFA $\mathcal{M}$ is the deterministic finite-state automata (DFA) given by the states Q, alphabet Σ, transitions δ, and initial state q_0 of $\mathcal{M}$. By the *structure* of a PDFA, we mean its structural components.[1] Each PDFA $\mathcal{M}$ defines a family of distributions given by the possible instantiations of T and F satisfying Equation 1. These distributions have at most $|Q| \cdot (|\Sigma| + 1)$ parameters (since for each state there are $|\Sigma|$ possible transitions plus the possibility of finality.) These are, for all $q \in Q$ and $\sigma \in \Sigma$, the probabilities $T(q, \sigma)$ and $F(q)$. To make the connection to probability theory, we sometimes write these as $Pr(\sigma \mid q)$ and $Pr(\# \mid q)$, respectively.

We define the product of PDFAs in terms of *co-emission probabilities* (Vidal et al., 2005a). Let $\mathcal{M}_1 = \langle Q_1, \Sigma_1, q_{01}, \delta_1, F_1, T_1 \rangle$ and $\mathcal{M}_2 =$

[1] This is up to the renaming of states so PDFA with isomorphic structural components are said to have the same structure.

$\langle Q_2, \Sigma_2, q_{02}, \delta_2, F_2, T_2 \rangle$ be PDFAs. The probability that σ_1 is emitted from $q_1 \in Q_1$ at the same moment σ_2 is emitted from $q_2 \in Q_2$ is $CT(\sigma_1, \sigma_2, q_1, q_2) = T_1(q_1, \sigma_1) \cdot T_2(q_2, \sigma_2)$. Similarly, the probability that a word simultaneously ends at $q_1 \in Q_1$ and at $q_2 \in Q_2$ is $CF(q_1, q_2) = F_1(q_1) \cdot F_2(q_2)$.

Definition 1 *The* normalized co-emission product *of PDFAs $\mathcal{M}_1$ and $\mathcal{M}_2$ is $\mathcal{M} = \mathcal{M}_1 \times \mathcal{M}_2 = \langle Q, \Sigma, q_0, \delta, F, T \rangle$ where*

1. *Q, q_0, and F are defined in terms of the standard DFA product over the state space $Q_1 \times Q_2$ (Hopcroft et al., 2001).*

2. *$\Sigma = \Sigma_1 \times \Sigma_2$*

3. *For all $\langle q_1, q_2 \rangle \in Q$ and $\langle \sigma_1, \sigma_2 \rangle \in \Sigma$, $\delta(\langle q_1, q_2 \rangle, \langle \sigma_1, \sigma_2 \rangle) = \langle q_1', q_2' \rangle$ iff $\delta_1(q_1, \sigma_1) = q_1'$ and $\delta_2(q_2, \sigma_2) = q_2'$.*[2]

4. *For all $\langle q_1, q_2 \rangle \in Q$,*

   (a) *let $Z(\langle q_1, q_2 \rangle) = CF(\langle q_1, q_2 \rangle) + \sum_{\langle \sigma_1, \sigma_2 \rangle \in \Sigma} CT(\sigma_1, \sigma_2, q_1, q_2)$ be the* normalization term*; and*

   (b) *$F(\langle q_1, q_2 \rangle) = \frac{CF(q_1, q_2)}{Z}$; and*

   (c) *for all $\langle \sigma_1, \sigma_2 \rangle \in \Sigma$, $T(\langle q_1, q_2 \rangle, \langle \sigma_1, \sigma_2 \rangle) = \frac{CT(\langle \sigma_1, \sigma_2, q_1, q_2 \rangle)}{Z}$*

In other words, the numerators of T and F are defined to be the co-emission probabilities, and division by Z ensures that $\mathcal{M}$ defines a well-formed probability distribution.[3] The normalized co-emission product effectively adopts a statistical independence assumption between the states of $\mathcal{M}_1$ and $\mathcal{M}_2$. If S is a list of PDFAs, we write $\bigotimes S$ for their product (note order of product is irrelevant up to renaming of the states).

The maximum likelihood (ML) estimation of regular deterministic distributions is a solved problem when the structure of the PDFA is known (Vidal et al., 2005a; Vidal et al., 2005b; de la Higuera, 2010). Let S be a finite sample of words drawn from a regular deterministic distribution $\mathcal{D}$. The problem is to estimate parameters T and F of $\mathcal{M}$ so that $\mathcal{D}_\mathcal{M}$ approaches $\mathcal{D}$ using the widely-adopted ML criterion (Equation 3).

$$(\hat{T}, \hat{F}) = \underset{T,F}{\text{argmax}} \left(\prod_{w \in S} Pr_\mathcal{M}(w) \right) \quad (3)$$

It is well-known that if $\mathcal{D}$ is generated by some PDFA $\mathcal{M}'$ with the same structural components as $\mathcal{M}$, then the *ML estimate of S with respect to $\mathcal{M}$* guarantees that $\mathcal{D}_\mathcal{M}$ approaches $\mathcal{D}$ as the size of S goes to infinity (Vidal et al., 2005a; Vidal et al., 2005b; de la Higuera, 2010).

Finding the ML estimate of a finite sample S with respect to $\mathcal{M}$ is simple provided $\mathcal{M}$ is deterministic with known structural components. Informally, the corpus is passed through the PDFA, and the paths of each word through the corpus are tracked to obtain counts, which are then normalized by state. Let $\mathcal{M} = \langle Q, \Sigma, \delta, q_0, F, T \rangle$ be the PDFA whose parameters F and T are to be estimated. For all states $q \in Q$ and symbols $\sigma \in \Sigma$, The ML estimation of the probability of $T(q, \sigma)$ is obtained by dividing the number of times this transition is used in parsing the sample S by the number of times state q is encountered in the parsing of S. Similarly, the ML estimation of $F(q)$ is obtained by calculating the relative frequency of state q being final with state q being encountered in the parsing of S. For both cases, the division is *normalizing*; i.e. it guarantees that there is a well-formed probability distribution at each state. Figure 1 illustrates the counts obtained for a machine $\mathcal{M}$ with sample $S = \{abca\}$.[4] Figure 1 shows a DFA with counts and the PDFA obtained after normalizing these counts.

3 Strictly local distributions

In formal language theory, *strictly k-local* languages occupy the bottom rung of a subregular hierarchy which makes distinctions on the basis of contiguous subsequences (McNaughton and Papert, 1971; Rogers and Pullum, to appear; Rogers et al., 2009). They are also the categorical counterpart to stochastic languages describable with n-gram models (where $n = k$) (Garcia et al., 1990; Jurafsky and Martin, 2008). Since stochastic languages are distributions, we refer to strictly k-local stochastic languages as strictly k-local distri-

[2]Note that restricting δ to cases when $\sigma_1 = \sigma_2$ obtains the standard definition of $\delta = \delta_1 \times \delta_2$ (Hopcroft et al., 2001). The reason we maintain two alphabets becomes clear in §4.

[3]$Z(\langle q_1, q_2 \rangle)$ is less than one whenever either $F_1(q_1)$ or $F_2(q_2)$ are neither zero nor one.

[4]Technically, $\mathcal{M}$ is neither a simple DFA or PDFA; rather, it has been called a Frequency DFA. We do not formally define them here, see de la Higuera (2010).

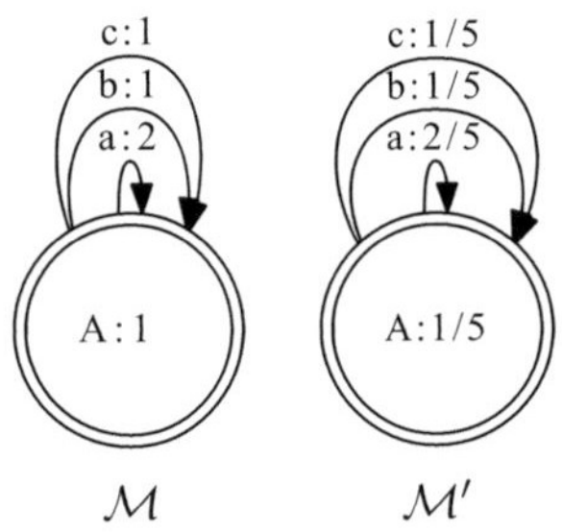

Figure 1: $\mathcal{M}$ shows the counts obtained by parsing it with sample $S = \{abca\}$. $\mathcal{M}'$ shows the probabilities obtained after normalizing those counts.

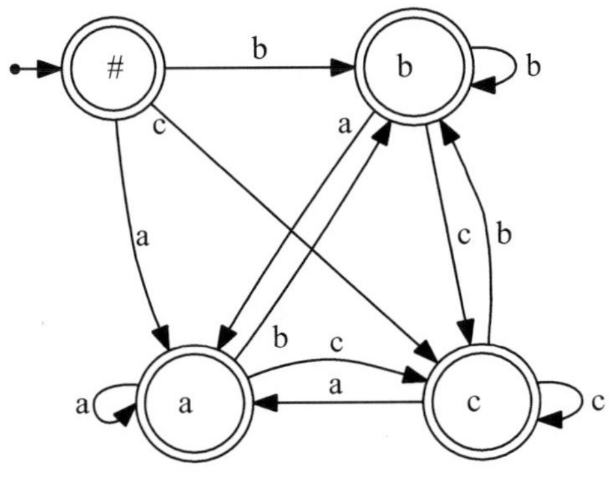

Figure 2: $\mathcal{M}_{\mathrm{SL}2}(\{a, b, c\})$ represents the structure of SL_2 distributions when $\Sigma = \{a, b, c\}$.

	F	G
a	+	-
b	+	+
c	-	+

Table 1: An example of a feature system with $\Sigma = \{a, b, c\}$ and two features F and G.

butions (SLD_k). We illustrate with SLD_2 (bigram models) for ease of exposition.

For an alphabet Σ, SL_2 distributions have $(|\Sigma| + 1)^2$ parameters. These are, for all $\sigma, \tau \in \Sigma \cup \{\#\}$, the probabilities $Pr(\sigma \mid \tau)$. The probability of $w = \sigma_1 \ldots \sigma_n$ is given in Equation 4.

$$Pr(w) \stackrel{\text{def}}{=} Pr(\sigma_1 \mid \#) \times Pr(\sigma_2 \mid \sigma_1) \times \ldots \times Pr(\# \mid \sigma_n) \quad (4)$$

PDFA representations of SL_2 distributions have the following structure: $Q = \Sigma \cup \{\#\}$, $q_0 = \#$, and for all $q \in Q$ and $\sigma \in \Sigma$, it is the case that $\delta(q, \sigma) = \sigma$.

As an example, the DFA in Figure 2 provides the structure of PDFAs which recognize SL_2 distributions with $\Sigma = \{a, b, c\}$. Plainly, the parameters of the model are given by assigning probabilities to each transition and to the ending at each state. In fact, for all $\sigma \in \Sigma$ and $\tau \in \Sigma \cup \{\#\}$, $Pr(\sigma \mid \tau)$ is $T(\tau, \sigma)$ and $Pr(\# \mid \tau)$ is $F(\tau)$. It follows that the probability of a particular path through the model corresponds to Equation 4. The structure of a SL_2 distribution for alphabet Σ is given by $\mathcal{M}_{\mathrm{SL}2}(\Sigma)$.

Additionally, given a finite sample $S \subset \Sigma^*$, the ML estimate of S with respect to the family of distributions describable with $\mathcal{M}_{\mathrm{SL}2}(\Sigma)$ is given by counting the parse of S through $\mathcal{M}_{\mathrm{SL}2}(\Sigma)$ and then normalizing as described in §2. This is equivalent to the procedure described in Jurafsky and Martin (2008, chap. 4).

4 Feature-based distributions

This section first introduces feature systems. Then it defines feature-based SL_2 distributions which make the strong independence assumption that no two features interact. It explains how to find the ML estimate of samples with respect to such distributions. This section closes by identifying kinds of featural interactions in phonotactic patterns, and discusses how such interactions can be addressed within this framework.

4.1 Feature systems

Assume the elements of the alphabet share properties, called features. For concreteness, let each feature be a total function $F : \Sigma \rightarrow \mathbb{V}_F$, where the codomain $\mathbb{V}_F$ is a finite set of *values*. A finite vector of features $\mathbb{F} = \langle F_1, \ldots, F_n \rangle$ is called a *feature system*. Table 1 provides an example of a feature system with $\mathbb{F} = \langle F, G \rangle$ and values $\mathbb{V}_F = \mathbb{V}_G = \{+, -\}$.

We extend the domain of all features $F \in \mathbb{F}$ to Σ^+, so that $F(\sigma_1 \ldots \sigma_n) = F(\sigma_1) \ldots F(\sigma_n)$. For example, using the feature system in Table 1, $F(abc) = + + -$ and $G(abc) = - + +$. We also extend the domain of F to all languages: $F(L) = \cup_{w \in L} f(w)$. We also extend the notation so that $\mathbb{F}(\sigma) = \langle F_1(\sigma), \ldots, F_n(\sigma) \rangle$. For example, $\mathbb{F}(c) = \langle -F, +G \rangle$ (feature indices are included for readability).

For feature $F : \Sigma \rightarrow \mathbb{V}_F$, let F^{-1} be the inverse function with domain V_F and codomain $\mathcal{P}(\Sigma)$. For example in Table 1, $G^{-1}(+) = \{b, c\}$. $\mathbb{F}^{-1}$ is similarly defined, i.e. $\mathbb{F}^{-1}(\langle -F, +G \rangle) = \{c\}$.

If, for all arguments $\vec{v}$, $\mathbb{F}^{-1}(\vec{v})$ is nonempty then the feature system is *exhaustive*. If, for all arguments $\vec{v}$ such that $\mathbb{F}^{-1}(\vec{v})$ is nonempty, it is the case that $|\mathbb{F}^{-1}(\vec{v})| = 1$ then the feature system is *distinctive*. E.g. the feature system in Table 1 in not exhaustive since $\mathbb{F}^{-1}(\langle -F, -G\rangle) = \emptyset$, but it is distinctive since where $\mathbb{F}^{-1}$ is nonempty, it picks out exactly one element of the alphabet.

Generally, phonological feature systems for a particular language are distinctive but not exhaustive. Any feature system $\mathbb{F}$ can be made exhaustive by adding finitely many symbols to the alphabet (since $\mathbb{F}$ is finite). Let Σ' denote an alphabet obtained by adding to Σ the fewest symbols which make $\mathbb{F}$ exhaustive.

Each feature system also defines a set of indicator functions $\mathbb{VF} = \bigcup_{f\in\mathbb{F}}(\mathbb{V}_f \times \{f\})$ with domain Σ such that $\langle v, f\rangle(\sigma) = 1$ iff $f(\sigma) = v$ and 0 otherwise. In the example in Table 1, $\mathbb{VF} = \{+F, -F, +G, -G\}$ (omitting angle braces for readability). For all $f \in \mathbb{F}$, the set $\mathbb{VF}_f$ is the $\mathbb{VF}$ restricted to f. So continuing our example, $\mathbb{VF}_F = \{+F, -F\}$.

4.2 Feature-based distributions

We now define feature-based SL_2 distributions under the strong independence assumption that no two features interact. For feature system $\mathbb{F} = \langle F_1 \dots F_n\rangle$, there are n PDFAs, one for each feature. The normalized co-emission product of these PDFAs essentially defines the distribution. For each F_i, the structure of its PDFA is given by $\mathcal{M}_{SL2}(\mathbb{V}_{F_i})$. For example, $\mathcal{M}_F = \mathcal{M}_{SL2}(\mathbb{V}_F)$ and $\mathcal{M}_G = \mathcal{M}_{SL2}(\mathbb{V}_G)$ in figures 3 and 4 illustrate the finite-state representation of feature-based SL_2 distributions given the feature system in Table 1.[5] The states of each machine make distinctions according to features F and G, respectively. The parameters of these distributions are given by assigning probabilities to each transition and to the ending at each state (except for $Pr(\# \mid \#)$).[6]

Thus there are $2|\mathbb{VF}| + \sum_{F\in\mathbb{F}} |\mathbb{VF}_F|^2 + 1$ parameters for feature-based SL_2 distributions. For example, the feature system in Table 1 defines a distribution with $2\cdot 4 + 2^2 + 2^2 + 1 = 17$ parameters, which include $Pr(\# \mid +F)$, $Pr(+F \mid \#)$, $Pr(+F \mid +F)$, $Pr(+F \mid -F), \dots$, the G equivalents, and $Pr(\# \mid \#)$. Let $SLD2_{\mathbb{F}}$ be the family of distributions given by all possible parameter settings (i.e. all possible probability assignments for each $\mathcal{M}_{SL2}(\mathbb{V}_{F_i})$ in accordance with Equation 1.)

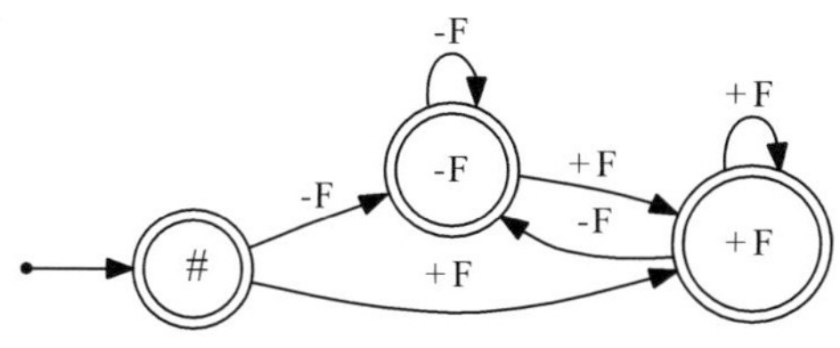

Figure 3: $\mathcal{M}_F$ represents a SL_2 distribution with respect to feature F.

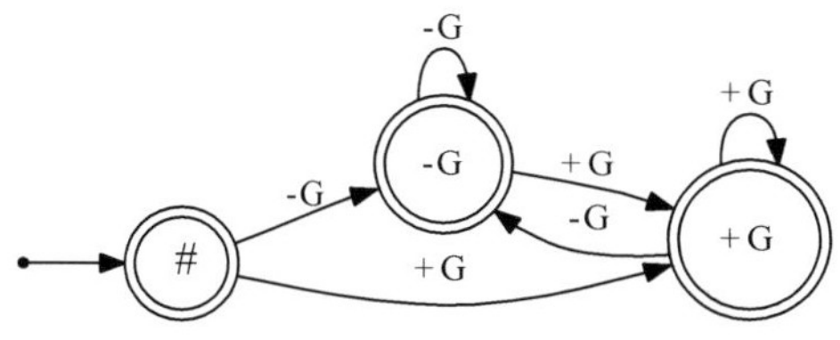

Figure 4: $\mathcal{M}_G$ represents a SL_2 distribution with respect to feature G.

The normalized co-emission product defines the feature-based distribution. For example, the structure of the product of $\mathcal{M}_F$ and $\mathcal{M}_G$ is shown in Figure 5.

As defined, the normalized co-emission product can result in states and transitions that cannot be interpreted by non-exhaustive feature systems. An example of this is in Figure 5 since $\langle -F, -G\rangle$ is not interpretable by the feature system in Table 1. We make the system exhaustive by letting $\Sigma' = \Sigma \cup \{d\}$ and setting $\mathbb{F}(d) = \langle -F, -G\rangle$.

What is the probability of a given b in the feature-based model? According to the normalized co-emission product (Defintion 1), it is

$$Pr(a \mid b) = Pr(\langle +F, -G\rangle \mid \langle +F, +G\rangle) = \frac{Pr(+F \mid +F)\cdot Pr(-G \mid +G)}{Z}$$

where $Z = Z(\langle +F, +G\rangle)$ equals

$$\sum_{\sigma\in\Sigma'} \Pr(F(\sigma) \mid +F)\cdot \Pr(G(\sigma) \mid +G)$$
$$+ (\Pr(\# \mid +F)\cdot \Pr(\# \mid +G)$$

Generally, for an *exhuastive* distinctive feature system $\mathbb{F} = \langle F_1, \dots, F_n\rangle$, and for all $\sigma, \tau \in \Sigma$,

[5] For readability, featural information in the states and transitions is included in these figures. By definition, the states and transitions are only labeled with elements of $\mathbb{V}_F$ and $\mathbb{V}_G$, respectively. In this case, that makes the structures of the two machines identical.

[6] It is possible to replace $Pr(\# \mid \#)$ with two parameters, $Pr(\# \mid \#_F)$ $Pr(\# \mid \#_G)$, but for ease of exposition we do not pursue this further.

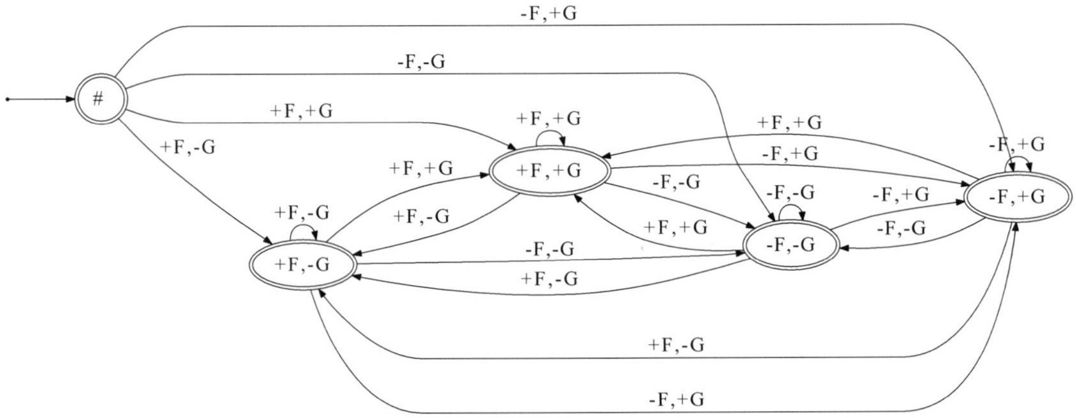

Figure 5: The structure of the product of $\mathcal{M}_F$ and $\mathcal{M}_G$.

the $Pr(\sigma \mid \tau)$ is given by Equation 5. First, the normalization term is provided. Let

$$Z(\tau) = \sum_{\sigma\in\Sigma} \left(\prod_{1\leq i\leq n} Pr(F_i(\sigma) \mid F_i(\tau)) \right) + \prod_{1\leq i\leq n} Pr(\# \mid F_i(\tau))$$

Then

$$Pr(\sigma \mid \tau) = \frac{\prod_{1\leq i\leq n} Pr(F_i(\sigma) \mid F_i(\tau))}{Z(\tau)} \quad (5)$$

The probabilities $Pr(\sigma \mid \#)$ and $Pr(\# \mid \tau)$ are similarly decomposed into featural parameters. Finally, like SL_2 distributions, the probability of a word $w \in \Sigma^*$ is given by Equation 4. We have thus proved the following.

Theorem 1 *The parameters of a feature-based* SL_2 *distribution define a well-formed probability distribution over* Σ^*.

Proof It is sufficient to show for all $\tau \in \Sigma \cup \{\#\}$ that $\sum_{\sigma\in\Sigma\cup\{\#\}} Pr(\sigma \mid \tau) = 1$ since in this case, Equation 4 yields a well-formed probability distribution over Σ^*. This follows directly from the definition of the normalized co-emission product (Definition 1). □

The normalized co-emission product adopts a statistical independence assumption, which here is between features since each machine represents a single feature. For example, consider $Pr(a \mid b) = Pr(\langle -F, +G\rangle \mid \langle +F, +G\rangle)$. The probability $Pr(\langle -F, +G\rangle \mid \langle +F, +G\rangle)$ cannot be arbitrarily different from the probabilities $Pr(-F \mid +F)$ and $Pr(+G \mid +G)$; it is not an independent parameter. In fact, because $Pr(a \mid b)$ is computed directly as the normalized product of parameters $Pr(-F \mid +F)$ and $Pr(+G \mid +G)$, the assumption is that the features F and G do not interact. In other words, this model describes exactly the state of affairs one expects if there is no statistical interaction between phonological features. In terms of inference, this means if one sound is observed to occur in some context (at least contexts distinguishable by SL_2 models), then similar sounds (i.e. those that share many of its featural values) are expected to occur in this context as well.

4.3 ML estimation

The ML estimate of feature-based SL_2 distributions is obtained by counting the parse of a sample through each feature machine, and normalizing the results. This is because the parameters of the distribution are the probabilities on the feature machines, whose product determines the actual distribution. The following theorem follows immediately from the PDFA representation of feature-based SL_2 distributions.

Theorem 2 *Let* $\mathbb{F} = \langle F_1, \ldots F_n\rangle$ *and let* $\mathcal{D}$ *be described by* $\mathcal{M} = \bigotimes_{1\leq i\leq n} \mathcal{M}_{\mathrm{SL2}}(\mathbb{V}_{Fi})$. *Consider a finite sample* S *drawn from* $\mathcal{D}$. *Then the ML estimate of* S *with respect to* $\mathrm{SLD2}_{\mathbb{F}}$ *is obtained by finding, for each* $F_i \in \mathbb{F}$, *the ML estimate of* $F_i(S)$ *with respect to* $\mathcal{M}_{\mathrm{SL2}}(\mathbb{V}_{Fi})$.

Proof The ML estimate of S with respect to $\mathrm{SLD2}_{\mathbb{F}}$ returns the parameter values that maximize the likelihood of S within the family $\mathrm{SLD2}_{\mathbb{F}}$. The parameters of $\mathcal{D} \in \mathrm{SLD2}_{\mathbb{F}}$ are found on the states of each $\mathcal{M}_{\mathrm{SL2}}(\mathbb{V}_{F_i})$. By definition, each $\mathcal{M}_{\mathrm{SL2}}(\mathbb{V}_{F_i})$ describes a probability distribution over $F_i(\Sigma^*)$, as well as a family of distributions. Therefore finding the MLE of S with respect to $\mathrm{SLD2}_{\mathbb{F}}$ means finding the MLE estimate of $F_i(S)$ with respect to each $\mathcal{M}_{\mathrm{SL2}}(\mathbb{V}_{F_i})$.

Optimizing the ML estimate of $F_i(S)$ for each $\mathcal{M}_i = \mathcal{M}_{\mathrm{SL2}}(\mathbb{V}_{F_i})$ means that as $|F_i(S)|$ increases, the estimates $\hat{T}_{\mathcal{M}_i}$ and $\hat{F}_{\mathcal{M}_i}$ approach the true values $T_{\mathcal{M}_i}$ and $F_{\mathcal{M}_i}$. It follows that as $|S|$ increases, $\hat{T}_{\mathcal{M}}$ and $\hat{F}_{\mathcal{M}}$ approach the true values of $T_{\mathcal{M}}$ and $F_{\mathcal{M}}$ and consequently $\mathcal{D}_{\mathcal{M}}$ approaches $\mathcal{D}$. □

4.4 Discussion

Feature-based models can have significantly fewer parameters than segment-based models. Consider binary feature systems, where $|\mathbb{VF}| = 2|\mathbb{F}|$. An exhaustive feature system with 10 binary features describes an alphabet with 1024 symbols. Segment-based bigram models have $(1024+1)^2 = 1,050,625$ parameters, but the feature-based one only has $40 + 40 + 1 = 81$ parameters! Consequently, much less training data is required to accurately estimate the parameters of the model.

Another way of describing this is in terms of expressivity. For given feature system, feature-based SL_2 distributions are a proper subset of SL_2 distributions since, as the the PDFA representations make clear, every feature-based distribution can be described by a segmental bigram model, but not vice versa. The fact that feature-based distributions have potentially far fewer parameters is a reflection of the restrictive nature of the model. The statistical independence assumption constrains the system in predictable ways. The next section shows exactly what feature-based generalization looks like under these assumptions.

5 Examples

This section demonstrates feature-based generalization by comparing it with segment-based generalization, using a small corpus $S = \{aaab, caca, acab, cbb\}$ and the feature system in Table 1. Tables 2 and 3 show the results of ML estimation of S with respect to segment-based SL_2 distributions (unsmoothed bigram model) and feature-based SL_2 distributions, respectively. Each table shows the $Pr(\sigma \mid \tau)$ for all $\sigma, \tau \in \{a, b, c, d, \#\}$ (where $\mathbb{F}(d) = \langle -F, -G \rangle$), for ease of comparison.

P(σ | τ)		σ				
		a	b	c	d	#
τ	a	0.29	0.29	0.29	0.	0.14
	b	0.	0.25	0.	0.	0.75
	c	0.75	0.25	0.	0.	0.
	d	0.	0.	0.	0.	0.
	#	0.5	0.	0.5	0.	0.

Table 2: ML estimates of parameters of segment-based SL_2 distributions.

P(σ | τ)		σ				
		a	b	c	d	#
τ	a	0.22	0.43	0.17	0.09	0.09
	b	0.32	0.21	0.09	0.13	0.26
	c	0.60	0.40	0.	0	0.
	d	0.33	0.67	0	0	0
	#	0.25	0.25	0.25	0.25	0.

Table 3: ML estimates of parameters of feature-based SL_2 distributions.

Observe the sharp divergence between the two models in certain cells. For example, no words begin with b in the sample. Hence the segment-based ML estimates of $Pr(b \mid \#)$ is zero. Conversely, the feature-based ML estimate is nonzero because b, like a, is +F, and b, like c, is +G, and both a and c begin words. Also, notice nonzero probabilities are assigned to d occuring after a and b. This is because $\mathbb{F}(d) = \langle -F, -G \rangle$ and the following sequences all occur in the corpus: [+F][-F] (ac), [+G][-G] (ca), and [-G][-G] (aa). On the other hand, zero probabilities are assigned to d ocurring after c and d because there are no cc sequences in the corpus and hence the probability of [-F] occuring after [-F] is zero.

This simple example demonstrates exactly how the model works. Generalizations are made on the basis of individual features, not individual symbols. In fact, segments are truly epiphenomenal in this model, as demonstrated by the nonzero probabilties assigned to segments outside the original feature system (here, this is d). To sum up, this model captures exactly the idea that the distribution of segments is conditioned on the distributions of its features.

6 Featural interaction

In many empirical cases of interest, features do interact, which suggests the strong independence assumption is incorrect for modeling phonotactic learning.

There are at least four kinds of featural interaction. First, different features may be prohibited from occuring simultaneously in certain contexts. As an example of the first type consider the fact that both velars and nasal sounds occur word-initially in English, but the velar nasal may not. Second, specific languages may prohibit different features from simultaneously occuring in all contexts. In English, for example, there are syllabic sounds and obstruents but no syllabic obstruents. Third, different features may be universally incompatible: e.g. no vowels are both [+high] and [+low]. The last type of interaction is that different features may be prohibited from occuring syntagmatically. For example, some languages prohibit voiceless sounds from occuring after nasals.

Although the independence assumption is too strong, it is still useful. First, it allows researchers to quantify the extent to which data can be explained without invoking featural interaction. For example, following Hayes and Wilson (2008), we may be interested in how well human acceptability judgements collected by Scholes (1966) can be explained if different features do not interact. After training the feature-based SL_2 model on a corpus of word initial onsets adapted from the CMU pronouncing dictionary (Hayes and Wilson, 2008, 395-396) and using a standard phonological feature system (Hayes, 2009, chap. 4), it achieves a correlation (Spearman's r) of 0.751.[7] In other words, roughly three quarters of the acceptability judgements are explained without relying on featural interaction (or segments).

Secondly, the incorrect predictions of the model are in principle detectable. For example, recall that English has word-inital velars and nasals, but no word-inital velar nasals. A one-cell chi-squared test can determine whether the observed number of [#ŋ] is significantly below the expected number according to the feature-based distribution, which could lead to a new parameter being adopted to describe the interaction of the [dorsal] and [nasal] features word-initially. The details of these procedures are left for future research and are likely to draw from the rich literature on Bayesian networks (Pearl, 1989; Ghahramani, 1998).

More important, however, is this framework allows researchers to construct the independence assumptions they want into the model in at least two ways. First, universally incompatible features can be excluded. For example, suppose [-F] and [-G] in the feature system in Table 1 are anatomically incompatible like [+low] and [+high]. If desired, they can be excluded from the model essentially by zeroing out any probability mass assigned to such combinations and re-normalizing.

Second, models can be defined where multiple features are permitted to interact. For example, suppose features F and G from Table 1 are embedded in a larger feature system. The machine in Figure 5 can be defined to be a *factor* of the model, and now interactions between F and G will be learned, including syntagmatic ones. The flexibility of the framework and the generality of the normalized co-emission product allow researchers to consider feature-based distributions which allow any two features to interact but which prohibit three-feature interactions, or which allow any three features to interact but which prohibit four-feature interactions, or models where only certain features are permitted to interact but not others (perhaps because they belong to the same node in a feature geometry (Clements, 1985; Clements and Hume, 1995).[8]

7 Hayes and Wilson (2008)

This section introduces the Hayes and Wilson (2008) (henceforth HW) phonotactic learner and shows that the contribution features play in generalization is not as clear as previously thought.

HW propose an inductive model which acquires a maxent grammar defined by weighted constraints. Each constraint is described as a sequence of natural classes using phonological features. The constraint format also allows reference to word boundaries and at most one complement class. (The complement class of $S \subseteq \Sigma$ is Σ/S.) For example, the constraint

*#[^ -voice,+anterior,+strident][-approximant]

means that in word-initial C_1C_2 clusters, if C_2 is a nasal or obstruent, then C_1 must be [s].

[7] We use the feature chart in Hayes (2009) because it contains over 150 IPA symbols (and not just English phonemes). Featural combinations not in the chart were assumed to be impossible (e.g. [+high,+low]) and were zeroed out.

[8] Note if all features are permitted to interact, this yields the segmental bigram model.

Hayes and Wilson maxent models	r
features & complement classes	0.946
no features & complement classes	0.937
features & no complement classes	0.914
no features & no complement classes	0.885

Table 4: Correlations of different settings versions of HW maxent model with Scholes data.

HW report that the model obtains a correlation (Spearman's r) of 0.946 with blick test data from Scholes (1966). HW and Albright (2009) attribute this high correlation to the model's use of natural classes and phonological features. HW also report that when the model is run without features, the grammar obtained scores an r value of only 0.885, implying that the gain in correlation is due specifically to the use of phonological features.

However, there are two relevant issues. The first is the use of complement classes. If features are not used but complement classes are (in effect only allowing the model to refer to single segments and the complements of single segments, e.g. [t] and [^t]) then in fact the grammar obtained scores an r value of 0.936, a result comparable to the one reported.[9] Table 4 shows the r values obtained by the HW learner under different conditions. Note we replicate the main result of $r = 0.946$ when using both features and complement classes.[10]

This exercise reveals that phonological features play a smaller role in the HW phonotactic learner than previously thought. Features are helpful, but not as much as complement classes of single segments (though features with complement classes yields the best result by this measure).

The second issue relates to the first: the question of whether additional parameters are worth the gain in empirical coverage. Wilson and Obdeyn (2009) provide an excellent discussion of the model comparison literature and provide a rigorous comparative analysis of computational modeleling of OCP restrictions. Here we only raise the questions and leave the answers to future research. Compare the HW learners in the first two rows in Table 4. Is the $\sim$ 0.01 gain in r score worth the additional parameters which refer to phonologically natural classes? Also, the feature-based SL_2 model in §4 only receives an r score of 0.751, much lower than the results in Table 4. Yet this model has far fewer parameters not only because the maxent models in Table 4 keep track of trigrams, but also because of its strong independence assumption. As mentioned, this result is informative because it reveals how much can be explained without featural interaction. In the context of model comparison, this particular model provides an inductive baseline against which the utility of additional parameters invoking featural interaction ought to be measured.

8 Conclusion

The current proposal explicitly embeds the Jakobsonian hypothesis that the primitive unit of phonology is the phonological feature into a phonotactic learning model. While this paper specifically shows how to integrate features into n-gram models to describe feature-based strictly n-local distributions, these techniques can be applied to other regular deterministic distributions, such as strictly k-piecewise models, which describe long-distance dependencies, like the ones found in consonant and vowel harmony (Heinz, to appear; Heinz and Rogers, 2010).

In contrast to models which assume that all features potentially interact, a baseline model was specifically introduced under the assumption that no two features interact. In this way, the "bottom-up" approach to feature-based generalization shifts the focus of inquiry to the featural interactions necessary (and ultimately sufficient) to describe and learn phonotactic patterns. The framework introduced here shows how researchers can study feature interaction in phonotactic models in a systematic, transparent way.

Acknowledgments

We thank Bill Idsardi, Tim O'Neill, Jim Rogers, Robert Wilder, Colin Wilson and the U. of Delaware's phonology/phonetics group for valuable discussion. Special thanks to Mark Ellison for helpful comments, to Adam Albright for illuminating remarks on the types of featural interaction in phonotactic patterns, and to Jason Eisner for bringing to our attention FHMMs and other related work.

---

[9] Examination of the output grammar reveals heavy reliance on the complement class [^s], which is not surprising given the discussion of [sC] clusters in HW.

[10] This software is available on Bruce Hayes' webpage: `http://www.linguistics.ucla.edu/people/hayes/Phonotactics/index.htm`.

References

Adam Albright. 2009. Feature-based generalisation as a source of gradient acceptability. *Phonology*, 26(1):9–41.

Noam Chomsky and Morris Halle. 1968. *The Sound Pattern of English*. Harper & Row, New York.

G.N. Clements and Elizabeth V. Hume. 1995. The internal organization of speech sounds. In John A. Goldsmith, editor, *The handbook of phonological theory*, chapter 7. Blackwell, Cambridge, MA.

George N. Clements. 1985. The geometry of phonological features. *Phonology Yearbook*, 2:225–252.

Colin de la Higuera. 2010. *Grammatical Inference: Learning Automata and Grammars*. Cambridge University Press.

Markus Dreyer and Jason Eisner. 2009. Graphical models over multiple strings. In *Proceedings of the Conference on Empirical Methods in Natural Language Processing (EMNLP)*, pages 101–110, Singapore, August.

Markus Dreyer, Jason R. Smith, and Jason Eisner. 2008. Latent-variable modeling of string transductions with finite-state methods. In *Proceedings of the Conference on Empirical Methods in Natural Language Processing (EMNLP)*, pages 1080–1089, Honolulu, October.

Pedro Garcia, Enrique Vidal, and José Oncina. 1990. Learning locally testable languages in the strict sense. In *Proceedings of the Workshop on Algorithmic Learning Theory*, pages 325–338.

Zoubin Ghahramani and Michael I. Jordan. 1997. Factorial hidden markov models. *Machine Learning*, 29(2):245–273.

Zoubin Ghahramani. 1998. Learning dynamic bayesian networks. In *Adaptive Processing of Sequences and Data Structures*, pages 168–197. Springer-Verlag.

Daniel Gildea and Daniel Jurafsky. 1996. Learning bias and phonological-rule induction. *Computational Linguistics*, 24(4).

Bruce Hayes and Colin Wilson. 2008. A maximum entropy model of phonotactics and phonotactic learning. *Linguistic Inquiry*, 39:379–440.

Bruce Hayes. 2009. *Introductory Phonology*. Wiley-Blackwell.

Jeffrey Heinz and James Rogers. 2010. Estimating strictly piecewise distributions. In *Proceedings of the 48th Annual Meeting of the Association for Computational Linguistics*, Uppsala, Sweden.

Jeffrey Heinz. to appear. Learning long-distance phonotactics. *Linguistic Inquiry*, 41(4).

John Hopcroft, Rajeev Motwani, and Jeffrey Ullman. 2001. *Introduction to Automata Theory, Languages, and Computation*. Boston, MA: Addison-Wesley.

Roman Jakobson, C. Gunnar, M. Fant, and Morris Halle. 1952. *Preliminaries to Speech Analysis*. MIT Press.

Daniel Jurafsky and James Martin. 2008. *Speech and Language Processing: An Introduction to Natural Language Processing, Speech Recognition, and Computational Linguistics*. Prentice-Hall, Upper Saddle River, NJ, 2nd edition.

Robert McNaughton and Seymour Papert. 1971. *Counter-Free Automata*. MIT Press.

Elliot Moreton. 2008. Analytic bias and phonological typology. *Phonology*, 25(1):83–127.

Judea Pearl. 1989. *Probabilistic Reasoning in Intelligent Systems: Networks of Plausible Inference*. Morgan Kauffman.

James Rogers and Geoffrey Pullum. to appear. Aural pattern recognition experiments and the subregular hierarchy. *Journal of Logic, Language and Information*.

James Rogers, Jeffrey Heinz, Gil Bailey, Matt Edlefsen, Molly Visscher, David Wellcome, and Sean Wibel. 2009. On languages piecewise testable in the strict sense. In *Proceedings of the 11th Meeting of the Assocation for Mathematics of Language*.

Lawrence K. Saul and Michael I. Jordan. 1999. Mixed memory markov models: Decomposing complex stochastic processes as mixtures of simpler ones. *Machine Learning*, 37(1):75–87.

Robert J. Scholes. 1966. *Phonotactic grammaticality*. Mouton, The Hague.

Enrique Vidal, Franck Thollard, Colin de la Higuera, Francisco Casacuberta, and Rafael C. Carrasco. 2005a. Probabilistic finite-state machines-part I. *IEEE Transactions on Pattern Analysis and Machine Intelligence*, 27(7):1013–1025.

Enrique Vidal, Frank Thollard, Colin de la Higuera, Francisco Casacuberta, and Rafael C. Carrasco. 2005b. Probabilistic finite-state machines-part II. *IEEE Transactions on Pattern Analysis and Machine Intelligence*, 27(7):1026–1039.

Colin Wilson and Marieke Obdeyn. 2009. Simplifying subsidiary theory: statistical evidence from arabic, muna, shona, and wargamay. Johns Hopkins University.

Colin Wilson. 2006. Learning phonology with substantive bias: An experimental and computational study of velar palatalization. *Cognitive Science*, 30(5):945–982.

A Method for Compiling Two-level Rules with Multiple Contexts

Kimmo Koskenniemi
University of Helsinki
Helsinki, Finland
kimmo.koskenniemi@helsinki.fi

Miikka Silfverberg
University of Helsinki
Helsinki, Finland
miikka.silfverberg@helsinki.fi

Abstract

A novel method is presented for compiling two-level rules which have multiple context parts. The same method can also be applied to the resolution of so-called right-arrow rule conflicts. The method makes use of the fact that one can efficiently compose sets of two-level rules with a lexicon transducer. By introducing variant characters and using simple pre-processing of multi-context rules, all rules can be reduced into single-context rules. After the modified rules have been combined with the lexicon transducer, the variant characters may be reverted back to the original surface characters. The proposed method appears to be efficient but only partial evidence is presented yet.

1 Introduction

Two-level rules can be compiled into length-preserving transducers whose intersection effectively reflects the constraints and the correspondences imposed by the two-level grammar. Two-level rules relate input strings (lexical representations) with output strings (surface representations). The pairs of strings are treated as character pairs `x:z` consisting of *lexical (input) characters* `x` and *surface (output) characters* `z`, and regular expressions based on such pairs. Two-level rule transducers are made length-preserving (epsilon-free) by using a place holder *zero* (0) within the rules and in the representations. The zero is then removed after the rules have been combined by (virtual) intersection, before the result is composed with the lexicon. There are four kinds of two-level rules:

1. *right-arrow rules* or restriction rules, (`x:z => LC _ RC`) saying that the correspondence pair is allowed only if immediately preceded by left context `LC` and followed by right context `RC`,
2. *left-arrow rules* or surface coercion rules, (`x:z <= LC _ RC`) which say that in this context, the lexical character `x` may only correspond to the surface character `z`,
3. *double-arrow rules* (<=>), a shorthand combining these two requirements, and
4. *exclusion rules* (`x:z /<= LC _ RC`) which forbid the pair `x:z` to occur in this context.

All types of rules may have more than one context part. In particular, the right-arrow rule `x:z => LC1 _ RC1; LC2 _ RC2` would say that the pair `x:z` (which we call the *centre* of the rule) may occur in either one of these two contexts. For various formulations of two-level rules, see e.g. (Koskenniemi, 1983), (Grimley-Evans et al., 1996), (Black et.al., 1987), (Ruessink, 1989), (Ritchie, 1992), (Kiraz, 2001) and a comprehensive survey on their formal interpretations, see (Vaillette, 2004).

Compiling two-level rules into transducers is easy in all other cases except for right-arrow rules with multiple context-parts; see e.g. Koskenniemi (1983). Compiling right-arrow rules with multiple context parts is more difficult because the compilation of the whole rule is not in a simple relation to the component expressions in the rule; see e.g. Karttunen et al. (1987).

The method proposed here reduces multi-context rules into a set of separate simple rules, one for each context, by introducing some auxiliary variant characters. These auxiliary characters are then normalized back into the original surface characters after the intersecting composition of the lexicon and the modified rules. The method is presented in section 3. The compilation of multiple contexts using the proposed scheme appears to be very simple and fast. Preliminary results and discussion about the computational complexity are presented in section 4.

Proceedings of the 11th Meeting of the ACL-SIGMORPHON, ACL 2010, pages 38–45,
Uppsala, Sweden, 15 July 2010.

1.1 The compilation task with an example

We make use of a simplified linguistic example where a stop k is realized as v between identical rounded close vowels (u, y). The example resembles one detail of Finnish consonant gradation but it is grossly simplified. According to the rule in the example, the lexical representation pukun would be realized as the surface representation puvun. This correspondence is traditionally represented as:

```
p u k u n
p u v u n
```

where the upper tier represents the lexical or morphophonemic representation which we interpret as the input, and the lower one corresponds to the surface representation which we consider as the output.[1] This two-tier representation is usually represented on a single line as a sequence of input and output character pairs where pairs of identical characters, such as p:p are abbreviated as a single p. E.g. the above pair of strings becomes a string of pairs:

```
p u k:v u n
```

In our example we require that the correspondence k:v may occur only between two identical rounded close vowels, i.e. either between two letters u or between two letters y. Multiple contexts are needed in the right-arrow rule which expresses this constraint. As a two-level grammar, this would be:

```
Alphabet a b … k … u v w …
 k:v;
Rules
k:v => u _ u;
       y _ y;
```

This grammar would permit sequences such as:

```
p u k:v u n
k y k:v y n
p u k:v u k:v u n
l u k:v u n k y k:v y n
t u k k u
```

but it would exclude sequences:

```
p u k:v y n
t u k:v a n
```

[1] In Xerox terminology, the input or lexical characters are called the upper characters, and the output or surface characters are called the lower characters. Other orientations are used by some authors.

Whereas one can always express multi-context left-arrow rules (<=) and exclusion rules (/<=) equivalently as separate rules, this does not hold for right-arrow rules. The two separate rules

```
k:v => u _ u;
k:v => y _ y;
```

would be in conflict with each other permitting no occurrences of k:v at all, (unless we apply so-called conflict resolution which would effectively combine the two rules back to a single rule with two context parts).

2 Previous compilation methods

The first compiler of two-level rules was implemented by the first author in 1985 and it handled also multi-context rules (Koskenniemi, 1985). The compiler used a finite-state package written by Ronald Kaplan and Martin Kay at Xerox PARC, and a variant of a formula they used for compiling cascaded rewrite rules. Their own work was not published until 1994. Koskenniemi's compiler was re-implemented in LISP by a student in her master's thesis (Kinnunen, 1987).

Compilation of two-level rules in general requires some care because the centres may occur several times in pair strings, the contexts may overlap and the centres may act as part of a context for another occurrence of the same centre. For other rules than right-arrow rules, each context is yet another condition for excluding ungrammatical strings of pairs, which is how the rules are related to each other. The context parts of a right-arrow rule are, however, permissions, one of which has to be satisfied. Expressing unions of context parts was initially a problem which required complicated algorithms.

Some of the earlier compilation methods are mentioned below. They all produce a single transducer out of each multi-context right-arrow rule.

2.1 Method based on Kaplan and Kay

Kaplan and Kay (1994) developed a method around 1980 for compiling rewriting rules into finite-state transducers[2]. The method was adapted by Koskenniemi to the compilation of two-level rules by modifying the formula

[2] Douglas Johnson (1972) presented a similar technique earlier but his work was not well known in early 1980s.

slightly. In this method, auxiliary left and right bracket characters (`<1, >1, <2, >2, ...`) were freely added in order to facilitate the checking of the context conditions. A unique left and right bracket was dedicated for each context part of the rule. For each context part of a rule, sequences with freely added brackets were then filtered with the context expressions so that only such sequences remained where occurrences of the brackets were delimited with the particular left or right context (allowing free occurrence of brackets for other context parts). Thereafter, it was easy to check that all occurrences of the centre (i.e. the left hand part of the rule before the rule operator) were delimited by some matching pair of brackets. As all component transducers in this expression were length-preserving (epsilon-free), the constraints could be intersected with each other resulting in a single rule transducer for the multi-context rule (and finally the brackets could be removed).

2.2 Method of Grimley-Evans, Kiraz and Pulman

Grimley-Evans, Kiraz and Pulman presented a simpler compilation formula for two-level rules (1996). The method is prepared to handle more than two levels of representation, and it does not need the freely added brackets in the intermediate stages. Instead, it uses a marker for the rule centre and can with it express disjunctions of contexts. Subtracting such a disjunction from all strings where the centre occurs expresses all pair strings which violate the multi-context rule. Thus, the negation of such a transducer is the desired result.

2.3 Yli-Jyrä's method

Yli-Jyrä (Yli-Jyrä et al., 2006) introduced a concept of Generalized Restriction (GR) where expressions with auxiliary boundary characters ♦ made it possible to express context parts of rules in a natural way, e.g. as:

```
Pi* LC ♦ Pi ♦ RC Pi*
```

Here `Pi` is the set of feasible pairs of characters and `LC` and `RC` are the left and right contexts. The two context parts of our example would correspond to the following two expressions:

```
Pi* u ♦ Pi ♦ u Pi*
Pi* y ♦ Pi ♦ y Pi*
```

Using such expressions, it is easy to express disjunctions of contexts as unions of the above expressions. This makes it logically simple to compile multi-context right-arrow rules. The rule centre `x:z` can be expressed simply as:

```
Pi* ♦ x:z ♦ Pi*
```

The right-arrow rule can be expressed as an implication where the expression for the centre implies the union of the context parts. Thereafter, one may just remove the auxiliary boundary characters, and the result is the rule-transducer. (It is easy to see that only one auxiliary character is needed when the length of the centres is one.)

The compilation of rules with centres whose length is one using the GR seems very similar to that of Grimley-Evans et al. The nice thing about GR is that one can easily express various rule types, including but not limited to the four types listed above.

2.4 Intersecting compose

It was observed somewhere around 1990 at Xerox that the rule sets may be composed with the lexicon transducers in an efficient way and that the resulting transducer was roughly similar in size as the lexicon transducer itself (Karttunen et al., 1992). This observation gives room to the new approach presented below.

At that time, it was not practical to intersect complete two-level grammars if they contained many elaborate rules (and this is still a fairly heavy operation). Another useful observation was that the intersection of the rules could be done in a joint single operation with the composition (Karttunen, 1994). Avoiding the separate intersection made the combining of the lexicon and rules feasible and faster. In addition to Xerox LEXC program, e.g. the HFST finite-state software contains this operation and it is routinely used when lexicons and two-level grammars are combined into lexicon transducers (Lindén et al., 2009).

Måns Huldén has noted (2009) that the composing of the lexicon and the rules is sometimes a heavy operation, but can be optimized if one first composes the output side of the lexicon transducer with the rules, and thereafter the original lexicon with this intermediate result.

3 Proposed method for compilation

The idea is to modify the two-level grammar so that the rules become simpler. The modified grammar will contain only simple rules with single context parts. This is done at the cost that the grammar will transform lexical representations into slightly modified surface representations.

The surface representations are, however, fixed after the rules have been combined with the lexicon so that the resulting lexicon transducer is equivalent to the result produced using earlier methods.

3.1 The method through the example

Let us return to the example in the introduction. The modified surface representation differs from the ultimate representation by having a slightly extended alphabet where some surface characters are expressed as their variants, i.e. there might be `v1` or `v2` in addition to `v`. In particular, the first variant `v1` will be used exactly where the first context of the original multi-context rule for `k:v` is satisfied, and `v2` where the second context is satisfied. After extending the alphabet and splitting the rule, our example grammar will be as follows:

```
Alphabet a b … k … u v w x y …
  k:v1 k:v2;
Rules
k:v1 => u _ u;
k:v2 => y _ y;
```

These rules would permit sequences such as:

```
p u k:v1 u n
k y k:v2 y n
p u k:v1 u k:v1 u n
```

but exclude a sequence

```
p u k:v2 u n
```

The output of the modified grammar is now as required, except that it includes these variants `v1` and `v2` instead of `v`. If we first perform the intersecting composition of the rules and the lexicon, we then can compose the result with a trivial transducer which simply transforms both `v1` and `v2` into `v`.

It should be noted that here the context expressions of these example rules do not contain `v` on the output side, and therefore the introduction of the variants `v1` and `v2` causes no further complications. In the general case, the variants should be added as alternatives of `v` in the context expressions, see the explanation below.

3.2 More general cases

The strategy is to pre-process the two-level grammar in steps by splitting more complex constructions into simpler ones until we have units whose components are trivial to compile. The intersection of the components will have the desired effect when composed with a lexicon and a trivial correction module. Assume, for the time being, that all centres (i.e. the left-hand parts) of the rules are of length one.

(1) Split double-arrow (<=>) rules into one right-arrow (=>) rule and one left-arrow (<=) rule with centres and context parts identical to those of the original double-arrow rule.

(2) Unfold the iterative `where` clauses in left-arrow rules by establishing a separate left-arrow rule for each value of the iterator variable, e.g.

```
V:Vb <= [a | o | u] ?* _;
 where V in (A O U)
       Vb in (a o u) matched;
```

becomes

```
A:a <= [a | o | u] ?* _;
O:o <= [a | o | u] ?* _;
U:u <= [a | o | u] ?* _;
```

Unfold the `where` clauses in right-arrow rules in either of the two ways: (a) If the `where` clauses create disjoint centres (as above), then establish a separate right-arrow rule for each value of the variable, and (b) if the clause does not affect the centre, then create a single multi-context right-arrow rule whose contexts consist of the context parts of the original rule by replacing the `where` clause variable by its values, one value at a time, e.g.

```
k:v => Vu _ Vu; where Vu in (u y);
```

becomes

```
k:v => u _ u;
       y _ y;
```

If there are set symbols or disjunctions in the centres of a right-arrow rule, then split the rule into separate rules where each rule has just a single pair as its centre, and the context part is identical to the context part (after the unfolding of the `where` clauses).

Note that these two first steps would probably be common to any method of compiling multi-context rules. After these two steps, we have right-arrow, left-arrow and exclusion rules. The right-arrow rules have single pairs as their centres.

(3) Identify the right-arrow rules which, after the unfolding, have multiple contexts, and record each pair which is the centre of such a rule. Suppose that the output character (i.e. the surface character) of such a rule is z and there are n context parts in the rule, then create n new auxiliary characters $z_1, z_2, \ldots, z_n$ and denote the set consisting of them by $S(z)$.

Split the rule into n distinct single-context right-arrow rules by replacing the z of the centre by each z_i in turn.

Our simple example rule becomes now.

```
k:v1 => u _ u;
k:v2 => y _ y;
```

(4) When all rules have been split according to the above steps, we need a post-processing phase for the whole grammar. We have to extend the alphabet by adding the new auxiliary characters in it. If original surface characters (which now have variants) were referred to in the rules, each such reference must be replaced with the union of the original character and its variants. This replacement has to be done throughout the grammar. For any existing pairs $x:z$ listed in the alphabet, we add there also the pairs $x:z_1, ..., x:z_n$. The same is done for all declarations of sets where z occurs (as an output character). Insert a declaration for a new character set corresponding to $S(z)$. In all define clauses and in all rule-context expressions where z occurs as an output character, it is replaced by the set $S(z)$. In all centres of left-arrow rules where z occurs as the output character, it is replaced by $S(z)$.

The purpose of this step is just to make the modified two-level grammar consistent in terms of its alphabet, and to make the modified rules treat the occurrence of any of the output characters $z_1, z_2, ..., z_n$ in the same way as the original rule treated z wherever it occurred in its contexts.

After this pre-processing we only have right-arrow, left-arrow and exclusion rules with a single context part. All rules are independent of each other in such a way that their intersection would have the effect we wish the grammar to have. Thus, we may compile the rule set as such and each of these simple rules separately. Any of the existing compilation formulas will do.

After compiling the individual rules, they have to be intersected and composed with the lexicon transducer which transforms base forms and inflectional feature symbols into the morphophonemic representation of the word-forms. The composing and intersecting is efficiently done as a single operation because it then avoids the possible explosion which can occur if intermediate result of the intersection is computed in full.

The rules are mostly independent of each other, capable of recurring freely. Therefore something near the worst case complexity is likely to occur, i.e. the size of the intersection would have many states, roughly proportional to the product of the numbers of the states in the individual rule transducers.

The composition of the lexicon and the logical intersection of the modified rules is almost identical to the composition of the lexicon and the logical intersection of the original rules. The only difference is that the output (i.e. the surface) representation contains some auxiliary characters z_i instead of the original surface characters z. A simple transducer will correct this. (The transducer has just one (final) state and identity transitions for all original surface characters and a reduction $z_i:z$ for each of the auxiliary characters.) This composition with the correcting transducer can be made only after the rules have been combined with the lexicon.

3.3 Right-arrow conflicts

Right-arrow rules are often considered as permissions. A rule could be interpreted as "this correspondence pair may occur if the following context condition is met". Further permissions might be stated in other rules. As a whole, any occurrence must get at least one permission in order to be allowed.

The right-arrow conflict resolution scheme presented by Karttunen implemented this through an extensive pre-processing where the conflicts were first detected and then resolved (Karttunen et al., 1987). The resolution was done by copying context parts among the rules in conflict. Thus, what was compiled was a grammar with rules extended with copies of context parts from other rules.

The scenario outlined above could be slightly modified in order to implement the simple right-arrow rule conflict resolution in a way which is equivalent to the solution presented by Karttunen. All that is needed is that one would first split the right-arrow rules with multiple context parts into separate rules. Only after that, one would consider all right-arrow rules and record rules with identical centres. For groups of rules with identical centres, one would introduce the further variants of the surface characters, a separate variant for each rule. In this scheme, the conflict resolution of right-arrow rules is implemented fairly naturally in a way analogous to the handling of multi-context rules.

3.4 Note on longer centres in rules

In the above discussion, the left-hand parts of rules, i.e. their centres, were always of length one. In fact, one may define rules with longer centres by a scheme which reduces them into rules with length one centres. It appears that the basic rule types (the left and right-arrow rules) with longer centres can be expressed in terms of length one centres, if we apply conflict resolution for the right-arrow rules.

We replace a right-arrow rule, e.g.

$x_1{:}z_1\ x_2{:}z_2\ \ldots\ x_k{:}z_k$ => LC _ RC;

with k separate rules

$x_1{:}z_1$ => LC _ $x_2{:}z_2\ \ldots\ x_k{:}z_k$ RC;
$x_2{:}z_2$ => LC $x_1{:}z_1$ _ $\ldots\ x_k{:}z_k$ RC;
...
$x_k{:}z_k$ => LC $x_1{:}z_1\ x_2{:}z_2\ \ldots$ _ RC;

Effectively, each input character may be realized according to the original rule only if the rest of the centre will also be realized according to the original rule.

Respectively, we replace a left-arrow rule, e.g.

$x_1{:}z_1\ x_2{:}z_2\ \ldots\ x_k{:}z_k$ <= LC _ RC;

with k separate rules

$x_1{:}z_1$ <= LC _ $x_2{:}\ \ldots\ x_k{:}$ RC;
$x_2{:}z_2$ <= LC $x_1{:}$ _ $\ldots\ x_k{:}$ RC;
...
$x_k{:}z_k$ <= LC $x_1{:}\ x_2{:}\ \ldots$ _ RC;

Here the realization of the surface string is forced for each of its character of the centre separately, without reference to what happens to other characters in the centre. (Otherwise the contexts of the separate rules would be too restrictive, and allow the default realization as well.)

4 Complexity and implementation

In order to implement the proposed method, one could write a pre-processor which just transforms the grammar into the simplified form, and then use an existing two-level compiler. Alternatively, one could modify an existing compiler, or write a new compiler which would be somewhat simpler than the existing ones. We have not implemented the proposed method yet, but rather simulated the effects using existing two-level rule compilers. Because the pre-processing would be very fast anyway, we decided to estimate the efficiency of the proposed method through compiling hand-modified rules with the existing HFST-TWOLC (Lindén et al., 2009) and Xerox TWOLC[3] two-level rule compilers. The HFST tools are built on top of existing open source finite-state packages OpenFST (Allauzen et al., 2007) and Helmut Schmid's SFST (2005).

It appears that all normal morphographemic two-level grammars can be compiled with the methods of Kaplan and Kay, Grimley-Evans and Yli-Jyrä.

Initial tests of the proposed scheme are promising. The compilation speed was tested with a grammar of consisting of 12 rules including one multi-context rule for Finnish consonant gradation with some 8 contexts and a full Finnish lexicon. When the multi-context rule was split into separate rules, the compilation was somewhat faster (12.4 sec) to than when the rule was compiled a multi-context rule using the GR formula (13.9 sec). The gain in the speed by splitting was lost at the additional work needed in the intersecting compose of the rules and the full lexicon and the final fixing of the variants. On the whole, the proposed method had no advantage over the GR method.

In order to see how the number of context parts affects the compilation speed, we made tests with an extreme grammar simulating Dutch hyphenation rules. The hyphenation logic was taken out of TeX hyphenation patterns which had been converted into two-level rules. The first grammar consisted of a single two-level rule which had some 3700 context parts. This grammar could not be compiled using Xerox TWOLC which applies the Kaplan and Kay method because more than 5 days on a dedicated Linux machine with 64 GB core memory was not enough for completing the computation. When using of GR method of HFST-TWOLC, the compilation time was not a problem (34 minutes). The method of Grimley-Evans et al. would probably have been equally feasible.

Compiling the grammar after splitting it into separate rules as proposed above was also feasible: about one hour with Xerox TWOLC and about 20 hours with HFST-TWOLC. The difference between these two implementations depends most likely on the way they handle alphabets. The Xerox tool makes use of a so-called 'other' symbol which stands for characters not mentioned in the rule. It also optimizes the computation by using equivalence classes of character pairs. These make the compilation less sensitive to the 3700 new symbols added to the alphabet than what happens in the HFST routines.

Another test was made using a 50 pattern subset of the above hyphenation grammar. Using

[3] We used an old version 3.4.10 (2.17.7) which we thought would make use of the Kaplan and Kay formula. We suspected that the most recent versions might have gone over to the GR formula.

the Xerox TWOLC, the subset compiled as a multi-context rule in 28.4 seconds, and when split according to the method proposed here, it compiled in 0.04 seconds. Using the HFST-TWOLC, the timings were 3.1 seconds and 5.4 seconds, respectively. These results corroborate the intuition that the Kaplan and Kay formula is sensitive to the number of context parts in rules whereas the GR formula is less sensitive to the number of context parts in rules.

There are factors which affect the speed of HFST-TWOLC, including the implementation detail including the way of treating characters or character pairs which are not specifically mentioned in a particular transducer. We anticipate that there is much room for improvement in treating larger alphabets in HFST internal routines and there is no inherent reason why it should be slower than the Xerox tool. The next release of HFST will use Huldén's FOMA finite-state package. FOMA implements the 'other' symbol and is expected to improve the processing of larger alphabets.

Our intuition and observation is that the proposed compilation phase requires linear time with respect to the number of context parts in a rule. Whether the proposed compilation method has an advantage over the compilation using the GR or Grimley-Evans formula remains to be seen.

5 Acknowledgements

Miikka Silfverberg, a PhD student at Finnish graduate school Langnet and the author of HFST-TWOLC compiler. His contribution consists of making all tests used here to estimate and compare the efficiency of the compilation methods.

The current work is part of the FIN-CLARIN infrastructure project at the University of Helsinki funded by the Finnish Ministry of Education.

References

Cyril Allauzen, Michael Riley, Johan Schalkwyk, Wojciech Skut and Mehryar Mohri. 2007. OpenFst: A General and Efficient Weighted Finite-State Transducer Library. In *Implementation and Application of Automata*, Lecture Notes in Computer Science. Springer, Vol. 4783/2007, 11-23.

Alan Black, Graeme Ritchie, Steve Pulman, and Graham Russell. 1987. "Formalisms for morphographemic description". In *Proceedings of the Third Conference of the European Chapter of the Association for Computational Linguistics*, 11–18.

Edmund Grimley-Evans, Georg A. Kiraz, Stephen G. Pulman. 1996. Compiling a Partition-Based Two-Level Formalism. In *COLING 1996, Volume 1: The 16th International Conference on Computational Linguistics*, pp. 454-459.

Huldén, Måns. 2009. *Finite-State Machine Construction Methods and Algorithms for Phonology and Morphology*. PhD Thesis, University of Arizona.

Douglas C. Johnson. 1972. *Formal Aspects of Phonological Description*. Mouton, The Hague.

Ronald M. Kaplan and Martin Kay. 1994. Regular Models of Phonological Rule Systems. *Computational Linguistics* 20(3): 331–378.

Lauri Karttunen. 1994. Constructing lexical transducers. In Proceedings of the 15th conference on Computational linguistics, Volume 1. pp. 406-411.

Lauri Karttunen, Ronald M. Kaplan, and Annie Zaenen. 1992. Two-Level Morphology with Composition. *Proceedings of the 14th conference on Computational linguistics, August 23-28, 1992, Nantes, France.* 141-148.

Lauri Karttunen, Kimmo Koskenniemi, and Ronald. M. Kaplan. 1987. A Compiler for Two-level Phonological Rules. In Dalrymple, M. et al. *Tools for Morphological Analysis*. Center for the Study of Language and Information. Stanford University. Palo Alto.

Maarit Kinnunen. 1987. *Morfologisten sääntöjen kääntäminen äärellisiksi automaateiksi*. (Translating morphological rules into finite-state automata. Master's thesis.). Department of Computer Science, University of Helsinki

George Anton Kiraz. 2001. *Computational Nonlinear Morphology: With Emphasis on Semitic Languages*. Studies in Natural Language Processing. Cambridge University Press, Cambridge.

Kimmo Koskenniemi. 1983. *Two-Level Morphology: A General Computational Model for Word-form Recognition and Production*. University of Helsinki, Department of General Linguistics, Publications No. 11.

Kimmo Koskenniemi. 1985. Compilation of automata from morphological two-level rules. In F. Karlsson (ed.), *Papers from the fifth Scandinavian Conference of Computational Linguistics, Helsinki, December 11-12, 1985*. pp. 143-149.

Krister Lindén, Miikka Silfverberg and Tommi Pirinen. 2009. HFST Tools for Morphology – An Efficient Open-Source Package for Construction of Morphological Analyzers. In *State of the Art in Computational Morphology* (Proceedings of Workshop on Systems and Frameworks for Computational Morphology, SFCM 2009). Springer.

Graeme Ritchie. 1992. Languages generated by two-level morphological rules". *Computational Linguistics*, 18(1):41–59.

H. A. Ruessink. 1989. *Two level formalisms*. Utrecht Working Papers in NLP. Technical Report 5.

Helmut Schmid. 2005. A Programming Language for Finite State Transducers. In *Proceedings of the 5th International Workshop on Finite State Methods in Natural Language Processing (FSMNLP 2005)*. pp. 50-51.

Nathan Vaillette. 2004. *Logical Specification of Finite-State Transductions for Natural Language Processing*. PhD Thesis, Ohio State University.

Anssi Yli-Jyrä and Kimmo Koskenniemi. 2006. Compiling Generalized Two-Level Rules and Grammars. *International Conference on NLP: Advances in natural language processing*. Springer. 174 – 185.

Exploring dialect phonetic variation using PARAFAC

Jelena Prokić
University of Groningen
The Netherlands
j.prokic@rug.nl

Tim Van de Cruys
University of Groningen
The Netherlands
t.van.de.cruys@rug.nl

Abstract

In this paper we apply the multi-way decomposition method PARAFAC in order to detect the most prominent sound changes in dialect variation. We investigate various phonetic patterns, both in stressed and unstressed syllables. We proceed from regular sound correspondences which are automatically extracted from the aligned transcriptions and analyzed using PARAFAC. This enables us to analyze simultaneously the co-occurrence patterns of all sound correspondences found in the data set and determine the most important factors of the variation. The first ten dimensions are examined in more detail by recovering the geographical distribution of the extracted correspondences. We also compare dialect divisions based on the extracted correspondences to the divisions based on the whole data set and to the traditional scholarship as well. The results show that PARAFAC can be successfully used to detect the linguistic basis of the automatically obtained dialect divisions.

1 Introduction

Dialectometry is a multidisciplinary field that uses quantitative methods in the analysis of dialect data. From the very beginning, most of the research in dialectometry has been focused on the identification of dialect groups and development of methods that would tell us how similar (or different) one variety is when compared to the neighboring varieties. Dialect data is usually analyzed on the aggregate level by summing up the differences between various language varieties into a single number. The main drawback of aggregate analyses is that it does not expose the underlying linguistic structure, i.e. the specific linguistic elements that contributed to the differences between the dialects. In recent years there have been several attempts to automatically extract linguistic basis from the aggregate analysis, i.e. to determine which linguistic features are responsible for which dialect divisions. Although interesting for dialectology itself, this kind of research is very important in the investigation of sound variation and change, both on the synchronic and diachronic level.

The paper is structured as follows. In the next section, we discuss a number of earlier approaches to the problem of identifying underlying linguistic structure in dialect divisions. In section 3, we give a description of the dialect data used in this research. Section 4 then describes the methodology of our method, explaining our data representation using tensors, our three-way factorization method, and the design of our data set. In section 5, the results of our method are discussed, examining the values that come out of our factorization method in a number of ways. Section 6, then, draws conclusions and gives some pointers for future work.

2 Previous work

In order to detect the linguistic basis of dialect variation Nerbonne (2006) applied factor analysis to the results of the dialectometric analysis of southern American dialects. The analysis is based on 1132 different vowels found in the data. 204 vowel positions are investigated, where a vowel position is, e.g., the first vowel in the word 'Washington' or the second vowel in the word 'thirty'. Factor analysis has shown that 3 factors are most important, explaining 35% of the total amount of variation. However, this approach is based only on vowel positions in specific words.

Prokić (2007) extracted the 10 most frequent non-identical sound correspondences from the aligned word transcriptions. Based on the relative frequency of each of these correspondences each site in the data set was assigned a *correspondence index*. Higher value of this index indicates sites

Proceedings of the 11th Meeting of the ACL-SIGMORPHON, ACL 2010, pages 46–53,
Uppsala, Sweden, 15 July 2010.

where the presence of a certain sound is dominant with respect to some sound alternation. Although successful in describing some important sound alternations in the dialect variation, it examines only the 10 most frequent sound alternations without testing patterns of variation between different sound correspondences.

Shackleton (2007) applies principal component analysis (PCA) to a group of self constructed articulation-based features. All segments found in the data are translated into vectors of numerical features and analyzed using PCA. Based on the component scores for features, different groups of varieties (in which a certain group of features is present) are identified. We note that the main drawback of this approach is the subjectivity of the feature selection and segment quantification.

Wieling and Nerbonne (2009) used a bipartite spectral graph partitioning method to simultaneously cluster dialect varieties and sound correspondences. Although promising, this method compares the pronunciation of every site only to the reference site, rather than comparing it to all other sites. Another drawback of this method is that it does not use any information on the frequencies of sound correspondences, but instead employs binary features to represent whether a certain correspondence is present at a certain site or not.

In this paper we present an approach that tries to overcome some of the problems described in the previous approaches. It proceeds from automatically aligned phonetic transcriptions, where pronunciations of every site are compared to the corresponding pronunciations for all other sites. Extracted sound correspondences are analyzed using the multi-way decomposition method PARAFAC. The method allows us to make generalizations over multi-way co-occurrence data, and to look simultaneously at the co-occurrence patterns of all sound correspondences found in the data set.

3 Data description

The data set used in this paper consists of phonetic transcriptions of 152 words collected at 197 sites evenly distributed all over Bulgaria. It is part of the project *Buldialect – Measuring Linguistic unity and diversity in Europe.* Phonetic transcriptions include various diacritics and suprasegmentals, making the total number of unique phones in the data set 95: 43 vowels and 52 consonants.[1] The sign for primary stress is moved to a corresponding vowel, so that there is a distinction between stressed and unstressed vowels. Vowels are also marked for their length. Sonorants /r/ and /l/ have a mark for syllabicity and for stress in case they are syllabic. Here we list all phones present in the data set:

ˈɑ, e, i, ˈe, ə, ˈɛ, ɤ, ˈɒ, ɑ, ɪ, o, ˈo, u, ˈɑː, ʊ, ˈuː, ˈɤ, ˈə, ˈa, ˈi, ˈɪ, ˈeː, ɛ, ˈɔ, ˈʌ, ˈiː, ˈu, eː, ɨ, ˈɨ, ˈoː, ˈɛː, ˈɤː, uː, ɑː, y, ˈaː, a, oː, ɤː, ˈʊ, ˈy, ˈɪː, j̰, ɡ, n, nʲ, ɟ, r, w, x, rʲ, h, ɕ, f, s, v̰, ç, ɸ, p̰, t͡ʃ, m, k, t͡ɕ, pʲ, c, l, lʲ, t, tʲ, ʃ, d, dʲ, ˈr̩, vʲ, d͡ʑ, ʒ, ʑ, t͡s, r̩, cʲ, z, sʲ, b, ɡʲ, mʲ, l̩, zʲ, ˈl̩, kʲ, bʲ, d͡ʑ, d͡ʑ, fʲ, ɰ

Each of the 152 words in the data set shows phonetic variation, with some words displaying more than one change. There are in total 39 different dialectal features that are represented in the data set, with each of the features being present in a similar number of words. For example, the reflexes of Old Bulgarian vowels that show dialect variation are represented with the same or nearly the same number of words. A more detailed description of all features can be found in Prokić et al. (2009). For all villages only one speaker was recorded. In the data set, for some villages there were multiple pronunciations of the same word. In this reasearch we have randomly picked only one per every village.

4 Methodology

4.1 Tensors

Co-occurrence data (such as the sound correspondences used in this research) are usually represented in the form of a *matrix*. This form is perfectly suited to represent two-way co-occurrence data, but for co-occurrence data beyond two modes, we need a more general representation. The generalization of a matrix is called a *tensor*. A tensor is able to encode co-occurrence data of any n modes. Figure 1 shows a graphical comparison of a matrix and a tensor with three modes – although a tensor can easily be generalized to more than three modes.

Tensor operations come with their own algebraic machinery. We refer the interested reader to Kolda and Bader (2009) for a thorough and insightful introduction to the subject.

[1] The data is publicly available and can be downloaded from `http://www.bultreebank.org/BulDialects/index.html`

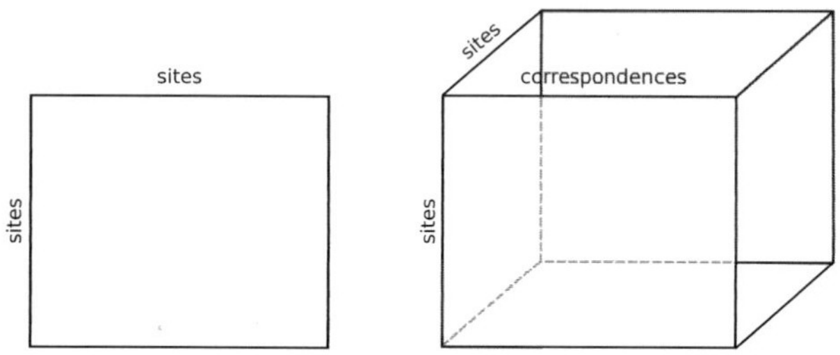

Figure 1: Matrix representation vs. tensor representation.

4.2 PARAFAC

In order to create a succinct and generalized model, the co-occurrence data are often analyzed with dimensionality reduction techniques. One of the best known dimensionality reduction techniques is principal component analysis (PCA, Pearson (1901)). PCA transforms the data into a new coordinate system, yielding the best possible fit in a least squares sense given a limited number of dimensions. Singular value decomposition (SVD) is the generalization of the eigenvalue decomposition used in PCA (Wall et al., 2003).

To be able to make generalizations among the three-way co-occurrence data, we apply a statistical dimensionality reduction technique called parallel factor analysis (PARAFAC, Harshman (1970); Carroll and Chang (1970)), a technique that has been sucessfully applied in areas such as psychology and bio-chemistry. PARAFAC is a multilinear analogue of SVD. The key idea is to minimize the sum of squares between the original tensor and the factorized model of the tensor. For the three mode case of a tensor $T \in \mathbb{R}^{D_1 \times D_2 \times D_3}$ this gives the objective function in 1, where k is the number of dimensions in the factorized model and $\circ$ denotes the outer product.

$$\min_{x_i \in \mathbb{R}^{D1}, y_i \in \mathbb{R}^{D2}, z_i \in \mathbb{R}^{D3}} \| T - \sum_{i=1}^{k} x_i \circ y_i \circ z_i \|_F^2 \tag{1}$$

The algorithm results in three matrices, indicating the loadings of each mode on the factorized dimensions. The model is represented graphically in Figures 2 and 3. Figure 2 visualizes the fact that the PARAFAC decomposition consists of the summation over the outer products of n (in this case three) vectors. Figure 3 represents the three resulting matrices that come out of the factorization, indicating the loadings of each mode on the factorized dimensions. We will be using the latter representation in our research.

Computationally, the PARAFAC model is fitted by applying an alternating least-squares algorithm. In each iteration, two of the modes are fixed and the third one is fitted in a least squares sense. This process is repeated until convergence.[2]

4.3 Sound correspondences

In order to detect the most important sound variation within Bulgarian dialects, we proceed from extracting all sound correspondences from the automatically aligned word transcriptions. All transcriptions were pairwise aligned using the Levenshtein algorithm (Levenshtein, 1965) as implemented in the program L04.[3] The Levenshtein algorithm is a dynamic programming algorithm used to measure the differences between two strings. The distance between two strings is the smallest number of insertions, deletions, and substitutions needed to transform one string to the other. In this work all three operations were assigned the same value, namely 1. The algorithm is also directly used to align two sequences. An example showing two aligned pronunciations of the word вълна /vɤlna/ 'wool' is given in Figure 4.[4]

v	'ɤ	-	n	ɑ
v	'ɑ	l	n	ə

Figure 4: Example of two pairwise aligned word transcriptions.

From the aligned transcriptions for all words and all villages in the data set we first extracted

[2]The algorithm has been implemented in MATLAB, using the Tensor Toolbox for sparse tensor calculations (Bader and Kolda, 2009).

[3]`http://www.let.rug.nl/kleiweg/L04`

[4]For some pairs of transcriptions there are two or more possible alignments, i.e. alignments that have the same cost. In these cases we have randomly picked only one of them.

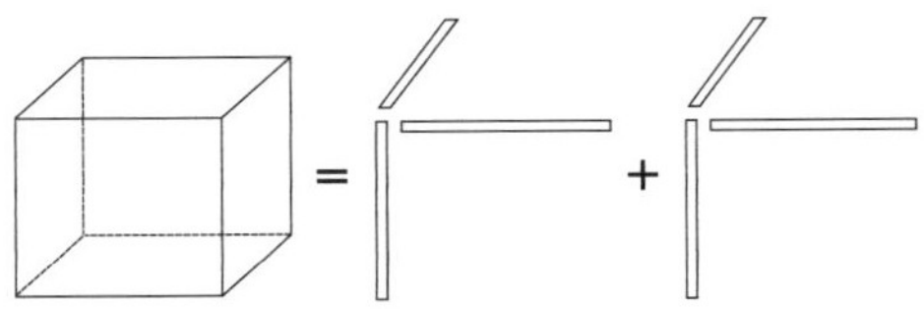

Figure 2: Graphical representation of PARAFAC as the sum of outer products.

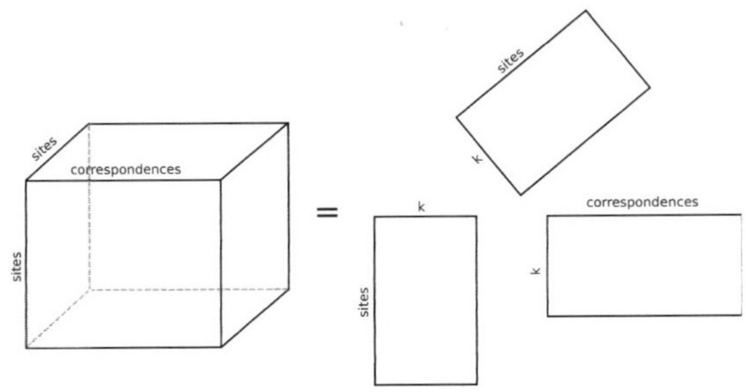

Figure 3: Graphical representation of the PARAFAC as three loadings matrices.

all corresponding non-identical sounds. For example, from the aligned transcriptions in Figure 4 we would extract the following sound pairs: [ˈɤ]-[ˈɑ], [-]-[l], [ɑ]-[ə]. The hyphen ('-') stands for a missing (i.e. inserted or deleted) sound, and in further analyses it is treated the same as any sound in the data set. For each pair of corresponding sounds from the data set we counted how often it appeared in the aligned transcriptions for each pair of villages separately. In total we extracted 907 sound correspondences and stored the information on each of them in a separate matrix. Every matrix records the distances between each two villages in the data set, measured as the number of times a certain phonetic alternation is recorded while comparing pronunciations from these sites.

Since we are interested in analyzing all sound correspondences simultaneously, we merged the information from all 907 two-mode matrices into a three-mode tensor $n \times n \times v$, where n represents the sites in the data set, and v represents the sound alternations. By arranging our data in a cube instead of a matrix, we are able to look into several sets of variables simultaneously. We are especially interested in the loadings for the third mode, that contains the values for the sound correspondences.

5 Results

In order to detect the most prominent sound correspondences we analyzed the three-mode tensor described in the previous section using a PARAFAC factorization with $k = 10$ dimensions. In Table 5 we present only the first five dimensions extracted by the algorithm. The final model fits 44% of the original data. The contribution of the first extracted dimension (dim1) to the final fit of the model is the largest – 23.81 per cent – while the next four dimensions contribute to the final fit with similar percentages: dim2 with 10.63 per cent, dim3 with 9.50 per cent, dim4 with 9.26 per cent, and dim5 with 9.09 per cent. Dimensions six to ten contribute in the range from 8.66 per cent to 6.98 per cent.

For every dimension we extracted the twenty sound correspondences with the highest scores. In the first dimension we find 11 pairs involving vowels and 9 involving consonant variation. The three sound correspondences with the highest scores are the [ɑ]-[ə], [o]-[u], and [e]-[i] alternations. This finding corresponds well with the traditional scholarly views on Bulgarian phonetics (Wood and Pettersson, 1988; Barnes, 2006) where we find that in unstressed syllables mid vowels [e] and [o] raise to neutralize with the high vowels [i] and [u]. The low vowel [a] raises to merge with [ə].

For every sound alternation we also check their geographical distribution. We do so by applying the following procedure. From the aligned pairs of transcriptions we extract corresponding pairs of sounds for every alternation. We count how many times each of the two sounds appears in the transcriptions for every village. Thus, for every pair of sound correspondences, we can create two maps that show the distribution of each of the sounds separately. On the map of Bulgaria these values

Table 1: First five dimensions for the sound correspondences.

dim1	dim2	dim3	dim4	dim5
[ɑ]-[ə]	[ə]-[ɤ]	[u]-[o]	[ɑ]-[ə]	[e]-[i]
[u]-[o]	[e]-[i]	[ɑ]-[ɤ]	[ə]-[ɤ]	[i]-[ˈe]
[e]-[i]	[ˈe]-[ˈɛ]	[ɑ]-[ə]	[ʊ]-[o]	[e]-[ə]
[-]-[j]	[-]-[j]	[ɤ]-[e]	[e]-[ə]	[r]-[rʲ]
[e]-[ˈe]	[ʃ]-[ɕ]	[e]-[ˈe]	[d]-[dʲ]	[d]-[dʲ]
[ʃ]-[ɕ]	[t͡ʃ]-[t͡ɕ]	[ˈe]-[ˈɛ]	[v]-[vʲ]	[ˈe]-[ˈɑ]
[t͡ʃ]-[t͡ɕ]	[ˈɑ]-[ˈɛ]	[-]-[j]	[n]-[nʲ]	[-]-[j]
[ˈe]-[ˈɛ]	[r]-[rʲ]	[ˈe]-[ˈɑ]	[-]-[j]	[ˈo]-[u]
[n]-[nʲ]	[l]-[lʲ]	[e]-[i]	[ˈe]-[ˈɛ]	[l]-[lʲ]
[ɑ]-[ɤ]	[e]-[ə]	[n]-[nʲ]	[l]-[lʲ]	[v]-[vʲ]
[e]-[ə]	[d]-[dʲ]	[r]-[rʲ]	[t]-[tʲ]	[u]-[o]
[ˈɑ]-[ˈɛ]	[n]-[nʲ]	[t͡ʃ]-[t͡ɕ]	[ˈe]-[ˈɑ]	[n]-[nʲ]
[ˈe]-[ˈɑ]	[u]-[ʊ]	[ˈɤ]-[ˈɑ]	[e]-[ˈe]	[-]-[v]
[d]-[dʲ]	[ˈɤ]-[ˈɔ]	[-]-[r]	[ʃ]-[ɕ]	[ˈɤ]-[ə]
[ɤ]-[e]	[ə]-[ˈɑ]	[ʃ]-[ɕ]	[t͡ʃ]-[t͡ɕ]	[u]-[ʊ]
[l]-[lʲ]	[ɤ]-[e]	[l]-[lʲ]	[r]-[rʲ]	[t͡ʃ]-[t͡ɕ]
[v]-[vʲ]	[ˈo]-[u]	[u]-[e]	[p]-[pʲ]	[ˈɑ]-[ˈɛ]
[r]-[rʲ]	[ʒ]-[ʑ]	[-]-[ˈɤ]	[ʒ]-[ʑ]	[ɑ]-[ˈɤ]
[ʒ]-[ʑ]	[i]-[ə]	[v]-[-]	[ə]-[ˈɑ]	[ə]-[ˈɑ]
[ˈɤ]-[ˈɔ]	[v]-[vʲ]	[ɑ]-[ˈɤ]	[e]-[i]	[b]-[bʲ]

are represented using a gradual color, which enables us to see not only the geographic distribution of a certain sound but also how regular it is in a given sound alternation. The highest scoring sites are coloured black and the lowest scoring sites are coloured white.

In Figure 5 we see the geographical distribution of the first three extracted correspondences. The first two alternations [ɑ]-[ə] and [o]-[u] have almost the same geographical distribution and divide the country into west and east. While in the west there is a clear presence of vowels [ɑ] and [o], in the east those vowels would be pronounced as [ə] and [u]. The division into east and west corresponds well with the so-called *jat* line, which is, according to traditional dialectologists (Stojkov, 2002) the main dialect border in Bulgaria. On the maps in Figure 5 we represent it with the black line that roughly divides Bulgaria into east and west. The third correspondence follows a slightly different pattern: mid vowel [e] is present not only west of the *jat* line, but also in the southern part of the country, in the region of Rodopi mountains. In the central and northeastern areas this sound is pronounced as high vowel [i]. For all three sound correspondences we see a clear two-way division of the country, with almost all sites being characterized by one of the two pronunciations, which, as we shall see later, is not always the case due to multiple reflections of some sounds at certain positions.

We also note that the distribution of the sound correspondences that involve soft consonants and their counterparts have the same east-west distribution (see Figure 6). In the first dimension we find the following consonants and their palatal counterparts [n], [d], [l], [v] and [r], but because of space limitations we show maps only for three correspondences. The east-west division also emerges with respect to the distribution of the [ɑ]-[ɤ] and [ˈe]-[ˈɑ] sounds.

Unlike the correspondences mentioned before, the [ʃ]-[ɕ], [t͡ʃ]-[t͡ɕ], and [ʒ]-[ʑ] pairs are defining the south part of the country as a separate zone. As shown on the maps in Figure 7, the southern part of the country (the region of Rodopi mountains) is characterized by a soft pronunciation of [ʃ], [t͡ʃ] and [ʒ]. In traditonal literature on Bulgarain dialectology (Stojkov, 2002), we also find that soft pronunciation of [ʃ], [t͡ʃ] and [ʒ] is one of the most important phonetic features of the varieties in the Rodopi zone. Based on the correspondences extracted in the first dimension, this area is also defined by the presence of the vowel [ˈɛ] in stressed syllables ([ˈe]-[ˈɛ] and [ˈɑ]-[ˈɛ] correspondences).

In some extracted correspondences, only one of the sounds has a geographically coherent distribution, like in the case of the [ɤ]-[e] pair where [e] is found in the west and south, while the [ɤ] sound is only sporadically present in the central region. This kind of asymmetrical distribution is also found with respect to the pair [ɑ]-[ɤ].

Most of the sound correspondences in the first dimension either divide the country along the *jat* line or separate the Rodopi area from the rest of the varieties. The only two exceptions are the [-]-[j] and [ˈɤ]-[ˈɔ] pairs. They both define the southwest area as a separate zone, while the northwest shares its pronunciation of the sound in question with the eastern part of the country.

We use the first 20 correspondences from the first dimension and perform *k-means* clustering in order to check which dialect areas would emerge based on this limited set of sound correspond-

Figure 5: [ɑ]-[ə] (left), [o]-[u] (middle), [e]-[i] (right) sound correspondences.

Figure 6: [d]-[d^j] (left), [v]-[v^j] (middle), [r]-[r^j] (right) sound correspondences.

ences. The results of the 2-way, 3-way and 4-way clustering are given in Figure 8.

In two-way clustering the algorithm detects an east-west split approximately along the *jat* line, slightly moved to the east. This fully corresponds to the traditional dialectology but also to the results obtained using Levenshtein algorithm on the whole data set where only east, west and south varieties could be asserted with great confidence (Prokić and Nerbonne, 2008). In Figure 9 we present the dialect divisions that we get if the distances between the sites are calculated using whole word transcriptions instead of only the 20 most prominent sound correspondences. We notice a high correspondence between the two analyses at the two- and three-level division. On the level of four and more groups, the two analyses start detecting different groups. In the analysis based on 20 sound correspondences, southern dialects are divided into smaller and smaller groups, while in the analysis based on the whole data set, the area in the west – near the Serbian border – emerges as the fourth group. This is no surprise, as the first 20 extracted correspondences do not contain any sounds typical only for this western area.

In order to compare two divisions of sites, we calculated the adjusted Rand index (Hubert and Arabie, 1985). The adjusted Rand index (ARI) is used in classification for comparing two different partitions of a finite set of objects. It is based on the Rand index (Rand, 1971), one of the most popular measures for comparing the degree to which partitions agree (in classification). Value 1 of the ARI indicates that two classifications match perfectly, while value 0 means that two partitions do not agree on any pair of points. For both two-level and three-level divisions of the sites the ARI for two classifications is 0.84. We also compared

Figure 7: [ʃ]-[ɕ] (left), [t͡ʃ]-[t͡ɕ] (middle), [ʒ]-[ʑ] (right) sound correspondences.

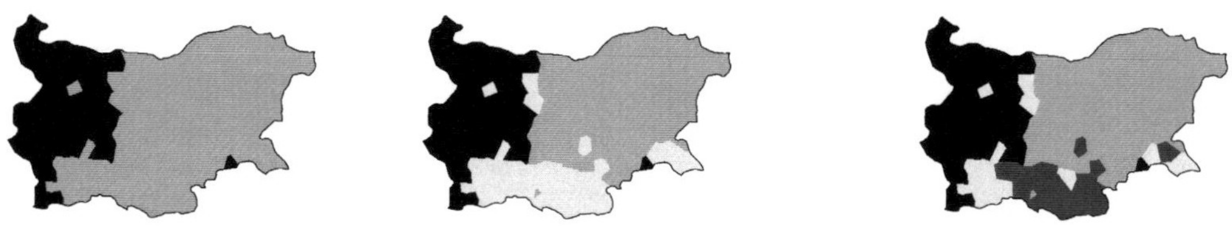

Figure 8: Dialect varieties detected by k-means clustering algorithm based on the first 20 sound correspondences in the first dimension.

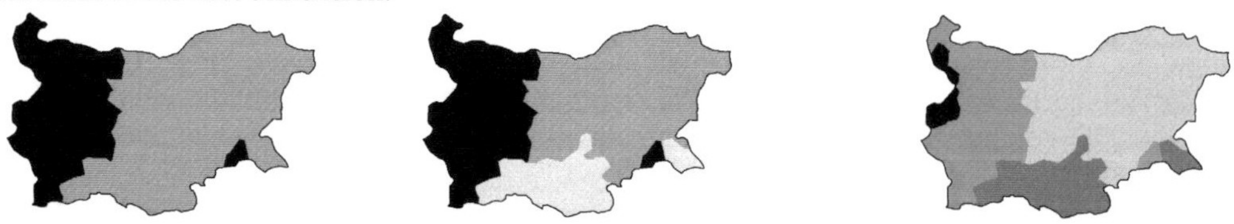

Figure 9: Dialect varieties detected by k-means clustering algorithm based on all word transcriptions.

both of the classifications to the classification of the sites done by Stojkov (2002). For the classification based on the first dimension extracted by PARAFAC, ARI is 0.73 for two-way and 0.64 for the three-way division. ARI score for the classification based on whole word transcriptions is 0.69 for two-way and 0.62 for three-way. As indicated by ARI the two classifications correspond with a high degree to each other, but to the traditional classification as well. We note that two-way classification based on the extracted sound correspondences corresponds higher to the traditional classification than classification that takes all sounds into account.

We conclude that the sound correspondences detected by PARAFAC form the linguistic basis of the two-way and three-way divisions of Bulgarian dialect area. Using the PARAFAC method we are able to detect that the most important sound changes on which two-way division is based are [o]-[u], [ɑ]-[ə] and palatal pronunciation of consonants. In the three-way division of sites done by *k-means*, the area in the south of the country appears as the third most important dialect zone. In the twenty investigated sound correspondences we find that the soft pronunciation of [ʃ],[t͡ʃ] and [ʒ] sounds is typical only for the varieties in this area. Apart from divisions that divide the country into west and east, including the southern varieties, we also detect sound correspondences whose distribution groups together western and southern areas.

We also analyzed in more depth sound correspondences extracted in other dimensions by the PARAFAC algorithm. Most of the correspondences found in the first dimension, also reappear in the following nine dimensions. Closer inspection of the language groups obtained using information from these dimensions show that eastern, western and southern varieties are the only three that are identified. No other dialect areas were detected based on the sound correspondences from these nine dimensions.

6 Conclusion

In this paper we have applied PARAFAC in the task of detecting the linguistic basis of dialect phonetic variation. The distances between varieties were expressed as a numerical vector that records information on all sound correspondences found in the data set. Using PARAFAC we were able to extract the most important sound correspondences. Based on the 20 most important sound correspondences we performed clustering of all sites in the data set and were able to detect three groups of sites. As found in traditional literature on Bulgarian dialects, these three dialects are the main dialect groups in Bulgaria. Using the aggregate approach on the same data set, the same three dialects were the only groups in the data that could be asserted with high confidence. We conclude that this approach is successful in extracting underlying linguistic structure in dialect variation, while at the same time overcoming some of the problems found in the earlier approaches to this problem.

In future work sounds in the data set could be defined in a more sophisticated way, using some kind of feature representation. Also, the role of stress should be examined in more depth, since there are different patterns of change in stressed in unstressed syllables. We would also like to extend the method and examine more than just two sound correspondences at a time.

References

Brett W. Bader and Tamara G. Kolda. 2009. Matlab tensor toolbox version 2.3. `http://csmr.ca.sandia.gov/~tgkolda/TensorToolbox/`, July.

Jonathan Barnes. 2006. *Strength and Weakness at the Interface: Positional Neutralization in Phonetics and Phonology*. Walter de Gruyter GmbH, Berlin.

J. Douglas Carroll and Jih-Jie Chang. 1970. Analysis of individual differences in multidimensional scaling via an n-way generalization of "eckart-young" decomposition. *Psychometrika*, 35:283–319.

Richard A. Harshman. 1970. Foundations of the parafac procedure: models and conditions for an "explanatory" multi-mode factor analysis. In *UCLA Working Papers in Phonetics*, volume 16, pages 1–84, Los Angeles. University of California.

Lawrence Hubert and Phipps Arabie. 1985. Comparing partitions. *Journal of Classification*, 2:193–218.

Tamara G. Kolda and Brett W. Bader. 2009. Tensor decompositions and applications. *SIAM Review*, 51(3), September.

Vladimir Levenshtein. 1965. Binary codes capable of correcting deletions, insertions and reversals. *Doklady Akademii Nauk SSSR*, 163:845–848.

John Nerbonne. 2006. Identifying linguistic structure in aggregate comparison. *Literary and Linguistic Computing*, 21(4):463–476.

Karl Pearson. 1901. On lines and planes of closest fit to systems of points in space. *Philosophical Magazine*, 2(6):559–572.

Jelena Prokić and John Nerbonne. 2008. Recognizing groups among dialects. *International Journal of Humanities and Arts Computing*, Special Issue on *Language Variation* ed. by John Nerbonne, Charlotte Gooskens, Sebastian Kürschner, and Renée van Bezooijen:153–172.

Jelena Prokić, John Nerbonne, Vladimir Zhobov, Petya Osenova, Krili Simov, Thomas Zastrow, and Erhard Hinrichs. 2009. The Computational Analysis of Bulgarian Dialect Pronunciation. *Serdica Journal of Computing*, 3:269–298.

Jelena Prokić. 2007. Identifying linguistic structure in a quantitative analysis of dialect pronunciation. In *Proceedings of the ACL 2007 Student Research Workshop*, pages 61–66.

William M. Rand. 1971. Objective criteria for the evaluation of clustering methods. *Journal of American Statistical Association*, 66(336):846–850, December.

Robert G. Shackleton. 2007. Phonetic variation in the traditional English dialects. *Journal of English Linguistics*, 35(1):30–102.

Stojko Stojkov. 2002. *Bulgarska dialektologiya*. Sofia, 4th ed.

Michael E. Wall, Andreas Rechtsteiner, and Luis M. Rocha, 2003. *Singular Value Decomposition and Principal Component Analysis*, chapter 5, pages 91–109. Kluwer, Norwell, MA, Mar.

Martijn Wieling and John Nerbonne. 2009. Bipartite spectral graph partitioning to co-cluster varieties and sound correspondences in dialectology. In *Text Graphs 4, Workshop at the 47th Meeting of the Association for Computational Linguistics*, pages 14–22.

Sidney A. J. Wood and Thore Pettersson. 1988. Vowel reduction in Bulgarian: the phonetic data and model experiments. *Folia Linguistica*, 22(3-4):239–262.

Quantitative evaluation of competing syllable parses

Jason A. Shaw
New York University/
Haskins Laboratories
New York, NY/New Haven, CT, USA
jason.shaw@nyu.edu

Adamantios I. Gafos
New York University/
Haskins Laboratories
New York, NY/New Haven, CT, USA
adamantios.gafos@nyu.edu

Abstract

This paper develops computational tools for evaluating competing syllabic parses of a phonological string on the basis of temporal patterns in speech production data. This is done by constructing models linking syllable parses to patterns of coordination between articulatory events. Data simulated from different syllabic parses are evaluated against experimental data from American English and Moroccan Arabic, two languages claimed to parse similar strings of segments into different syllabic structures. Results implicate a tautosyllabic parse of initial consonant clusters in English and a heterosyllabic parse of initial clusters in Arabic, in accordance with theoretical work on the syllable structure of these languages. It is further demonstrated that the model can correctly diagnose syllable structure even when previously proposed phonetic heuristics for such structure do not clearly point to the correct diagnosis.

1 Introduction

Languages are claimed to differ in how word-initial consonant clusters are parsed into higher level phonological structures. For example, English (Kahn, 1976) and Georgian (Vogt, 1971) are claimed to parse initial clusters into complex syllable onsets. In contrast, Berber and Moroccan Arabic are claimed to parse initial clusters heterosyllabically, [#C.CV-], because the syllable structure of these languages allows at most one consonant (simplex onset) per syllable onset (Dell & Elmedlaoui, 2002).

Of direct relevance to these claims are patterns of temporal stability in the production of initial clusters. In those cases where speech production data are available, languages that allow complex onsets exhibit patterns of temporal stability that differ from languages that allow only syllables with simplex syllable onsets.

These observed temporal differences have been quantified in terms of the relative stability of intervals as calculated across words beginning with one, two and three initial consonants (Browman & Goldstein, 1988; Byrd, 1995; Honorof & Browman, 1995; Shaw, Gafos, Hoole, & Zeroual, 2009). Figure 1 schematizes temporal differences between simplex and complex onsets. The figure shows three temporal intervals left-delimited by landmarks in the consonant cluster, the left edge of the cluster, the center of the cluster and the right edge of the cluster, and right-delimited by a common anchor point.

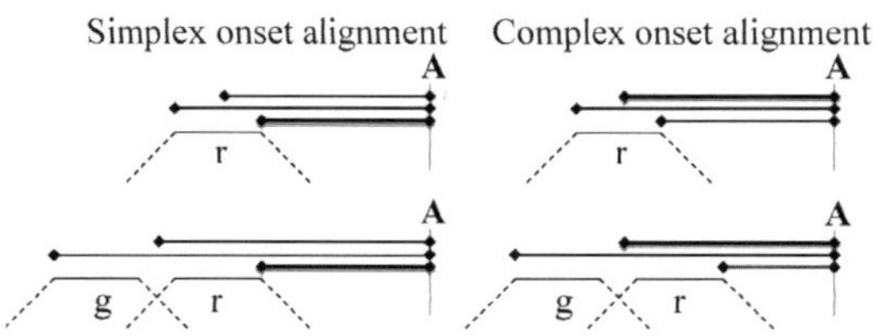

Figure 1. Schematic representation of three intervals, left edge to anchor, center to anchor and right edge to anchor, delineated by points in an initial single consonant or consonant cluster and a common anchor (A). The alignment schema on the left/right represents experimentally observed temporal manifestations of the simplex/complex onset parse. Such patterns have been used as phonetic heuristics in diagnosing syllable structure in experimental data.

When clusters are parsed into simplex syllable onsets (Figure 1: left), the duration of the right edge to anchor interval is unperturbed by the addition of consonants to the word. Consequently, this interval remains stable across #CVX and

Proceedings of the 11th Meeting of the ACL-SIGMORPHON, ACL 2010, pages 54–62,
Uppsala, Sweden, 15 July 2010.

#CCVX words. In contrast, when clusters are parsed into a complex onset (Figure 1: right), the duration of the right edge to anchor interval shrinks to make room for the addition of a consonant to the syllable. Under this temporal alignment schema, the center to anchor interval remains more stable across #CVX and #CCVX words than both the right edge to anchor interval and the left edge to anchor interval.

Experimental results showing temporal patterns consistent with the schema on the right side of Figure 1 include Browman and Goldstein (1988), Honorof and Browman (1995), and Marin and Pouplier (2008) on American English, Goldstein, Chitoran, & Selkirk (2007) on Georgian and Hermes, Grice, Muecke and Niemann (2008) on Italian. Results showing the temporal pattern on the left side of Figure 1 include Goldstein *et al.* (2007) on Berber, Shaw *et al.* (2009) on Moroccan Arabic and Hermes *et al.* (2008) on Italian.

We briefly review representative quantitative results illustrating the different temporal organizations in Figure 1. For a language with complex onsets, Browman and Goldstein (1988) show that the standard deviation calculated across English word sets such as *pot~sot~spot~lot~plot~splot* is smaller for the center to anchor interval, 15.8 ms, than for the left edge to anchor interval, 37.7 ms, and the right edge to anchor interval, 33.6 ms. In contrast, for a simplex onset language, Shaw *et al.* (2009) show that across similar Moroccan Arabic word sets, e.g., *bati~sbati,* the right edge to anchor interval has a lower standard deviation, 14 ms, than the center to anchor interval, 27 ms, and the left edge to anchor interval, 77 ms.

Although the experimental work reviewed above shows that stability comparisons among the right edge to anchor, center to anchor and left edge to anchor intervals can provide good heuristics for testing syllabification hypotheses in experimental data, such heuristics stated in terms of inequalities are known to break down under some conditions. For example, simulations with a model reported in Shaw *et al.* (2009) demonstrated that when the overall variability in the intervals is high, the simplex onset parse can generate intervals exhibiting *stability reversals* whereby the center to anchor interval is more stable than the right/left edge to anchor interval (contra the heuristic which states that the right edge to anchor interval should be the most stable; again, see Figure 1: left). This result indicates the frailty of phonetic heuristics in the form of inequalities, e.g. a simplex onset parse implies that the right edge to anchor interval *is more stable than* the center to anchor interval and the left edge to anchor interval. Such heuristics may be too coarse or even in some cases misleading in distinguishing competing syllabic parses using experimental data.

This paper advances a quantitative method for evaluating competing syllable parses that aims to improve on previously proposed phonetic heuristics and, by doing so, sharpen the interpretation of temporal stability patterns in terms of syllabic structure. In mediating between phonological theory and experimental data, the computational model makes it possible to discover syllabification rules from phonetic patterns. The model provides a new understanding of languages with known syllable structure and the analytical tools to deduce syllabification rules in less-studied languages.

2 Model

The general plan is to simulate data from models encoding competing syllabic parses, to quantify in the simulated data the pattern of stability in the intervals shown in Figure 1, and to evaluate the goodness of fit between the pattern of stability in the simulated data and the pattern of stability in experimental data. Our modeling paradigm capitalizes on structurally revealing temporal patterns in experimental data but improves on past work by modeling competing syllabic structures (both simplex and complex onset parses of initial clusters) and replacing hypotheses stated in the form of inequalities with quantitative indices of goodness of fit between syllable parses and experimental data.

Given a string of consonants and vowels, e.g. CCV, the models map the simplex and complex onset parse of that string to distinct coordination topologies. The coordination topologies reflect the temporal relations underlying the segmental sequence (Gafos, 2002: p. 316). Differences in temporal structure at this level yield the distinct temporal alignment patterns schematized in Figure 1.

Figure 2 shows how the syllable parse, simplex or complex, determines the relative temporal alignment of the segments involved. The boxes at the bottom of the figure (V rectangles) represent the temporal extent of the syllable nucleus, the vowel, which depends on the syllable parse. On a simplex onset parse (Figure 2a) the vowel is aligned to the midpoint of the immediately prevocalic consonant regardless of the number of preceding consonants. On a complex onset parse (Figure 2b) the vowel is aligned to the midpoint of the entire cluster of prevocalic consonants. These temporal alignment schemas have been proposed to underlie the experimental results we reviewed in Section 1.

The model simulates the temporal organization of words with one, two, and sometimes three initial consonant clusters on the basis of a probabilistic interpretation of the temporal structure encoded in the syllable parse (simplex or complex). In addition, the model has three phonetic parameters, k^p, k^{ipi}, and V, which determine, respectively, consonant plateau duration, the duration between consonant plateaus, and vowel duration. These latter parameters can be set using estimates from the phonetic record.

As summarized in Figure 2, word simulation proceeds from the immediately prevocalic consonant, C_n. The timestamp of the release of this consonant, C_n^{Rel}, is drawn from a Gaussian distribution. The timestamp of the achievement of target of this consonant, C_n^{Tar}, is determined by subtracting consonant plateau duration, k^p, from C_n^{Rel} and adding an error term. Additional prevocalic consonants, e.g. C_1 in #C_1C_2V, are determined with reference to the immediately preceding consonant. For example, the timestamp of the release of C_{n-1}, C_{n-1}^{Rel}, is determined by subtracting the inter-plateau interval, k^{ipi}, from C_n^{Tar} and adding a noise term. As noted above, the alignment of the vowel relative to the prevocalic consonant(s) is dictated by the syllable parse.

Once the temporal structure of the input segmental strings was generated, the stability of each target interval, the left edge to anchor, center to anchor and right edge to anchor interval was calculated across words in the simulated data. For these intervals, the offset of the vowel was used as the anchor point.

In light of past work indicating that phonetic heuristics for syllable structure may change as the level of variability in the data increases (Shaw *et al.*, 2009), we also manipulated the variability of the simulated intervals. We did this by varying the standard deviation of the vowel offset (from 0 to 70 ms in 15 discrete 5 ms increments such that anchors 1, 2, 3…15 have a standard deviation of 0 ms, 5 ms, 10 ms…70 ms, respectively). Since the vowel offset serves as an anchor in right-delimiting all of the measured intervals, increasing the standard deviation of this point is one way to increase the level of variability in all of the simulated intervals uniformly. This effectively allows the level of variability in simulated data to match the level of variability in experimental data.

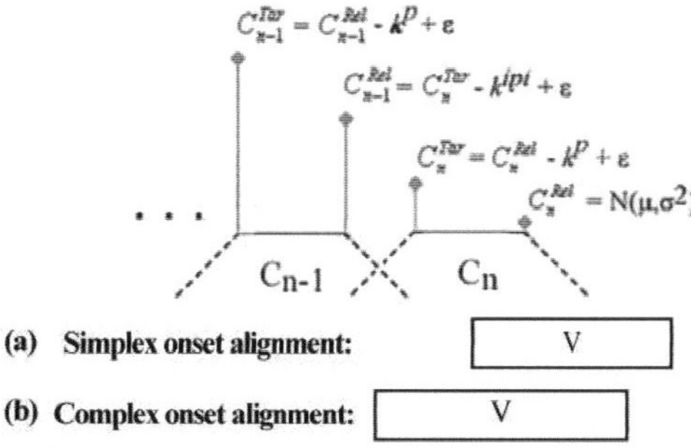

Figure 2: Summary of word simulation in the model. Consonant landmarks are generated from the release of the immediately prevocalic consonant. The alignment of the vowel is determined by the syllable parse (simplex or complex).

To sum up the central idea, the task of evaluating syllable parses with experimental data has been formulated here as the task of fitting abstract coordination topologies to the experimental data. This fitting can be expressed using two types of variables, coordination topologies and anchor variability. In the study of biological coordination and complex systems more generally, these two variables correspond respectively to the so-called essential and non-essential variables describing the behavior of complex systems (Kugler, Kelso, & Turvey, 1980: p. 13).

Essential variables specify the qualitative form of the system under study. For us, this corresponds to the syllabic parse of the phonological string. The fundamental hypothesis entailed in positing an abstract phonological organization isomorphic to syllable structure is that a syllable parse is a macroscopic organization uniform across a variegated set of segmental identities, lexical statistics and rate conditions, e.g. ‘plea’, ‘tree’, ‘glee’ are single syllables independent of speech rate, frequency or phonotactic probability (see Catford 1977: p. 13 on ‘phonological form’).

All of the above factors, however, have left imprints on the articulatory patterns registered in the experimental data. Crucially, we do not know and it may not be possible to predict for any given stimulus how each such factor or combination of factors has affected the intervals quantified. Taken together, then, these and other yet unknown factors have introduced noise in the intervals that will be measured. Therefore, in formulating the modeling problem of diagnosing syllable structure in experimental data, we let variability be one of the non-essential variables manipulated in the fitting process. The anchor offers a convenient location for introducing this variability into the intervals. In the discussion that follows, the non-essential variable of anchor index will be used to refer to the amount of variability introduced into the intervals through the anchor.

3 Syllable parse evaluation

Our models allow syllabic parses of the same string to be compared directly and evaluated quantitatively by determining which parse results in a better fit to the data.

As an index of interval stability, we employ the relative standard deviation of the three intervals shown in Figure 1, calculated across sets of words with one, two, and sometimes three initial consonants. Relative standard deviation, henceforth RSD, is calculated by dividing the standard deviation of an interval by its mean duration. Substantive reasons for using RSD as a dependent variable and not the standard deviation or mean duration of the intervals are described, respectively, in Shaw *et al.* (2009: p. 203) and Shaw (2010: p. 111-112).

Model performance was evaluated on the basis of two test statistics: the R^2 statistic and the F statistic. The R^2 statistic provides a measure of *goodness of fit* capable of detecting gradient improvement (or degradation) in model performance as a function of parameter values. The F statistic, on the other hand, is used to evaluate model performance in the following way. *Hits* or *misses* for each pairing of simulated RSDs and data RSDs will be determined based upon p values generated from the F statistic. The criterion of $p < .01$ will be interpreted as successful rejection of the null hypothesis (that the RSD of all intervals is equal) and constitute a *hit* while failure to reject the null hypothesis constitutes a *miss*. This method of interpreting the F statistic provides a direct way to evaluate model performance for each run of the simulation. Across multiple runs of the simulation, the ratio of hits to total runs (hits + misses) provides a *hit rate* which summarizes the performance of a syllable parse in matching the experimental data.

This method of model evaluation has a conceptual antecedent in other work in probabilistic grammar. The *hit rate* as described above plays a similar role in model evaluation as the confidence scores employed in Albright and Hayes (2003). The probabilistic rules of English past tense formation developed in that paper are associated with a reliability index. Albright and Hayes (2003) refer to this as a *raw confidence* score. The raw confidence score of a rule is the likelihood that the rule applies when its environment is met. The score is the ratio of the number of times that a particular rule applies, *hits*, by the number of times in which the environment for the rule is present in the data, the rule's *scope*. For example, the rule for the English past tense [ɪ] → [ʌ]/ {l,r}___ŋ correctly derives forms such as *sprung* from *spring* and *flung* from *fling*, but makes the wrong prediction, *brung* and not *brought*, for *bring*. Of the 4253 verbs employed in the Albright and Hayes (2003) learning set, the environment of the *spring-sprung* rule occurs 9 times and the rule applies correctly in 6 of those cases yielding a raw confidence score of .667. In contrast, the most general rule for the English past tense ∅ → d / X ____ has a scope identical to the size of the data set, 4253, and applies in 4034 cases yielding a raw confidence score of .949. In the case at hand, that of syllable structure, the *hit rate* proposed above plays a similar role to that of the confidence score. It provides a simple statistic summarizing the fit of a syllable parse to data.

The value of the non-essential variable (anchor index) that maximizes the R^2 statistic is also informative in evaluating syllable structure. When the syllable parse is correct, then large amounts of noise added to the intervals may be harmful, pushing the model output away from patterns dictated by the essential variable. On the other hand, when the syllable parse is wrong, then increases in noise may improve model performance by pushing the intervals in the direction of the correct syllable parse on some trials. Since noise is inserted into the intervals through the anchor, comparing the anchor indices that maximize R^2 may be informative in evaluating syllable parses. A lower anchor index indicates a better-fitting syllable parse.

The F and R^2 statistics used to provide quantitative evaluation of syllabic structure as described above are obtained by plotting RSDs measured in the data (x-axis) against corresponding RSDs simulated by the model (y-axis), and fitting a regression line to these coordinates using the least squares method. A representative plot is shown in Figure 3. The x-axis shows the RSD of the three intervals of interest for the *bulha~sbulha~ksbulha* triad as reported in Shaw *et al.* (2009). These are plotted against RSDs simulated by the model given a simplex onset parse and different levels of anchor variability. For simplicity in presentation, just four of the fifteen anchors simulated are shown in the figure. The standard deviation of these representative anchors is as follows: anchor 1 = 0 ms, anchor 7 = 30 ms, anchor 11 = 50 ms, and anchor 14 = 65 ms.

Figure 3 shows that R^2 is highest when the simplex onset parse is paired with anchor 7. At this level of anchor variability, the simplex onset parse provides a perfect fit to the data. At both lower (anchor 1) and higher (anchor 11) levels of anchor variability, the fit to the data is degraded.

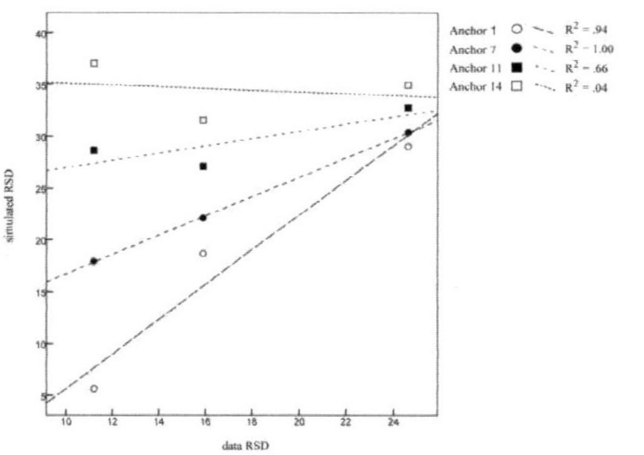

Figure 3. Fit between model and data. The RSD of three intervals in the data (x-axis) are plotted against the RSD of simulated intervals (y-axis) at different levels of anchor variability (anchor 1, anchor 7, anchor 11, anchor 14).

As illustrated in Figure 3, model performance is assessed by calculating the regression line on the basis of all three measured intervals at once. In doing so, the regression line captures the *relationship* between different measured intervals, or the *pattern* of interval stability. Since it is not the absolute value of the RSD of an interval but rather the relations between the RSDs of different intervals that is of theoretical interest, this is an important aspect of the fitting procedure.

For simulations reported below, the phonetic parameters discussed around Figure 2 are based on typical values for the languages under consideration. For American English, the values of these parameters used in the simulations were: k^p = 45 ms; k^{ipi} = 0 ms, and V = 230 ms. The error term, ε, associated with each consonantal landmark has a standard deviation of 14 ms. For Moroccan Arabic, the parameter values were: k^p = 42 ms; k^{ipi} = 66 ms, V = 196 ms. The error term was set to 20 ms. The results below are based on 1000 runs of the simulation for each word set.

4 Results

The simpex and complex onset parses were evaluated against three corpora using the procedure described above. The first two corpora are reported in Browman and Goldstein (1988) and Shaw *et al.* (2009) and provide relevant data on American English and Moroccan Arabic, respectively. Each of these studies reports articulatory data on just one speaker. The third corpus is a subset of the Wisconsin X-ray Microbeam Speech Production Database (Westbury, 1994). The sample analyzed here contains data from thirty-three speakers of American English.

4.1 American English (single speaker)

Our first American English data set draws from work of Browman and Goldstein (1988) which provides measurements of the stability of three relevant temporal intervals, left edge to anchor, right edge to anchor, and center to anchor, calculated over the following word set: [pɔt], [sɔt], [lɔt], [spɔt], [splɔt], [plɔt]. Interval stability was reported in terms of the standard deviation of each interval calculated across the word set.

In order to make these results directly comparable to those for Moroccan Arabic to be discussed in the next section, the relative standard deviation (RSD) of the English productions was calculated by dividing the standard deviation of each interval by the mean of that interval. Although Browman and Goldstein (1988) do not report the mean duration of the intervals, they provide a figure for each word and a scale (1 cm = 135 ms) for the figures allowing the relevant intervals to be measured. For each word, the duration of the three intervals of interest was measured from the figure and the standard deviation of the intervals was calculated across words. The resulting RSD values are shown in Table 1.

The RSDs from the data were compared to values output from model simulations based on a simplex onset parse, e.g., [sp.lɔt]~[p.lɔt]~[lɔt], and a complex onset parse, e.g., [splɔt]~[plɔt]~[lɔt], of the target strings. One run of the simulation generates ten repetitions of each of three word types, i.e., words beginning with one, two and three initial consonants. These words are generated based on a value for the essential variable (syllable structure) and a range of values of the non-essential variable (anchor index).

pot~sot~spot *lot~plot~splot*	Interval statistics		
	LE-A	CC-A	RE-A
mean	267	197	146
SD	37.7	15.8	33.6
RSD	14.0%	8.0%	23.0%

Table 1: The mean, standard deviation, and relative standard deviation of three intervals, left edge to anchor (LE-A), center to anchor (CC-A), right edge to anchor (RE-A), calculated across productions of *pot, sot, spot, lot, plot*, and *splot* by one speaker of American English.

The hit rate for the complex onset parse was 95.5% compared to just 57.7% for the simplex onset parse. This indicates that the complex onset parse provides a better fit to this data than the simplex onset parse. Moreover, the anchor index that maximizes R^2 for the complex onset parse is lower (anchor 3) than for the simplex parse (anchor 12). This further indicates that the complex onset parse outperforms the simplex onset parse on this data.

4.2 Moroccan Arabic (single speaker)

The results above indicate that the complex onset parse provides a better fit to the English data than the simplex onset parse. This section evaluates Moroccan Arabic data against these same syllabic parses. The data come from Shaw *et al.* (2009) which reports the RSD of the intervals of interest for seven word sets containing dyads or triads differing only in the number of initial consonants, e.g. *bulha~sbulha~ksbulha*. The word sets and the reported RSD of the intervals are summarized in Table 2.

For each word set, the model simulated corresponding word types. That is, for triads, e.g., *bulha~sbulha~ksbulha,* the model simulated 10 repetitions of words beginning with one, two, and three initial consonants, and, for dyads, e.g. *tab~ktab*, 10 repetitions of words beginning with one and two consonants. The model simulated word sets under each of the competing syllabic parses and evaluated the fit of each syllabic parse to the experimental data.

The resulting hit rates are summarized in Table 3. For each of the target word sets, the simplex onset parse shows a clear advantage in fitting the data. Hit rates for the simplex parse are above 75.4% in all cases and the hit rate for the complex onset parse never rises above 00.0%. Moreover, the anchor indices that maximize R^2 for the simplex onset parse are low, ranging from anchor 1 to anchor 7. For the complex onset parse, the highest variability anchor (anchor 15) provides the best fit to the data in all cases.

Word set	Interval RSD		
	LE-A	CC-A	RE-A
bulha~sbulha~ksbulha	24.6%	15.9%	11.2%
dulha~kdulha~bkdulha	22.2%	17.7%	10.7%
bal~dbal	20.5	9.7%	5.1%
tab~ktab	6.8%	5.7%	5.5%
bati~sbati	20.9%	9.1%	5.8%
bula~sbula	22.0%	11.1%	7.3%
lih~glih	18.5%	10.7%	2.7%

Table 2. Relative standard deviation of three intervals, left edge to anchor (LE-A), center to anchor (CC-A), right edge to anchor (RE-A) calculated across productions of word sets by one native speaker of Moroccan Arabic.

Word set	Hit rate	
	Simplex	Complex
bulha~sbulha~ksbulha	99.2% (7)	00.0% (15)
dulha~kdulha~bkdulha	99.9% (1)	00.0% (15)
bal~dbal	92.4% (3)	00.0% (15)
tab~ktab	75.4% (4)	00.0% (15)
bati~sbati	84.7% (4)	00.0% (15)
bula~sbula	88.5% (4)	00.0% (15)
lih~glih	98.3.0% (1)	00.0% (15)

Table 3. Hit rate for each syllable parse when evaluated against various Moroccan Arabic word sets. The anchor index that maximized R^2 for each syllable parse is given in parenthesis.

In sum, the simplex onset parse outperforms the complex onset parse on Moroccan Arabic data. The opposite result was obtained for American English. For English, it was the complex onset parse that achieved a higher hit rate with a lower anchor index.

Each of the data sets evaluated thus far were contributed by a single speaker. In these data the patterns of interval stability clearly reveal temporal organization in terms of syllables. To evaluate whether the model continues to distinguish syllabic parses when phonetic heuristics break down, we now turn to a corpus of less controlled stimuli from multiple speakers with a high degree of inter-speaker variability.

4.3 American English (multi-speaker data)

Under some conditions, stability-based phonetic heuristics break down as reliable indicators of syllable structure. This is known to occur, for example, when the level of overall variability in the intervals is high (Shaw *et al.*, 2009).

In controlled experimental studies, as can be seen in Figure 1, neither of the two syllabic parses, simplex or complex, has been observed to show the left edge to anchor interval as more stable than the center to anchor and right edge to anchor intervals. At high levels of variability, however, the probabilistic model developed in our work can produce patterns whereby the left edge to anchor interval is more stable than the other two intervals. This occurs regardless of the syllable parse when the anchor index is high (e.g. 15), which represents a high degree of variability in the intervals (the reason why high interval variability results in this pattern is explained in Shaw *et al.* 2009). Under these conditions of high variability, both values of the essential variable (simplex and complex onset parses) generate a pattern whereby the left edge to anchor interval has a lower RSD than the center to anchor interval and the right edge to anchor interval. Thus, at this level of variability, stability-based phonetic heuristics, i.e., *center to anchor stability implies a complex onset parse*, are rendered ineffective in distinguishing syllabic parses.

When variability leads competing syllable parses to the same predictions in terms of inequalities (both models show left edge to anchor stability), is our modeling paradigm still capable of distinguishing syllabic parses? To address this question, we need a corpus with the requisite level of variability.

The Wisconsin X-ray Microbeam Speech Production Database provides recordings of a variety of tasks including production of sentences, passages and word lists from fifty-seven speakers of American English (Westbury, 1994). Although not all speakers completed all tasks and some tokens have missing data which make them unusable for this analysis, it remains an archive of articulatory data that is extremely impressive in size. Within this archive there are various near-minimal pairs that can be used to evaluate syllable structure using the methods employed above. Here we report on thirty-three speakers' productions of the dyad *row~grows*. Calculating interval stability across multiple speaker samples of this word dyad is one way to introduce variability into the intervals and, by doing so, provide an interesting test case for our proposed methods.

The target word *row* was produced in the sentence *Things in a **row** provide a sense of order.* This sentence is one of several unrelated sentences included in Task #60 within the X-ray microbeam corpus. The word *grows* was produced in the sentence *That noise problem **grows** more annoying each day*, which is included in Task #56. Although these target words were produced in different syntactic frames and occur in different phrasal positions, we assume, following standard phonological assumptions, that all instances of /gr/ and /r/ were syllabified identically, namely, that they are parsed into complex syllable onsets. To test this assumption, we ask whether the models converge on the same result.

In all respects except for the determination of the anchor point, the quantification of the X-ray microbeam data followed the same procedure described for Electromagnetic Articulometry data in Shaw *et al.* (2009). To determine the anchor point, we followed past work on English (Browman and Goldstein 1988, Honorof and Browman 1995) by using an acoustic landmark, the offset of voicing in the vowel, as the anchor point right-delimiting the intervals of interest. This was done for the following reason. The target words in this case are not matched at the right edge of the syllable (*grows* ends in *s* while row ends in a vowel) and this makes it difficult to determine a common articulatory anchor across words. The articulatory landmarks that left-delimit the intervals of interest were the same as for the English and Arabic data discussed above.

The duration of the three intervals, left edge to anchor, center to anchor and right edge to anchor, were measured for one repetition of each word, *row* and *grows*, for thirty-three speakers. The variation across speakers in the duration of these intervals was substantial. As an example, the left edge to anchor interval of *row* ranges from 193 ms (Subject 44) to 518 ms (Subject 53). The mean, standard deviation and relative standard deviation of the intervals calculated across *row* and *grows* are provided in Table 4.

In this data the RSD of the left edge to anchor interval is lower than the RSD of both the center to anchor and right edge to anchor intervals. From the perspective of phonetic heuristics of syllable structure, this fact by itself is not particularly revealing. Both syllabic parses predict this should be the case at very high levels of variability. This data set therefore provides a challenge to phonetic heuristics stated in the form of directional inequalities and an appropriate test of the quantitative methods developed here.

row~grows	Interval statistics		
	LE-A	CC-A	RE-A
mean	302	269	233
SD	55.3	49.9	52.3
RSD	18.3%	18.6%	22.5%

Table 4. Mean, standard deviation, and relative standard deviation of three intervals, left edge to anchor (LE-A), center to anchor (CC-A), right edge to anchor (RE-A), calculated across productions of *row* and *grows* by thirty-three speakers of American English

Simulations with the simplex and complex onset models generated RSD values that were fitted to the RSD values of the three intervals of interest in the English *row~grows* data. On each run, the model simulated 10 repetitions of words beginning with one and two consonants. The same values of the constants used for the other English simulations were employed here as well, and the same range of anchor variability was produced for each parse. Anchor 1 has a standard deviation of zero and the standard deviation of each subsequent anchor increases by 5 ms so that anchor 15 has a standard deviation of 70 ms. Table 5 reports the results of 1000 runs of the simulation.

Word set	Hit rate	
	Simplex	Complex
row~grows	91.8% (11)	99.0% (6)

Table 5: Hit rate for each syllable parse when evaluated against the English dyad *row~grows*. The anchor index that maximized R^2 for each syllable parse is given in parenthesis.

The results of the model fitting reveal that the complex onset parse provides a superior fit to the data. The complex onset parse achieves a higher hit rate (99.0% vs. 91.8%) with a less variable anchor (anchor 6 vs. anchor 11) than the simplex onset parse. This result demonstrates that the model can distinguish syllabic parses even in noisy data contributed by multiple speakers.

Since the target words, *row* and *grows*, were produced in different environments, there are potentially a number of interacting factors influencing the pattern of temporal stability in the data. A model incorporating, for example, prosodic structure above the level of the syllable may identify interactions between syllable and higher levels of prosodic structure. We plan to explore models of this sort in future work. It remains an important result of the current model that competing parses of a given string can be distinguished in the data even at levels of variability that obscure phonetic heuristics for syllable structure.

5 Conclusion

There is a growing body of evidence indicating that the temporal dimension provides a rich source of information revealing phonological structure. In the domain syllables, the relation between temporal patterns in experimental data and qualitative aspects of phonological structure has often taken the form of statements expressing inequalities, e.g., a complex onset parse implies that the center to anchor interval *is more stable than* the right/left edge to anchor intervals. Phonetic heuristics of this sort are valid only under certain conditions. The models developed in this paper generate finer-grained quantitative predictions of syllabic structure based on a probabilistic interpretation of temporal organization. Our models make predictions not just about stability inequalities but also about *the permissible degree* to which interval stabilities may differ from one another under a given syllable parse. Crucially, these predictions allow for evaluation of competing syllable parses even when statements in the form of inequalities do not.

As the phonological literature is replete with debates regarding the syllabification of consonant clusters, the tools developed here have immediate application. They allow rigorous evaluation of syllable structure on the basis of experimental data.

Acknowledgments

The authors gratefully acknowledge support from NSF grant 0922437. This paper was improved by the comments and suggestions of three anonymous reviewers. Remaining errors are solely the responsibility of the authors.

References

Albright, A., & Hayes, B. (2003). Rules vs. analogy in English past tenses: a computational/experimental study. *Cognition, 90*, 119-161.

Browman, C. P., & Goldstein, L. (1988). Some Notes on Syllable Structure in Articulatory Phonology. *Phonetica, 45*, 140-155.

Byrd, D. (1995). C-centers revisited. *Phonetica, 52*, 285-306.

Catford, J. C. (1977). *Fundamental Problems in Phonetics*. Bloomington: Indiana University Press.

Dell, F., & Elmedlaoui, M. (2002). *Syllables in Tashlhiyt Berber and in Moroccan Arabic*. Dordrecht, Netherlands, and Boston, MA: Kluwer Academic Publishers.

Gafos, A. (2002). A grammar of gestural coordination. *Natural Language and Linguistic Theory, 20*, 269-337.

Goldstein, L. M., Chitoran, I., & Selkirk, E. (2007). *Syllable structure as coupled oscillator modes: evidence from Georgian vs. Tashlhiyt Berber.* Proceedings of the *XVIth International Congress of Phonetic Sciences*, 241-244, Saabrucken, Germany.

Hermes, A., Grice, M., Muecke, D., & Niemann, H. (2008). *Articulatory indicators of syllable affiliation in word initial consonant clusters in Italian.* In R. Stock, S. Fuchs & Y. Laprie (Eds.), Proceedings of the *8th International Seminar on Speech Production*, 433-436, Strasbourg, France.

Honorof, D., & Browman, C. (1995). *The center or the edge: how are consonant clusters organised with respect to the vowel?* In K. Elenius & P. Branderud (Eds.), Proceedings of the *XIIIth International Congress of Phonetic Sciences* Vol. 3, 552-555, Stockholm, Sweden.

Kahn, D. (1976). *Syllable-based generalizations in English phonology.* Unpublished Ph.D. Dissertation, MIT, Cambridge, MA.

Kugler, P. N., Kelso, J. A. S., & Turvey, M. T. (1980). On the concept of coordinative structures as dissipative structures: I. Theoretical lines of convergence. In G. E. Stelmach & J. Requin (Eds.), *Tutorials in Motor Behavior* (p. 3-47): North-Holland Publishing Company.

Marin, S., & Pouplier, M. (2008). *Organization of complex onsets and codas in American English: Evidence for a competitive coupling model.* In R. Sock, S. Fuchs & Y. Laprie (Eds.), Proceedings of the *8th International Seminar of Speech Production*, 437-440, Strasbourg, France.

Shaw, J. A. (2010). *The temporal organization of syllabic structure.* Unpublished Ph.D. Dissertation, NYU, New York, NY.

Shaw, J. A., Gafos, A., Hoole, P., & Zeroual, C. (2009). Syllabification in Moroccan Arabic: evidence from patterns of temporal stability in articulation. *Phonology, 26*, 187-215.

Vogt, H. (Ed.). (1971). *Grammaire de la langue Géorgienne.* Oslo: Universitetsforlaget.

Westbury, J. R. (1994). X-ray Microbeam Speech Production Database User's Handbook. University of Wisconsin.

Toward a Totally Unsupervised, Language-Independent Method for the Syllabification of Written Texts

Thomas Mayer
Department of Linguistics
University of Konstanz, Germany
thomas.mayer@uni-konstanz.de

Abstract

Unsupervised algorithms for the induction of linguistic knowledge should at best require as few basic assumptions as possible and at the same time in principle yield good results for any language. However, most of the time such algorithms are only tested on a few (closely related) languages. In this paper, an approach is presented that takes into account typological knowledge in order to induce syllabic divisions in a fully automatic manner based on reasonably-sized written texts. Our approach is able to account for syllable structures of languages where other approaches would fail, thereby raising the question whether computational methods can really be claimed to be language-universal when they are not tested on the variety of structures that are found in the languages of the world.

1 Introduction

Many approaches developed in the field of computational linguistics are only tested and optimized for one language (mostly English) or a small set of closely related languages, but at the same time are often claimed to be applicable to any natural language, cf. Bender (2009). Our aim is to stress the importance of having a more varied sample of languages that include the different types that can be found in the languages of the world in order to do justice to the range of variation in linguistic structures across languages. Furthermore, we want to point to the usefulness of using typological knowledge for a language-universal approach.

In this paper, we present an unsupervised, language-independent syllabification method based on raw unannotated texts in a phonemic transcription. The methods and procedures presented in this work rest upon insights from typological work and do not need any additional language-dependent information. The main purpose of this paper is not to present an improvement on already established statistical approaches to the problem of syllabification of an individual language, but to introduce data from languages that might constitute a problem for many syllabification methods that have been optimized on languages like English and therefore make it necessary to integrate an additional component that is able to handle such cases.

The remainder of the paper is organized as follows. First, it is argued in Section 2 that orthographic texts (in any alphabetic script) can be used for the induction of phonological patterns if the spelling system is reasonably close to a phonemic transcription. The syllabification process can be divided into two steps. In Section 3, we present and evaluate an algorithm for an unsupervised classification of all symbols in the input texts into vowels and consonants. Based on this classification, a syllabification procedure is discussed that makes use of distributional information of clusters in order to break up vowel and consonant sequences into syllables (Section 4). Finally, we conclude with a discussion of the advantages and disadvantages of the present approach and its implications for future research.

2 Learning phonological patterns on the basis of written texts?

Most studies that are based on original texts are concerned with research questions that do not make use of phonological knowledge that has been extracted from the texts. The reason for this is obvious. The orthographies of many well-studied modern languages contain many idiosyncratic rules and exceptions that would make it difficult to use them for dealing with phonological aspects of the languages under consideration. On

Proceedings of the 11th Meeting of the ACL-SIGMORPHON, ACL 2010, pages 63–71,
Uppsala, Sweden, 15 July 2010.

the other hand, in order to be able to use distributional information for phonological problems there are not enough reasonably-sized phonetically transcribed corpora, especially for a wider range of languages.

However, many spelling systems do not suffer from these shortcomings and thus can be used for these purposes. When looking at languages whose orthographies have been conceived or standardized only recently it can be noted that many of them are pretty close to a phonemic transcription. Provided the size of the corpus is big enough, smaller inconsistencies in the spelling system can be considered to be noise in the data.

Phonemic orthographies as they are usually devised for a new spelling system also show an advantage that phonetic transcriptions lack, namely that they already group together those symbols that represent the same phoneme in the language.[1] Moreover, obligatory phonological processes such as final devoicing are mostly not represented in the written form (Turkish being a notable exception), thereby providing a sort of underlying representation that is useful to induce which sequences can be grouped together to morphemes.

For these reasons written texts can in our view also be used for the induction of phonological knowledge for languages with phonemic spelling systems, even though their results have to be analyzed with great care.

3 Sukhotin's algorithm

Sukhotin's algorithm (Sukhotin, 1962, 1973) is a totally unsupervised method to discriminate vowels from consonants on the basis of a phonemic transcription. The approach relies on two fundamental assumptions that are grounded on typological insights. First, vowels and consonants in words tend to alternate rather than being grouped together. Second, the most frequent symbol in the corpus is a vowel. The latter assumption is used to initialize the classification step by claiming that the most frequent symbol is the first member of the vowel class, with the rest of the symbols initially all classified as consonants. With the help of the first assumption the other vowels are then classified by iteratively checking which symbol is less frequently adjacent to the already detected vowels.

3.1 Typological basis

It has been noticed in the typological literature at least since Jakobson and Halle (1956) that there is a tendency in the languages of the world for having CV as the basic syllable structure. Of course, languages differ as to the number and types of syllables; there are languages that allow a huge variety of consonant (or vowel) clusters whereas others are stricter in their phonotactic possibilities. However, all languages seem to obey the universal law that CV is more basic than other syllable types and that "CV is the only universal model of the syllable." Evidence for this comes from different areas of linguistics, including the observation that no matter how small the number of syllable types in a language is, it always includes CV. This is also reflected in the Onset Maximization Principle (OMP), which states that an intervocalic consonant is attributed to the following syllable and is assumed to be a language-universal principle for syllabification.

We are not aware of any cross-linguistic study that investigated the token frequency of phonemes in larger samples of texts. Hence, the second assumption that the most frequent symbol in a text is always a vowel cannot be backed up by typological knowledge. However, this claim can be supported indirectly. In his study on consonant-vowel ratios in 563 languages, Maddieson (2008) states that the ratio ranges between 1.11 and 29. The lowest value has been calculated for the isolate language Andoke, which has 10 consonants and 9 vowels. The mean value is 4.25, though. Provided that it is always the case that languages have more consonants than vowel types, it can be argued that the fewer vowels have higher token frequencies in order to be able to contribute their share to the make-up of syllables.[2] Yet this generalization is untested and could be wrong for some languages (or rather corpora of those languages). In our sample of texts in different languages, nevertheless the most frequent symbol is always a vowel.

3.2 Description of the algorithm

Sukhotin's algorithm is computationally simple and can even be illustrated with a small toy cor-

[1] In the remainder of this paper we will use the term 'symbol' as a more neutral expression for all letters in the written texts in order not to be explicit whether the spelling system really lives up to the goal of representing phonemes by letters.

[2] In the French corpus that Goldsmith and Xanthos (2009) used in their studies, the most frequent phoneme turned out to be a consonant. However, the rest of the classification was not affected and all remaining phonemes were labelled correctly.

pus.[3] Given a corpus with the inventory of n symbols $S := \{s_1, \ldots, s_n\}$ we construct an $n \times n$ matrix M where the rows represent the first and the columns the second symbol in a bigram sequence and which indicates the number of times the sequences occur in the corpus.

$$M = \begin{pmatrix} m_{11} & \ldots & m_{1n} \\ \ldots & \ldots & \ldots \\ m_{n1} & \ldots & m_{nn} \end{pmatrix}$$

The main diagonal, i.e., the self-succession of symbols, is ignored by setting all its values to zero. For instance, given a sample corpus $C = \{saat, salat, tal, last, stall, lese, seele\}$ we obtain the following 5×5 matrix (for ease of understanding the symbols have been put in front of the cells of the matrix and the row sums in the last column):

$$M = \begin{pmatrix} & s & a & t & l & e & \text{Sum} \\ s & 0 & 3 & 2 & 0 & 3 & 8 \\ a & 3 & 0 & 3 & 4 & 0 & 10 \\ t & 2 & 3 & 0 & 0 & 2 & 7 \\ l & 0 & 4 & 0 & 0 & 3 & 7 \\ e & 3 & 0 & 2 & 3 & 0 & 8 \end{pmatrix}$$

Sukhotin's algorithm initially considers all symbols to be consonants before it enters an interative phase. In each cycle of the phase, the symbol with the highest row sum greater than zero is detected and classified as a vowel. The row sum for any symbol s_a is calculated by adding up all occurrences of the symbol s_a as a first or second member in a sequence $\sum_{i=1}^{n} m_{ai}$. After a new vowel has been detected, its row sum is set to zero and all other row sums are updated by subtracting from the sum of the row of each remaining symbol twice the number of times it occurs next to the new-found vowel. This process is repeated until no more symbols with positive row sums are left. In our example, the vectors of row sums ($RSum$) for all symbols in the individual steps of the iteration phase look as follows:

$$RSum_1 = \begin{pmatrix} s & a & t & l & e \\ 8 & 10 & 7 & 7 & 8 \end{pmatrix}$$

$$RSum_2 = \begin{pmatrix} s & a & t & l & e \\ 2 & 0 & 1 & -1 & 8 \end{pmatrix}$$

[3]More detailed descriptions can be found in Guy (1991) and Goldsmith and Xanthos (2009).

$$RSum_3 = \begin{pmatrix} s & a & t & l & e \\ -4 & 0 & -3 & -7 & 0 \end{pmatrix}$$

The rationale behind this algorithm with respect to its basic assumptions is as follows. The fact that initially the symbol with the highest sum is considered to be a vowel reflects the idea that the most frequent symbol in the corpus has to be a vowel. What the row sums after each step actually contain is the difference between the number of times a symbol is found next to a consonant and the number of times it is found next to a vowel. Whenever a new vowel has been detected all occurrences of this vowel have to be subtracted from the other symbols because this symbol is no longer considered to be a consonant.

3.3 Evaluation

To the best of our knowledge, the algorithm has never been tested on a larger cross-linguistic sample. There are results for a number of languages in Sukhotin's original papers, in Sassoon (1992) and in Goldsmith and Xanthos (2009), yet almost all languages in those samples belong to the Indo-European family (except for Georgian, Hungarian and Finnish) or do not fulfill the criterion of a phonemic transcription (Hebrew). It therefore still needs to be tested on a more cross-linguistic sample of languages. In particular, it is an interesting question to see if the algorithm works even for those languages that are notorious for having many consonant clusters. On the basis of his sample of five languages, Sassoon (1992) comes to the conclusion that it works very well on those languages that have only few consonant clusters but has problems when more complex clusters are involved. However, he also notices that this effect disappears with larger text samples. Table 1 provides an evaluation of Sukhotin's algorithm on the basis of Bible texts (NT) in our sample of 39 languages. The size of the corpora in Sassoon's sample range from 1641 to 3781 characters while the Bible texts contain more than 100,000 characters (e.g., English has 716,301 characters). On average, Sukhotin's algorithm classifies 95.66% of the symbols correctly. However, this percentage also includes those languages which do not fulfill the criterion of having a suitable phonemic writing system (e.g., Russian, English, German, French). When looking only at those languages whose spelling systems are close to a phonemic transcription (or where the digraphs have been substituted by single symbols), the results are even better.

Misclassified symbols are either very infrequent and happen to occur next to symbols of the same class or are part of one of the digraphs used in the spelling system of the language. In the Maltese case, the symbol *î* is classified as a consonant because it only occurs twice in the corpus in the word *eloî* where it stands next to a symbol that is clearly a vowel. For some languages, minor modifications to the original texts have been made in order to replace the most frequent digraphs. In Swahili, for instance, with the official orthography the symbol *c* is classified as a vowel because it only occurs in the digraph *ch*. After the digraph has been replaced by a single symbol, the classification is correct in all cases. Sometimes a symbol (e.g., *h* in Warlpiri) is misclassified because it does not occur in the writing system of the language but is part of a digraph in foreign words (mostly proper names of people or locations in the Bible texts). Another problem of the approach is with orthographies that use the same symbol for both vowels and consonants. Since the classification is global, symbols like English *y*, which is a consonant in *yoghurt* and a vowel in *lady*, are always treated as either a vowel or a consonant for the whole language independent of the context where they occur. Therefore symbols in the input text should always be able to be classified to one or the other category.

As the discussion of misclassified symbols shows, the main errors in the results are not due to the algorithm itself, but a problem of the spelling systems of the texts at hand. Our results confirm the findings of Sassoon (1992) that the algorithm is sensitive to the corpus size and the frequency of occurrence of individual symbols. Larger corpora, such as Bible texts, yield much better results for these languages. Even those languages with many and very complex consonant clusters (e.g., Georgian, Croatian and Czech) get an almost perfect classification. It is remarkable that the overall distribution of the symbols makes up for those cases where consonants frequently occur in clusters. Experiments with smaller corpus sizes also revealed that one of the first symbols that get wrongly classified is the sibilant *s*. This might be another indicator for the exceptional status of sibilants with respect to syllabification and their occurrence in consonant sequences where they can violate the sonority principle (e.g., in the sequence *str* in words like *string* the consonant *s* is to the left of the consonant *t* although higher in sonority).

4 Unsupervised syllabification

Based the classification of input symbols into vowels and consonants, the syllabification procedure can then be applied. Knowledge of syllable structure is not only relevant for a better understanding of the procedures and representations that are involved in both computer and human language learning but also interesting from an engineering standpoint, e.g., for the correct pronunciation of unknown words in text-to-speech systems or as an intermediate step for morphology induction.

Several methods have been proposed in the literature for an unsupervised language-independent syllabification (see Vogel, 1977 for an overview and Goldsmith and Larson, 1990 for an implementation of a more recent approach based on the sonority hierarchy). Some methods that have been suggested in the literature (going back to Herodotus, who observed this for Ancient Greek; cf. Kuryłowicz, 1948) rely on the observation that word-medial tautosyllabic consonant clusters mostly constitute a subset of word-peripheral clusters. Intervocalic consonant clusters can therefore be divided up into a word-final and word-initial cluster. Theoretically, two types of problems can be encountered. First, those where more than one division is possible and second, those in which no division is possible.

Several approaches have been suggested to resolve the first problem, i.e., word-medial consonant sequences where there are several possible divisions based on the occurrence of word-initial and word-final clusters. O'Connor and Trim (1953) and Arnold (1956) suggest that in cases of ambiguous word-medial clusters the preference for one syllable division over another can be determined by the frequency of occurrence of different types of word-initial and word-final clusters. For this purpose, they determine the frequency of occurrence of word-initial and word-final CV, VC, etc. syllable patterns. Based on these frequencies they calculate the probabilities of dividing a word-medial sequence by summing up the values established for the different word-peripheral syllable types. The candidate syllabification with the highest sum is then chosen as the optimal division.

The approach taken here is a slight modification of the proposal in O'Connor and Trim (1953) and

Language	Vowels	Consonants
Afrikaans	a c* e i o u y á é ê í ò ó ô ú	b d f g h j k l m n p q r s t v w x ä* ë* ï* ü*
Albanian	a e g* h* i o u y ç* é ë	b c d f j k l m n p q r s t v x z
Armenian (transl.)	a e e’ y’ i o ch* o’	b g d z t’ jh l x c’ k h d’ gh tw m y n sh p j r’ s v t r c w p’ q f
Basque	a e i o u v* á æ é í ó ö	b c d f g h k l m n p q r s t x y z à* ä* ç è* ü*
Breton	a c* e i o u ê	b d f g h j k l m n p r s t v w y z ñ ù* ü*
Chamorro	a e i o u á â é í ó ú	b c d f g h j l m n p q r s t v x y ã* ñ ü*
Croatian	a e i o u	b c d f g h j k l m n p r s t v z ä* ð ó* ć č đ š ž
Czech	a e i o u y á é í ó ú ý ě ů	b c d f g h j k l m n p q r s t v x z č ď ň ř š ť ž
Danish	a e i o u y å æ ø	b c d f g h j k l m n p r s t v x z
Dutch	a c* e i o u y	b d f g h j k l m n p q r s t v w x z
English	a e g* i o t* u	b c d f h j k l m n p q r s v w x y z
Finnish	a e i o u y ä ö	b c d f g h j k l m n p q r s t v x z
French	a e i o u à â è é ê î ô û	b c d f g h j k l m n p q r s t v x y z ç ë* ï* ù* ü* œ*
Georgian (transl.)	a e i o u h*	b g d v z t k’ l m n p’ zh r s t’ p k gh q sh ch ts dz ts’ ch’ kh j
German	a e h* i o p* u y ä ö ü	b c d f g j k l m n q r s t v w x z ß
Gothic	a e i o u v* x* û	b d f g h j k l m n p q r s t w z ï* þ
Greek	α ε η ι ο υ ω	β γ δ ζ θ κ λ μ ν ξ π ρ ς σ τ φ χ ψ
Hungarian	a c* e i o u y á é í ó õ ö ú û ü	b d f g h j k l m n p r s t v x z
Icelandic	a e i o u y á æ é í ó ö ú ý	b d f g h j k l m n p r s t v x ð þ
Italian	a e h* i o u à è ì ò ù	b c d f g j k l m n p q r s t v z é*
Latin	a e i o u y	b c d f g h l m n p q r s t v x z
Maltese (rev.)	a e g* i o u à â è ì í ò ù	b d f h j k l m n p q r s t v w x z î* ċ ġ ħ ż
Mandarin (toneless)	a e i o u	ng zh ch b c d f g h j k l m n p q r s t w x y z sh
Maori (rev.)	a e i o u	g h k m n p r t ng w wh
Norwegian (Bokmål)	a e i o u y å æ é ó ø	b c d f g h j k l m n p r s t v z ë*
Potawatomi (rev.)	a e i o u	c d g k l m n p s t w sh y
Romanian	a e i o u î ă	b c d f g h j l m n p r s t v x z ş ţ
Russian	а е и о у ы (ь*) э я	б в г д ж з й к л м н п р с т ф х ц ч ш щ (ъ*) (ю*)
Scots Gaelic	a h* i o u	b c d e* f g l m n p r s t
Spanish	a e i o u á â é ê í î ó ô ù ú	b c d f g h j l m n p q r s t v x y z ñ ü*
Swahili (rev.)	a e i o u	b d f g h j k l m n p r s t v w x y z
Swedish	a e i o u y ä å é ö	b c d f g h j k l m n p r s t v x
Tagalog (rev.)	a e i o u	ng b c d f g h j k l m n p q r s t v w x y z
Turkish	a e i o u â å î ö û ü ı	b c d f g h j k l m n p r s t v y z ç ğ ş
Ukrainian	і а е и о у ь ю я є і ї	с у б в г д ж з й к л м н п р с т ф х ц ч ш щ ґ
Uma	a e g* i o u	b c d f h j k l m n p r s t w y z ï*
Warlpiri (rev.)	a e h* i o u	c f j k l m n p q r s t v w x y z
Wolof	a e i o u à é ë ó	b c d f g j k l m n p q r s t w x y ñ ŋ
Xhosa	a e g* i o t* u â	b c d f h j k l m n p q r s v w x y z

Table 1: Results for Sukhotin’s algorithm on Bible texts in 39 languages. All symbols of the input Bible texts for the respective languages are listed even if they are very infrequent. For those languages marked as revised the most frequent digraphs have been replaced by a single symbol. Wrongly classified symbols are marked with an asterisk. Languages with spelling systems which notoriously contain many idiosyncratic rules are shaded. We decided to include them as a reference where the problems occur with these systems.

Arnold (1956). Instead of counting the frequency of occurrence of syllable types, the actual syllables are counted in order to determine the best split of word-medial consonant sequences. An example calculation for the German word *fasten* 'to abstain from food' is given in Table 2.

a)	fa st$_{142]}$ en	[fast.en]	sum: 142
b)	fa s$_{528]}$ $_{[216}$t en	[fas.ten]	sum: 744
c)	fa $_{[176}$st en	[fa.sten]	sum: 176

Table 2: Example calculations for the word-medial cluster in the German word *fasten*.

The example calculations in Table 2 show that the candidate syllabification in b) yields the highest sum and is therefore chosen as the correct syllabification of the word. One of the advantages of this approach (as well as the one proposed by O'Connor and Trim and Arnold) is that OMP follows from the fact that word-initial CV sequences are more frequent than word-final VC sequences and does not have to be stipulated independently.

The claim that CV is the unmarked syllable structure for all languages of the world (and OMP a universal principle) has been challenged by some Australian languages that seem to behave differently with respect to syllabification of VCV sequences (Breen and Pensalfini, 1999). In those languages VCV sequences are syllabified as VC.V instead of V.CV, as OMP would predict. The authors provide evidence from a number of processes in these languages (reduplication, language games) as well as historical and comparative evidence that support the analysis that VC seems to be more accurate as the basic syllable type for those languages.[4]

For cases where word-medial clusters cannot be broken up by sequences that are found at word edges (bad clusters), we decided to go back to the original method used by O'Connor and Trim and Arnold and calculate the frequency of occurrence of syllable types. However, bad clusters are not very frequent compared to the overall data in our experiments.

One additional problem when working with written texts[5] rather than transcribed corpora is the fact that diphthongs are not clearly distinguished from sequences of monophthongs. Yet this is vital for a correct syllabification procedure since the number of syllables of the word is different depending on this choice. In order to retrieve the diphthongs of the language from the distribution of vowel sequences in the corpus the following approach has been used.[6] For each bigram vowel sequence the number of times the first vowel v_1 is directly followed by the second vowel v_2 is compared with the number of times both vowels are separated by one consonant. If the frequency of direct adjacency is higher than the frequency of $v_1 c v_2$ the sequence is considered to be a "diphthong"; if not, the sequence is considered to be a case of hiatus and both vowels are attributed to different syllables. Similar to Sukhotin's algorithm the present syllabification algorithm is also global in the sense that the diphthong/monophthong distinction is always used in the same way no matter in which environment the sequence occurs.[7] Table 3 gives a list of the diphthongs extracted from the corpus for a number of languages in our sample based on this method.

Dutch	aa (772), oo (510), ie (440), ui (301), ou (155), eu (110), uu (27)
German	ei (1373), au (641), eu (216)
English	ea (336), ou (280), io (231), oo (79)
French	ai (863), ou (686), eu (397), io (339), ui (272), au (232), oi (232)
Greek	ου (1687), ει (1684), ευ (650), οι (616), αυ (287)
Wolof	aa (1027), ee (821), oo (656), ée (181), ii (158), óo (118)

Table 3: "Diphthongs" for a subset of the languages in the sample (in brackets the frequency of adjacent occurrence).

4.1 The problem of evaluating syllabification methods

There are several reasons why a gold standard for syllabification, with which the syllabification methods are compared, is difficult to establish.

[4]Note that this does not invalidate one of the basic assumptions of Sukhotin's algorithm, since C and V still alternate even though in the reverse order.

[5]Some linguists also believe that stress can lead to a violation of OMP by attracting an intervocalic consonant to the coda of the previous stressed syllable. Since stress is usually not reflected in most orthographies, we do not consider this option here.

[6]We thank Bernhard Wälchli (p.c.) for drawing our attention to this idea.

[7]In German, for instance, the vowel sequence *eu* can either be tautosyllabic and in that case constitute a diphthong as in *heute* 'today'; or it can be a case of hiatus and therefore be broken up by a syllable boundary as in *Museum* 'museum'.

Duanmu (2009) states that even for well-described languages like English linguists do not agree on the correct syllabification of comparatively straightforward cases. For the English word *happy*, for instance, four different analyses have been proposed:

[hæ.pi]	Hayes (1995), Halle (1998), Gussmann (2002)
[hæp.i]	Selkirk (1982), Hammond (1999)
[hæp̲i]	Kahn (1976), Giegerich (1992), Kreidler (2004)
[hæp.pi]	Burzio (1994)

Table 4: Analyses of *happy* (cited from Duanmu, 2009). Underlined consonants are ambisyllabic.

The correct syllabification of a word can best be established when there is some operation in the language that takes recourse on the syllable structure of the word. In the case of the Australian languages with no syllable onsets, Breen and Pensalfini (1999:6f) provide evidence from reduplication processes in Arrernte to support their analysis. If the Arrernte syllable shape is VC(C), rather than (C)CV, reduplication is most straightforwardly described in terms of syllables. The attenuative prefix is formed by /-elp/ preceded by the first syllable of the base if VC(C) syllabification is assumed. The attenuative form of the base *emp*^{w}*aṛ* 'to make' is therefore *emp*^{w}*elpemp*^{w}*aṛ*.[8] A similar argumentation can be put forward for languages that show phonological operations that are based on the structure of syllables, e.g., syllable-final devoicing. If a voiced obstruent is realized unvoiced, the syllabification might suggest its position to be in the coda.

Besides disagreement on the correct syllabification of words, another crucial aspect of evaluating syllabification methods is the question of whether the test set should consist of a random sample of words of the language or whether there should be any constraints on the composition of the evaluation data. If the evaluation consists of a huge number of monosyllabic words, the results are much better than with polysyllabic words because no consonant clusters have to be broken up. For the evaluation of their syllabification methods, Goldwater and Johnson (2005) distinguish words with any number of syllables from words with at least two syllables. Depending on the method that they test the differences in the percentage of correctly syllabified words range from a few to almost 30%. It is therefore easier to get better results when applying the syllabification methods to languages with a large number of monosyllabic words and fewer consonant clusters, like Mandarin Chinese, for instance.

4.2 Discussion and evaluation

One of the problems of a cross-linguistic investigation is the availability of gold standards for evaluation. Thus, instead of providing a comparative evaluation, we want to discuss the advantages and disadvantages of the procedure with respect to the more common sonority-based syllabification method. We tested our method on a manually created gold standard of 1,000 randomly selected words in Latin. The precision is 92.50% and the recall 94.96% (F-Score 0.94) for each transition from one symbol to another. Most misplaced syllable boundaries are due to the vowel cluster *io*, which has been treated as a diphthong by our method.

The most interesting aspect of our approach is that it is able to account for those languages where intervocalic consonants are better be analyzed as belonging to the previous syllable, thereby violating OMP. Approaches relying on the Onset Maximization Principle would get all of these syllable boundaries wrong. Breen and Pensalfini (1999) note that Arrernte also has only VC in word-initial position. Consequently, an approach that is based on word-peripheral clusters can predict the lack of word-medial onsets correctly. The importance of word-peripheral clusters is also supported by findings in Goldwater and Johnson (2005) where a bigram model improves after training with Expectation Maximization whereas a positional model does not, which might be due to the fact that a bigram model (unlike the positional model) can generalize whatever it learns about clusters no matter if they occur at word edges or word-medially.

Moreover, the influence of word-peripheral clusters on the syllabification of word-medial consonant sequences is not restricted to syllable types only, but sometimes also holds solely for individual consonants. In Chamorro, for instance, Topping (1973) describes the syllabification of intervocalic consonants as observing OMP. However,

[8] As one reviewer remarked, reduplication patterns are usually described in terms of a CV-template rather than syllable structures. However, in the case of Arrernte, a description in terms of syllables rather than VC(C) shapes would be more elegant and at the same time account for other operations as well.

this does not apply if the consonant is the glottal stop /'/, in which case the syllable division occurs after the consonant, leading to the syllabification /na'.i/ 'to give'. The interesting observation in this respect is that the glottal stop phonologically never occurs at the beginning of a word in Chamorro whereas all other consonants (with the exception of /w/) do occur word-initially,[9] which leads to the correct syllabification results with our approach.

Another advantage of the present method is that clusters with sibilant consonants that do not conform to the sonority principle (see the example of *str* in Section 3.3) do not have to be treated differently. They merely follow from the fact that these clusters are particularly frequent in word-peripheral position. The biggest disadvantage is the fact that the method is sensitive to frequencies of individual clusters and thereby sometimes breaks up clusters that should be tautosyllabic (one of the few examples in our Latin corpus was *teneb.rae*).

5 Conclusions and future work

A complete model of syllabification involves more than what has been presented in this paper. The method proposed here is restricted to single words and does not take into account resyllabification across word boundaries as well as some other criteria that might influence the actual syllable structure of words such as stress and morphological boundaries. Nevertheless, the discussion of our approach shows that expanding the range of languages to other families and areas of the world can challenge some of the well-established findings that are used for inferring linguistic knowledge.

The results of Sukhotin's algorithm show that the distinction between vowels and consonants, which is vital for any syllabification method, can be induced from raw texts on the basis of the simple assumptions that vowels and consonants tend to alternate and that a vowel is the most frequent symbol in a corpus. In contrast to previous studies of the algorithm (Sassoon, 1992), our results do not suffer from the fact that the input text is too short and therefore yield better results.

Based on the classifications of symbols into vowels and consonants with Sukhotin's algorithm our unsupervised syllabification method determines syllable boundaries on distributional information. In contrast to other unsupervised approaches to syllabification that are grounded on attributing a sonority value to each consonant and OMP, our procedure breaks up word-medial consonant sequences by considering the frequencies of all possible word-peripheral clusters in order to get the most probable division. We did not provide a comparative evaluation of our procedure but only discussed the problems that can be encountered when looking at a wider variety of languages and how they can be solved by our approach. The question that this paper wants to raise is therefore if it is more important to optimize a procedure on a single language (mostly English or related European languages) or whether it should be capable of dealing with the variety of structures that can be found in the languages of the world.

For future work we want to apply the present methods on phonetically transcribed corpora in order to be able to compare the results for the well-studied European languages to other methods. There are still some challenges remaining for a universal syllabification procedure, one of them being the detection of syllabic consonants. Ultimately, we also want to integrate a sonority hierarchy of the input symbols to combine the advantages of both approaches and to create a gradual value for syllabification that is able to account for the difference between clear-cut syllable boundaries and ambisyllabic consonants or other cases where a syllable boundary is harder to establish.

Acknowledgments

This work has been funded by the research initiative "Computational Analysis of Linguistic Development" and the DFG Sonderforschungsbereich 471 "Variation und Entwicklung im Lexikon" at the University of Konstanz. The author would like to thank the Australian Institute of Aboriginal and Torres Strait Islander Studies (AIATSIS) for the Warlpiri Bible sections as well as Miriam Butt, Frans Plank, Bernhard Wälchli and three anonymous reviewers for valuable comments and suggestions.

References

Gordon F. Arnold. 1955-1956. A phonological approach to vowel, consonant and syllable in modern french. *Lingua*, V:251–287.

[9] Topping notes that phonetically there is a glottal stop preceding every word-initial vowel, yet this is totally predictable in this position and therefore not phonemic.

Emily Bender. 2009. Linguistically naive != language independent: Why NLP needs linguistic typology. In *Proceedings of the EACL 2009 Workshop on the Interaction between Linguistics and Computational Linguistics*, pages 26–32.

Gavan Breen and Rob Pensalfini. 1999. Arrernte: A language with no syllable onsets. *Linguistic Inquiry*, 30(1):1–25.

Luigi Burzio. 1994. *Principles of English Stress*. Cambridge: Cambridge University Press.

San Duanmu. 2009. *Syllable Structure*. Oxford: Oxford University Press.

Heinz Giegerich. 1992. *English Phonology*. Cambridge: Cambridge University Press.

John Goldsmith and Gary Larson. 1990. Local modelling and syllabification. In Michael Ziolkowski, Manuela Noske, and Karen Deaton, editors, *The Parasession on the Syllable in Phonetics & Phonology*, volume 2 of *Papers from the 26th Regional Meeting of the Chicago Linguistic*, pages 130–141. Chicago Linguistic Society.

John Goldsmith and Aris Xanthos. 2009. Learning phonological categories. *Language*, 85(1):4–38.

Sharon Goldwater and Mark Johnson. 2005. Representational bias in unsupervised learning of syllable structure. In *Proceedings of the 9th Conference on Computational Natural Language Learning (CONLL), Ann Arbor*.

Edmund Gussmann. 2002. *Phonoloy: Analysis and Theory*. Cambridge: Cambridge University Press.

Jacques B. M. Guy. 1991. Vowel identification: an old (but good) algorithm. *Cryptologia*, XV(3):258–262, July.

Morris Halle. 1998. The stress of english words. *Linguistic Inquiry*, 29(4):539–568.

Michael Hammond. 1999. *The Phonology of English: A Prosodic Optimality Theoretic Approach*. Oxford: Oxford University Press.

Bruce Hayes. 1995. *Metrical Stress Theory: Principles and Case Studies*. Chicage: University of Chicage Press.

Roman Jakobson and Morris Halle. 1956. *Fundamentals of Language I. Phonology and Phonetics*. 's-Gravenhage: Mouton.

Daniel Kahn. 1976. *Syllable-based generalizations in English phonology*. Ph.D. thesis, Massachusetts Institute of Technology.

Charles W. Kreidler. 2004. *The Pronunciation of English: A Course Book*. Malden, MA: Blackwell.

Jerzy Kuryłowicz. 1948. Contribution à la théorie de la syllabe. *Bulletin de la Societe Polonaise de Linguistique*, 8:5–114.

Ian Maddieson. 2008. Consonant-vowel ratio. In Martin Haspelmath, Matthew S. Dryer, David Gil, and Bernard Comrie, editors, *The World Atlas of Language Structures Online*, chapter 3. Munich: Max Planck Digital Library. Available online at http://wals.info/feature/3. Accessed on 2010-04-23.

J. D. O'Connor and J. L. M. Trim. 1953. Vowel, consonant, and syllable - a phonological definition. *Word*, 9(2):103–122.

George T. Sassoon. 1992. The application of Sukhotin's algorithm to certain Non-English languages. *Cryptologia*, 16(2):165–173.

Elisabeth O. Selkirk. 1982. The syllable. In Harry van der Hulst and Norval Smith, editors, *The Structure of Phonological Representations, part II*, pages 337–383. Dordrecht: Foris.

Boris V. Sukhotin. 1962. Eksperimental'noe vydelenie klassov bukv s pomoşçju evm. *Problemy strukturnoj lingvistiki*, 234:189–206.

Boris V. Sukhotin. 1973. Méthode de déchiffrage, outil de recherche en linguistique. *T.A. Informations*, 2:1–43.

Donald M. Topping. 1980. *Chamorro Reference Grammar*. The University Press of Hawaii, Honolulu.

Irene Vogel. 1977. *The Syllable in Phonological Theory with Special Reference to Italian*. Ph.D. thesis, Stanford University.

Comparing Canonicalizations of Historical German Text

Bryan Jurish
Berlin-Brandenburg Academy of Sciences
Berlin, Germany
jurish@bbaw.de

Abstract

Historical text presents numerous challenges for contemporary natural language processing techniques. In particular, the absence of consistent orthographic conventions in historical text presents difficulties for any system requiring reference to a static lexicon accessed by orthographic form. In this paper, we present three methods for associating unknown historical word forms with synchronically active canonical cognates and evaluate their performance on an information retrieval task over a manually annotated corpus of historical German verse.

1 Introduction

Historical text presents numerous challenges for contemporary natural language processing techniques. In particular, the absence of consistent orthographic conventions in historical text presents difficulties for any system requiring reference to a fixed lexicon accessed by orthographic form, such as document indexing systems (Sokirko, 2003; Cafarella and Cutting, 2004), part-of-speech taggers (DeRose, 1988; Brill, 1992; Schmid, 1994), simple word stemmers (Lovins, 1968; Porter, 1980), or more sophisticated morphological analyzers (Geyken and Hanneforth, 2006; Clematide, 2008).

When adopting historical text into such a system, one of the most crucial tasks is the association of one or more *extant equivalents* with each word of the input text: synchronically active types which best represent the relevant features of the input word. Which features are considered "relevant" here depends on the application in question: for a lemmatization task only the root lexeme is relevant, whereas syntactic parsing may require additional morphosyntactic features. For current purposes, extant equivalents are to be understood as *canonical cognates*, preserving both the root(s) and morphosyntactic features of the associated historical form(s), which should suffice (modulo major grammatical and/or lexical semantic shifts) for most natural language processing tasks.

In this paper, we present three methods for automatic discovery of extant canonical cognates for historical German text, and evaluate their performance on an information retrieval task over a small gold-standard corpus.

2 Canonicalization Methods

In this section, we present three methods for automatic discovery of extant canonical cognates for historical German input: *phonetic conflation* (Pho), *Levenshtein edit distance* (Lev), and a heuristic *rewrite transducer* (rw). The various methods are presented individually below, and characterized in terms of the linguistic resources required for their application. Formally, each canonicalization method R is defined by a characteristic *conflation relation* $\sim_R$, a binary relation on the set $\mathcal{A}^*$ of all strings over the finite grapheme alphabet $\mathcal{A}$. Prototypically, $\sim_R$ will be a true equivalence relation, inducing a partitioning of $\mathcal{A}^*$ into equivalence classes or "conflation sets" $[w]_R = \{v \in \mathcal{A}^* : v \sim_R w\}$.

2.1 Phonetic Conflation

If we assume despite the lack of consistent orthographic conventions that historical graphemic forms were constructed to reflect phonetic forms, and if the phonetic system of the target language is diachronically more stable than the graphematic system, then the phonetic form of a word should provide a better clue to its extant cognates (if any) than a historical graphemic form alone. Taken together, these assumptions lead to the canonicaliza-

Proceedings of the 11th Meeting of the ACL-SIGMORPHON, ACL 2010, pages 72–77,
Uppsala, Sweden, 15 July 2010.

tion technique referred to here as *phonetic conflation*.

In order to map graphemic forms to phonetic forms, we may avail ourselves of previous work in the realm of text-to-speech synthesis, a domain in which the discovery of phonetic forms for arbitrary text is an often-studied problem (Allen et al., 1987; Dutoit, 1997), the so-called "letter-to-sound" (LTS) conversion problem. The phonetic conversion module used here was adapted from the LTS rule-set distributed with the IMS German Festival package (Möhler et al., 2001), and compiled as a finite-state transducer (Jurish, 2008).

In general, the phonetic conflation strategy maps each (historical or extant) input word $w \in \mathcal{A}^*$ to a unique phonetic form $\mathrm{pho}(w)$ by means of a computable function $\mathrm{pho} : \mathcal{A}^* \to \mathcal{P}^*$,[1] conflating those strings which share a common phonetic form:

$$w \sim_{\mathrm{Pho}} v :\Leftrightarrow \mathrm{pho}(w) = \mathrm{pho}(v) \qquad (1)$$

2.2 Levenshtein Edit Distance

Although the phonetic conflation technique described in the previous section is capable of successfully identifying a number of common historical graphematic variation patterns such as *ey/ei, œ/ö, th/t,* and *tz/z*, it fails to conflate historical forms with any extant equivalent whenever the graphematic variation leads to non-identity of the respective phonetic forms, as determined by the LTS rule-set employed. In particular, whenever a historical variation would effect a pronunciation difference in synchronic forms, that variation will remain uncaptured by a phonetic conflation technique. Examples of such phonetically salient variations with respect to the simplified IMS German Festival rule-set include *guot/gut* "good", *liecht/licht* "light", *tiuvel/teufel* "devil", and *wolln/wollen* "want".

In order to accommodate graphematic variation phenomena beyond those for which strict phonetic identity of the variant forms obtains, we may employ an approximate search strategy based on the simple *Levenshtein edit distance* (Levenshtein, 1966; Navarro, 2001). Formally, let $\mathrm{Lex} \subseteq \mathcal{A}^*$ be the lexicon of all extant forms, and let $d_{\mathrm{Lev}} : \mathcal{A}^* \times \mathcal{A}^* \to \mathbb{N}$ represent the Levenshtein distance over grapheme strings, then define for every input word $w \in \mathcal{A}^*$ the "best" synchronic equivalent $\mathrm{best}_{\mathrm{Lev}}(w)$ as the unique extant word $v \in \mathrm{Lex}$ with minimal edit-distance to the input word:[2]

$$\mathrm{best}_{\mathrm{Lev}}(w) = \arg\min_{v \in \mathrm{Lex}} d_{\mathrm{Lev}}(w, v) \qquad (2)$$

Ideally, the image of a word w under $\mathrm{best}_{\mathrm{Lev}}$ will itself be the canonical cognate sought,[3] leading to conflation of all strings which share a common image under $\mathrm{best}_{\mathrm{Lev}}$:

$$w \sim_{\mathrm{Lev}} v :\Leftrightarrow \mathrm{best}_{\mathrm{Lev}}(w) = \mathrm{best}_{\mathrm{Lev}}(v) \qquad (3)$$

The function $\mathrm{best}_{\mathrm{Lev}}(w) : \mathcal{A}^* \to \mathrm{Lex}$ can be computed using a variant of the Dijkstra algorithm (Dijkstra, 1959) even when the lexicon is infinite (as in the case of productive nominal composition in German) whenever the set Lex can be represented by a finite-state acceptor (Mohri, 2002; Allauzen and Mohri, 2009; Jurish, 2010). For current purposes, we used the (infinite) input language of the TAGH morphology transducer (Geyken and Hanneforth, 2006) stripped of proper names, abbreviations, and foreign-language material to approximate Lex.

2.3 Rewrite Transducer

While the simple edit distance conflation technique from the previous section is quite powerful and requires for its implementation only a lexicon of extant forms, the Levenshtein distance itself appears in many cases too coarse to function as a reliable predictor of etymological relations, since each edit operation (deletion, insertion, or substitution) is assigned a cost independent of the characters operated on and of the immediate context in the strings under consideration. This operand-independence of the traditional Levenshtein distance results in a number of spurious conflations such as those given in Table 1.

In order to achieve a finer-grained and thus more precise mapping from historical forms to extant canonical cognates while preserving some degree of the robustness provided by the relaxation of the strict identity criterion implicit in the edit-distance conflation technique, a non-deterministic weighted finite-state "rewrite" transducer was developed to replace the simple Levenshtein metric. The rewrite transducer was compiled from a

[1] $\mathcal{P}$ is a finite phonetic alphabet.

[2] We assume that whenever multiple extant minimal-distance candidate forms exist, one is chosen randomly.

[3] Note here that every extant form is its own "best" equivalent: $w \in \mathrm{Lex}$ implies $\mathrm{best}_{\mathrm{Lev}}(w) = w$, since $d_{\mathrm{Lev}}(w, w) = 0 < d_{\mathrm{Lev}}(w, v)$ for all $v \neq w$.

w	$\text{best}_{\text{Lev}}(w)$		Extant Equivalent	
aug	*aus*	"out"	*auge*	"eye"
faszt	*fast*	"almost"	*fasst*	"grabs"
ouch	*buch*	"book"	*auch*	"also"
ram	*rat*	"advice"	*rahm*	"cream"
vol	*volk*	"people"	*voll*	"full"

Table 1: Example spurious Levenshtein distance conflations

heuristic two-level rule-set (Karttunen et al., 1987; Kaplan and Kay, 1994; Laporte, 1997) whose 306 rules were manually constructed to reflect linguistically plausible patterns of diachronic variation as observed in the lemma-instance pairs automatically extracted from the full 5.5 million word DWB verse corpus (Jurish, 2008). In particular, phonetic phenomena such as *schwa deletion*, *vowel shift*, *voicing alternation*, and *articulatory location shift* are easily captured by such rules.

Of the 306 heuristic rewrite rules, 131 manipulate consonant-like strings, 115 deal with vowel-like strings, and 14 operate directly on syllable-like units. The remaining 46 rules define expansions for explicitly marked elisions and unrecognized input. Some examples of rules used by the rewrite transducer are given in Table 2.

Formally, the rewrite transducer Δ_{rw} defines a pseudo-metric $[\![\Delta_{\text{rw}}]\!] : \mathcal{A}^* \times \mathcal{A}^* \to \mathbb{R}_\infty$ on all string pairs (Mohri, 2009). Assuming the non-negative tropical semiring (Simon, 1987) is used to represent transducer weights, analagous to the transducer representation of the Levenshtein metric (Allauzen and Mohri, 2009), the rewrite pseudo-metric can be used as a drop-in replacement for the Levenshtein distance in Equations (2) and (3), yielding Equations (4) and (5):

$$\text{best}_{\text{rw}}(w) = \arg\min_{v \in \text{Lex}} [\![\Delta_{\text{rw}}]\!](w, v) \quad (4)$$

$$w \sim_{\text{rw}} v :\Leftrightarrow \text{best}_{\text{rw}}(w) = \text{best}_{\text{rw}}(v) \quad (5)$$

3 Evaluation

3.1 Test Corpus

The conflation techniques described above were tested on a corpus of historical German verse extracted from the quotation evidence in a single volume of the digital first edition of the dictionary *Deutsches Wörterbuch* "DWB" (Bartz et al., 2004). The test corpus contained 11,242 tokens of 4157 distinct word types, discounting non-alphabetic types such as punctuation. Each corpus type was manually assigned one or more extant equivalents based on inspection of its occurrences in the whole 5.5 million word DWB verse corpus in addition to secondary sources. Only extinct roots, proper names, foreign and other non-lexical material were not explicitly assigned any extant equivalent at all; such types were flagged and treated as their own canonical cognates, *i.e.* identical to their respective "extant" equivalents. In all other cases, equivalence was determined by direct etymological relation of the root in addition to matching morphosyntactic features. Problematic types were marked as such and subjected to expert review. 296 test corpus types representing 585 tokens were ambiguously associated with more than one canonical cognate. In a second annotation pass, these remaining ambiguities were resolved on a per-token basis.

3.2 Evaluation Measures

The three conflation strategies from Section 2 were evaluated using the gold-standard test corpus to simulate a document indexing and query scenario. Formally, let $G \subset \mathcal{A}^* \times \mathcal{A}^*$ represent the finite set of all gold-standard pairs $(w, \widetilde{w})$ with $\widetilde{w}$ the manually determined canonical cognate for the corpus type w, and let $Q = \{\widetilde{w} : \exists (w, \widetilde{w}) \in G\}$ be the set of all canonical cognates represented in the corpus. Then define for a binary conflation relation $\sim_R$ on $\mathcal{A}^*$ and a query string $q \in Q$ the sets $\text{relevant}(q), \text{retrieved}_R(q) \subseteq G$ of *relevant* and *retrieved* gold-standard pairs as:

$$\begin{aligned} \text{relevant}(q) &= \{(w, \widetilde{w}) \in G : \widetilde{w} = q\} \\ \text{retrieved}_R(q) &= \{(w, \widetilde{w}) \in G : w \sim_R q\} \end{aligned}$$

Type-wise precision and recall can then be defined directly as:

$$\begin{aligned} \text{pr}_G &= \frac{\left|\bigcup_{q \in Q} \text{retrieved}_R(q) \cap \text{relevant}(q)\right|}{\left|\bigcup_{q \in Q} \text{retrieved}_R(q)\right|} \\ \text{rc}_G &= \frac{\left|\bigcup_{q \in Q} \text{retrieved}_R(q) \cap \text{relevant}(q)\right|}{\left|\bigcup_{q \in Q} \text{relevant}(q)\right|} \end{aligned}$$

If $\text{tp}_R(q) = \text{retrieved}_R(q) \cap \text{relevant}(q)$ represents the set of *true positives* for a query q, then token-wise precision and recall are defined in terms of the gold-standard frequency function

From → To /	Left _ Right ⟨Cost⟩		Example(s)	
$\varepsilon \to e$ /	$(\mathcal{A}\backslash\{e\})$ _ #	⟨ 5 ⟩	*aug* ⇝ *auge*	"eye"
$z \to s$ /	s _	⟨ 1 ⟩	*faszt* ⇝ *fasst*	"grabs"
$o \to a$ /	_ u	⟨ 1 ⟩	*ouch* ⇝ *auch*	"also"
$\varepsilon \to h$ /	V _ C	⟨ 5 ⟩	*ram* ⇝ *rahm*	"cream"
$l \to ll$ /	_	⟨ 8 ⟩	*vol* ⇝ *voll*	"full"

Table 2: Some example heuristics used by the rewrite transducer. Here, ε represents the empty string, # represents a word boundary, and $\mathrm{V}, \mathrm{C} \subset \mathcal{A}$ are sets of vowel-like and consonant-like characters, respectively.

$f_G : G \to \mathbb{N}$ as:

$$\mathrm{pr}_{f_G} = \frac{\sum_{q \in Q, g \in \mathrm{tp}_R(q)} f_G(g)}{\sum_{q \in Q, g \in \mathrm{retrieved}_R(q)} f_G(g)}$$

$$\mathrm{rc}_{f_G} = \frac{\sum_{q \in Q, g \in \mathrm{tp}_R(q)} f_G(g)}{\sum_{q \in Q, g \in \mathrm{relevant}(q)} f_G(g)}$$

We use the unweighted harmonic precision-recall average F (van Rijsbergen, 1979) as a composite measure for both type- and token-wise evaluation modes:

$$\mathrm{F}(pr, rc) = \frac{2 \cdot pr \cdot rc}{pr + rc}$$

3.3 Results

The elementary canonicalization function for each of the conflation techniques[4] was applied to the entire test corpus to simulate a corpus indexing run. Running times for the various methods on a 1.8GHz Linux workstation using the `gfsmxl` C library are given in Table 3. The Levenshtein edit-distance technique is at a clear disadvantage here, roughly 150 times slower than the phonetic technique and 40 times slower than the specialized heuristic rewrite transducer. This effect is assumedly due to the density of the search space (which is maximal for an unrestricted Levenshtein editor), since the `gfsmxl` greedy k-best search of a Levenshtein transducer cascade generates at least $|\mathcal{A}|$ configurations per character, and a single backtracking step requires an additional $3|\mathcal{A}|$ heap extractions (Jurish, 2010). Use of specialized lookup algorithms (Oflazer, 1996) might ameliorate such problems.

Qualitative results for several conflation techniques with respect to the DWB verse test corpus are given in Table 4. An additional conflation relation "Id" using strict identity of grapheme strings

[4]pho, $\mathrm{best}_{\mathrm{Lev}}$ and $\mathrm{best}_{\mathrm{rw}}$ for the phonetic, Levenshtein, and heuristic rewrite transducer methods respectively

Method	Time	Throughput
Pho	1.82 sec	7322 tok/sec
Lev	278.03 sec	48 tok/sec
rw	7.02 sec	1898 tok/sec

Table 3: Processing time for elementary canonicalization functions

($w \sim_{\mathrm{Id}} v :\Leftrightarrow w = v$) was tested to provide a baseline for the methods described in Section 2.

As expected, the strict identity baseline relation was the most precise of all methods tested, achieving 99.9% type-wise and 99.1% token-wise precision. This is unsurprising, since the Id method yields false positives only when a historical form is indistinguishable from a non-equivalent extant form, as in the case of the mapping *wider* ⇝ *wieder* ("again") and the non-equivalent extant form *wider* ("against"). Despite its excellent precision, the baseline method's recall was the lowest of any tested method, which supports the claim that a synchronically-oriented lexicon cannot adequately account for a corpus of historical text. Type-wise recall was particularly low (70.8%), indicating that diachronic variation was more common in low-frequency types.

Surprisingly, the phonetic and Levenshtein edit-distance methods performed similarly for all measures except token-wise precision, in which Lev incurred 61.6% fewer errors than Pho. Given their near-identical type-wise precision, this difference can be attributed to a small number of phonetic misconflations involving high-frequency types, such as *wider*∼*wieder* ("against"∼"again"), *statt*∼*stadt*, ("instead"∼"city"), and *in*∼*ihn* ("in"∼"him"). Contrary to expectations, Lev did not yield any recall improvements over Pho, although the union of the two underlying conflation relations

	Type-wise %			Token-wise %		
R	pr_G	rc_G	F_G	pr_{f_G}	rc_{f_G}	F_{f_G}
Id	**99.9**	70.8	82.9	**99.1**	83.7	90.7
Pho	96.7	80.1	87.6	92.7	89.6	91.1
Lev	96.6	78.9	86.9	97.2	87.8	92.2
rw	98.5	88.4	**93.2**	98.2	93.4	**95.8**
Pho | Lev	94.1	84.3	88.9	91.3	91.6	91.5
Pho | rw	96.1	**89.8**	92.8	92.5	**94.5**	93.5

Table 4: Qualitative evaluation of various conflation techniques

($\sim_{\mathrm{Pho}\,|\,\mathrm{Lev}} = \sim_{\mathrm{Pho}} \cup \sim_{\mathrm{Lev}}$) achieved a type-wise recall of 84.3% (token-wise recall 91.6%), which suggests that these two methods complement one another when both an LTS module and a high-coverage lexicon of extant types are available.

Of the methods described in Section 2, the heuristic rewrite transducer Δ_{rw} performed best overall, with a type-wise harmonic mean F of 93.2% and a token-wise F of 95.8%. While Δ_{rw} incurred some additional precision errors compared to the naïve graphemic identity method Id, these were not as devastating as those incurred by the phonetic or Levenshtein distance methods, which supports the claim from Section 2.3 that a fine-grained context-sensitive pseudo-metric incorporating linguistic knowledge can more accurately model diachronic processes than an all-purpose metric like the Levenshtein distance.

Recall was highest for the composite phonetic-rewrite relation $\sim_{\mathrm{Pho}\,|\,\mathrm{rw}} = \sim_{\mathrm{Pho}} \cup \sim_{\mathrm{rw}}$, although the precision errors induced by the phonetic component outweighed the comparatively small gain in recall. The best overall performance is achieved by the heuristic rewrite transducer Δ_{rw} on its own, yielding a reduction of 60.3% in type-wise recall errors and of 59.5% in token-wise recall errors, while minimizing the number of newly introduced precision errors.

4 Conclusion & Outlook

We have presented three different methods for associating unknown historical word forms with synchronically active canonical cognates. The heuristic mapping of unknown forms to extant equivalents by means of linguistically motivated context-sensitive rewrite rules yielded the best results in an information retrieval task on a corpus of historical German verse, reducing type-wise recall errors by over 60% compared to a naïve text-matching strategy. Depending on the availability of linguistic resources (*e.g.* phonetization rule-sets, lexica), use of phonetic canonicalization and/or Levenshtein edit distance may provide a more immediately accessible route to improved recall for other languages or applications, at the expense of some additional loss of precision.

We are interested in verifying our results using larger corpora than the small test corpus used here, as well as extending the techniques described here to other languages and domains. In particular, we are interested in comparing the performance of the domain-specific rewrite transducer used here to other linguistically motivated language-independent metrics such as (Covington, 1996; Kondrak, 2000).

Acknowledgements

The work described above was funded by a *Deutsche Forschungsgemeinschaft* (DFG) grant to the project *Deutsches Textarchiv*. Additionally, the author would like to thank Jörg Didakowski, Oliver Duntze, Alexander Geyken, Thomas Hanneforth, Henriette Scharnhorst, Wolfgang Seeker, Kay-Michael Würzner, and this paper's anonymous reviewers for their helpful feedback and comments.

References

Cyril Allauzen and Mehryar Mohri. 2009. Linear-space computation of the edit-distance between a string and a finite automaton. In *London Algorithmics 2008: Theory and Practice*. College Publications.

Jonathan Allen, M. Sharon Hunnicutt, and Dennis Klatt. 1987. *From Text to Speech: the MITalk system*. Cambridge University Press.

Hans-Werner Bartz, Thomas Burch, Ruth Christmann, Kurt Gärtner, Vera Hildenbrandt, Thomas Schares, and Klaudia Wegge, editors. 2004. *Der Digitale*

Grimm. Deutsches Wörterbuch von Jacob und Wilhelm Grimm. Zweitausendeins, Frankfurt am Main.

Eric Brill. 1992. A simple rule-based part-of-speech tagger. In *Proceedings of ANLP-92, 3rd Conference on Applied Natural Language Processing*, pages 152–155, Trento, Italy.

Mike Cafarella and Doug Cutting. 2004. Building Nutch: Open source search. *Queue*, 2(2):54–61.

Simon Clematide. 2008. An OLIF-based open inflection resource and yet another morphological system for German. In Storrer et al. (Storrer et al., 2008), pages 183–194.

Michael A. Covington. 1996. An algorithm to align words for historical comparison. *Computational Linguistics*, 22:481–496.

Stephen DeRose. 1988. Grammatical category disambiguation by statistical optimization. *Computational Linguistics*, 14(1):31–39.

Edsger W. Dijkstra. 1959. A note on two problems in connexion with graphs. *Numerische Mathematik*, 1:269–271.

Thierry Dutoit. 1997. *An Introduction to Text-to-Speech Synthesis.* Kluwer, Dordrecht.

Alexander Geyken and Thomas Hanneforth. 2006. TAGH: A complete morphology for German based on weighted finite state automata. In *Proceedings FSMNLP 2005*, pages 55–66, Berlin. Springer.

Bryan Jurish. 2008. Finding canonical forms for historical German text. In Storrer et al. (Storrer et al., 2008), pages 27–37.

Bryan Jurish. 2010. Efficient online k-best lookup in weighted finite-state cascades. To appear in *Studia Grammatica*.

Ronald M. Kaplan and Martin Kay. 1994. Regular models of phonological rule systems. *Computational Linguistics*, 20(3):331–378.

Lauri Karttunen, Ronald M. Kay, and Kimmo Koskenniemi. 1987. A compiler for two-level phonological rules. In M. Dalrymple, R. Kaplan, L. Karttunen, K. Koskenniemi, S. Shaio, and M. Wescoat, editors, *Tools for Morphological Analysis*, volume 87-108 of *CSLI Reports*, pages 1–61. CSLI, Stanford University, Palo Alto, CA.

Gregorz Kondrak. 2000. A new algorithm for the alignment of phonetic sequences. In *Proceedings NAACL*, pages 288–295.

Éric Laporte. 1997. Rational transductions for phonetic conversion and phonology. In Emmanuel Roche and Yves Schabes, editors, *Finite-State Language Processing*. MIT Press, Cambridge, MA.

Vladimir I. Levenshtein. 1966. Binary codes capable of correcting deletions, insertions, and reversals. *Soviet Physics Doklady*, 10(1966):707–710.

Julie Beth Lovins. 1968. Development of a stemming algorithm. *Mechanical Translation and Computational Linguistics*, 11:22–31.

Mehryar Mohri. 2002. Semiring frameworks and algorithms for shortest-distance problems. *Journal of Automata, Languages and Combinatorics*, 7(3):321–350.

Mehryar Mohri. 2009. Weighted automata algorithms. In *Handbook of Weighted Automata*, Monographs in Theoretical Computer Science, pages 213–254. Springer, Berlin.

Gregor Möhler, Antje Schweitzer, and Mark Breitenbücher, 2001. *IMS German Festival manual, version 1.2.* Institute for Natural Language Processing, University of Stuttgart.

Gonzalo Navarro. 2001. A guided tour to approximate string matching. *ACM Computing Surveys*, 33(1):31–88.

Kemal Oflazer. 1996. Error-tolerant finite-state recognition with applications to morphological analysis and spelling correction. *Computational Linguistics*, 22(1):73–89.

Martin F. Porter. 1980. An algorithm for suffix stripping. *Program*, 14(3):130–137.

Helmut Schmid. 1994. Probabilistic part-of-speech tagging using decision trees. In *International Conference on New Methods in Language Processing*, pages 44–49, Manchester, UK.

Imre Simon. 1987. The nondeterministic complexity of finite automata. Technical Report RT-MAP-8073, Instituto de Matemática e Estatística da Universidade de São Paulo.

Alexey Sokirko. 2003. A technical overview of DWDS/dialing concordance. Talk delivered at the meeting *Computational linguistics and intellectual technologies*, Protvino, Russia.

Angelika Storrer, Alexander Geyken, Alexander Siebert, and Kay-Michael Würzner, editors. 2008. *Text Resources and Lexical Knowledge.* Mouton de Gruyter, Berlin.

C. J. van Rijsbergen. 1979. *Information Retrieval.* Butterworth-Heinemann, Newton, MA.

Semi-supervised learning of concatenative morphology

Oskar Kohonen and **Sami Virpioja** and **Krista Lagus**
Aalto University School of Science and Technology
Adaptive Informatics Research Centre
P.O. Box 15400, FI-00076 AALTO, Finland
{oskar.kohonen,sami.virpioja,krista.lagus}@tkk.fi

Abstract

We consider morphology learning in a semi-supervised setting, where a small set of linguistic gold standard analyses is available. We extend Morfessor Baseline, which is a method for unsupervised morphological segmentation, to this task. We show that known linguistic segmentations can be exploited by adding them into the data likelihood function and optimizing separate weights for unlabeled and labeled data. Experiments on English and Finnish are presented with varying amount of labeled data. Results of the linguistic evaluation of Morpho Challenge improve rapidly already with small amounts of labeled data, surpassing the state-of-the-art unsupervised methods at 1000 labeled words for English and at 100 labeled words for Finnish.

1 Introduction

Morphological analysis is required in many natural language processing problems. Especially, in agglutinative and compounding languages, where each word form consists of a combination of stems and affixes, the number of unique word forms in a corpus is very large. This leads to problems in word-based statistical language modeling: Even with a large training corpus, many of the words encountered when applying the model did not occur in the training corpus, and thus there is no information available on how to process them. Using morphological units, such as stems and affixes, instead of complete word forms alleviates this problem. Unfortunately, for many languages morphological analysis tools either do not exist or they are not freely available. In many cases, the problems of availability also apply to morphologically annotated corpora, making supervised learning infeasible.

In consequence, there has been a need for approaches for morphological processing that would require little language-dependent resources. Due to this need, as well as the general interest in language acquisition and unsupervised language learning, the research on unsupervised learning of morphology has been active during the past ten years. Especially, methods that perform morphological segmentation have been studied extensively (Goldsmith, 2001; Creutz and Lagus, 2002; Monson et al., 2004; Bernhard, 2006; Dasgupta and Ng, 2007; Snyder and Barzilay, 2008b; Poon et al., 2009). These methods have shown to produce results that improve performance in several applications, such as speech recognition and information retrieval (Creutz et al., 2007; Kurimo et al., 2008).

While unsupervised methods often work quite well across different languages, it is difficult to avoid biases toward certain kinds of languages and analyses. For example, in isolating languages, the average amount of morphemes per word is low, whereas in synthetic languages the amount may be very high. Also, different applications may need a particular bias, for example, not analyzing frequent compound words as consisting of smaller parts could be beneficial in information retrieval. In many cases, even a small amount of labeled data can be used to adapt a method to a particular language and task. Methodologically, this is referred to as semi-supervised learning.

In semi-supervised learning, the learning system has access to both labeled and unlabeled data. Typically, the labeled data set is too small for supervised methods to be effective, but there is a large amount of unlabeled data available. There are many different approaches to this class of problems, as presented by Zhu (2005). One approach is to use generative models, which specify a join distribution over all variables in the model. They can be utilized both in unsupervised

Proceedings of the 11th Meeting of the ACL-SIGMORPHON, ACL 2010, pages 78–86,
Uppsala, Sweden, 15 July 2010.

and supervised learning. In contrast, discriminative models only specify the conditional distribution between input data and labels, and therefore require labeled data. Both, however, can be extended to the semi-supervised case. For generative models, it is, in principle, very easy to use both labeled and unlabeled data. For unsupervised learning one can consider the labels as missing data and estimate their values using the Expectation Maximization (EM) algorithm (Dempster et al., 1977). In the semi-supervised case, some labels are available, and the rest are considered missing and estimated with EM.

In this paper, we extend the Morfessor Baseline method for the semi-supervised case. Morfessor (Creutz and Lagus, 2002; Creutz and Lagus, 2005; Creutz and Lagus, 2007, etc.) is one of the well-established methods for morphological segmentation. It applies a simple generative model. The basic idea, inspired by the Minimum Description Length principle (Rissanen, 1989), is to encode the words in the training data with a lexicon of morphs, that are segments of the words. The number of bits needed to encode both the morph lexicon and the data using the lexicon should be minimized. Morfessor does not limit the number of morphemes per word form, making it suitable for modeling a large variety of agglutinative languages irrespective of them being more isolating or synthetic. We show that the model can be trained in a similar fashion in the semi-supervised case as in the unsupervised case. However, with a large set of unlabeled data, the effect of the supervision on the results tends to be small. Thus, we add a discriminative weighting scheme, where a small set of word forms with gold standard analyzes are used for tuning the respective weights of the labeled and unlabeled data.

The paper is organized as follows: First, we discuss related work on semi-supervised learning. Then we describe the Morfessor Baseline model and the unsupervised algorithm, followed by our semi-supervised extension. Finally, we present experimental results for English and Finnish using the Morpho Challenge data sets (Kurimo et al., 2009).

1.1 Related work

There is surprisingly little work that consider improving the unsupervised models of morphology with small amounts of annotated data. In the related tasks that deal with sequential labeling (word segmentation, POS tagging, shallow parsing, named-entity recognition), semi-supervised learning is more common.

Snyder and Barzilay (2008a; 2008b) consider learning morphological segmentation with non-parametric Bayesian model from multilingual data. For multilingual settings, they extract 6 139 parallel short phrases from the Hebrew, Arabic, Aramaic and English bible. Using the aligned phrase pairs, the model can learn the segmentations for two languages at the same time. In one of the papers (2008a), they consider also semi-supervised scenarios, where annotated data is available either in only one language or both of the languages. However, the amount of annotated data is fixed to the half of the full data. This differs from our experimental setting, where the amount of unlabeled data is very large and the amount of labeled data relatively small.

Poon et al. (2009) apply a log-linear, undirected generative model for learning the morphology of Arabic and Hebrew. They report results for the same small data set as Snyder and Barzilay (2008a) in both unsupervised and semi-supervised settings. For the latter, they use somewhat smaller proportions of annotated data, varying from 25% to 100% of the total data, but the amount of unlabeled data is still very small. Results are reported also for a larger 120 000 word Arabic data set, but only for unsupervised learning.

A problem similar to morphological segmentation is word segmentation for the languages where orthography does not specify word boundaries. However, the amount of labeled data is usually large, and unlabeled data is just an additional source of information. Li and McCallum (2005) apply a semi-supervised approach to Chinese word segmentation where unlabeled data is utilized for forming word clusters, which are then used as features for a supervised classifier. Xu et al. (2008) adapt a Chinese word segmentation specifically to a machine translation task, by using the indirect supervision from a parallel corpus.

2 Method

We present an extension of the Morfessor Baseline method to the semi-supervised setting. Morfessor Baseline is based on a generative probabilistic model. It is a method for modeling concatenative morphology, where the morphs—i.e., the surface forms of morphemes—of a word are its non-overlapping segments. The model parameters $\boldsymbol{\theta}$ encode a morph lexicon, which includes the properties of the morphs, such as their string representations. Each morph m in the lexicon has a probability of occurring in a word, $P(M = m \mid \boldsymbol{\theta})$.[1] The probabilities are assumed to be independent. The model uses a prior $P(\boldsymbol{\theta})$, derived using the Minimum Description Length (MDL) principle, that controls the complexity of the model. Intuitively, the prior assigns higher probability to models that store fewer morphs, where a morph is considered stored if $P(M = m \mid \boldsymbol{\theta}) > 0$. During model learning, $\boldsymbol{\theta}$ is optimized to maximize the posterior probability:

$$\begin{aligned}\boldsymbol{\theta}^{\text{MAP}} &= \arg\max_{\boldsymbol{\theta}} P(\boldsymbol{\theta}|\boldsymbol{D}_W) \\ &= \arg\max_{\boldsymbol{\theta}} \{P(\boldsymbol{\theta})P(\boldsymbol{D}_W|\boldsymbol{\theta})\}, \qquad (1)\end{aligned}$$

where $\boldsymbol{D}_W$ includes the words in the training data. In this section, we first consider separately the likelihood $P(\boldsymbol{D}_W|\boldsymbol{\theta})$ and the prior $P(\boldsymbol{\theta})$ used in Morfessor Baseline. Then we describe the algorithms, first unsupervised and then semi-supervised, for finding optimal model parameters. Last, we shortly discuss the algorithm for segmenting new words after the model training.

2.1 Likelihood

The latent variable of the model, $\boldsymbol{Z} = (Z_1, \ldots, Z_{|\boldsymbol{D}_W|})$, contains the analyses of the words in the training data $\boldsymbol{D}_W$. An instance of a single analysis for the j:th word is a sequence of morphs, $z_j = (m_{j1}, \ldots, m_{j|z_j|})$. During training, each word w_j is assumed to have only one possible analysis. Thus, instead of using the joint distribution $P(\boldsymbol{D}_W, \boldsymbol{Z} \mid \boldsymbol{\theta})$, we need to use the likelihood function only conditioned on the analyses of the observed words, $P(\boldsymbol{D}_W \mid \boldsymbol{Z}, \boldsymbol{\theta})$. The conditional likelihood is

$$\begin{aligned}&P(\boldsymbol{D}_W \mid \boldsymbol{Z} = \boldsymbol{z}, \boldsymbol{\theta}) \\ &= \prod_{j=1}^{|\boldsymbol{D}_W|} P(W = w_j \mid \boldsymbol{Z} = \boldsymbol{z}, \boldsymbol{\theta}) \\ &= \prod_{j=1}^{|\boldsymbol{D}_W|} \prod_{i=1}^{|z_j|} P(M = m_{ji} \mid \boldsymbol{\theta}), \qquad (2)\end{aligned}$$

where m_{ij} is the i:th morph in word w_j.

[1] We denote variables with uppercase letters and their instances with lowercase letters.

2.2 Priors

Morfessor applies Maximum A Posteriori (MAP) estimation, so priors for the model parameters need to be defined. The parameters $\boldsymbol{\theta}$ of the model are:

- Morph type count, or the size of the morph lexicon, $\mu \in \mathbb{Z}_+$
- Morph token count, or the number of morphs tokens in the observed data, $\nu \in \mathbb{Z}_+$
- Morph strings $(\sigma_1, \ldots, \sigma_\mu)$, $\sigma_i \in \Sigma^*$
- Morph counts $(\tau_1, \ldots, \tau_\mu)$, $\tau_i \in \{1, \ldots, \nu\}$, $\sum_i \tau_i = \nu$. Normalized with ν, these give the probabilities of the morphs.

MDL-inspired and non-informative priors have been preferred. When using such priors, morph type count and morph token counts can be neglected when optimizing the model. The morph string prior is based on length distribution $P(L)$ and distribution $P(C)$ of characters over the character set Σ, both assumed to be known:

$$P(\sigma_i) = P(L = |\sigma_i|) \prod_{j=1}^{|\sigma_i|} P(C = \sigma_{ij}) \qquad (3)$$

We use the implicit length prior (Creutz and Lagus, 2005), which is obtained by removing $P(L)$ and using end-of-word mark as an additional character in $P(C)$. For morph counts, the non-informative prior

$$P(\tau_1, \ldots, \tau_\mu) = 1 / \binom{\nu - 1}{\mu - 1} \qquad (4)$$

gives equal probability to each possible combination of the counts when μ and ν are known, as there are $\binom{\nu-1}{\mu-1}$ possible ways to choose μ positive integers that sum up to ν.

2.3 Unsupervised learning

In principle, unsupervised learning can be performed by looking for the MAP estimate with the EM-algorithm. In the case of Morfessor Baseline, this is problematic, because the prior only assigns higher probability to lexicons where fewer morphs have nonzero probabilities. The EM-algorithm has the property that it will not assign a zero probability to any morph, that has a nonzero likelihood in the previous step, and this will hold for all morphs that initially have a nonzero probability. In consequence, Morfessor Baseline instead uses a local search algorithm, which will assign zero probability to a large part of the potential morphs. This is memory-efficient, since only the morphs with nonzero probabilities need to be stored in memory. The training algorithm of Morfessor Baseline, described by Creutz and Lagus (2005), tries to minimize the cost function

$$L(\boldsymbol{\theta}, \boldsymbol{z}, \boldsymbol{D}_W) = -\ln P(\boldsymbol{\theta}) - \ln P(\boldsymbol{D}_W \mid \boldsymbol{z}, \boldsymbol{\theta}) \tag{5}$$

by testing local changes to $\boldsymbol{z}$, modifying the parameters according to each change, and selecting the best one. More specifically, one word is processed at a time, and the segmentation that minimizes the cost function with the optimal model parameters is selected:

$$z_j^{(t+1)} = \arg\min_{z_j} \Big\{ \min_{\boldsymbol{\theta}} L(\boldsymbol{\theta}, \boldsymbol{z}^{(t)}, \boldsymbol{D}_W) \Big\}. \tag{6}$$

Next, the parameters are updated:

$$\boldsymbol{\theta}^{(t+1)} = \arg\min_{\boldsymbol{\theta}} \Big\{ L(\boldsymbol{\theta}, \boldsymbol{z}^{(t+1)}, \boldsymbol{D}_W) \Big\}. \tag{7}$$

As neither of the steps can increase the cost function, this will converge to a local optimum. The initial parameters are obtained by adding all the words into the morph lexicon. Due to the context independence of the morphs within a word, the optimal analysis for a segment does not depend on in which context the segment appears. Thus, it is possible to encode $\boldsymbol{z}$ as a binary tree-like graph, where the words are the top nodes and morphs the leaf nodes. For each word, every possible split into two morphs is tested in addition to no split. If the word is split, the same test is applied recursively to its parts. See, e.g., Creutz and Lagus (2005) for more details and pseudo-code.

2.4 Semi-supervised learning

A straightforward way to do semi-supervised learning is to fix the analyses $\boldsymbol{z}$ for the labeled examples. Early experiments indicated that this has little effect on the results. The Morfessor Baseline model only contains local parameters for morphs, and relies on the bias given by its prior to guide the amount of segmentation. Therefore, it may not be well suited for semi-supervised learning. The labeled data affects only the morphs that are found in the labeled data, and even their analyses can be overwhelmed by a large amount of unsupervised data and the bias of the prior.

We suggest a fairly simple solution to this by introducing extra parameters that guide the more general behavior of the model. The amount of segmentation is mostly affected by the balance between the prior and the model. The Morfessor Baseline model has been developed to ensure this balance is sensible. However, the labeled data gives a strong source of information regarding the amount of segmentation preferred by the gold standard. We can utilize this information by introducing the weight α on the likelihood. To address the problem of labeled data being overwhelmed by the large amount of unlabeled data we introduce a second weight β on the likelihood for the labeled data. These weights are optimized on a separate held-out set. Thus, instead of optimizing the MAP estimate, we minimize the following function:

$$\begin{aligned} L(\boldsymbol{\theta}, \boldsymbol{z}, \boldsymbol{D}_W, \boldsymbol{D}_{W\mapsto A}) = \\ & - \ln P(\boldsymbol{\theta}) \\ & - \alpha \times \ln P(\boldsymbol{D}_W \mid \boldsymbol{z}, \boldsymbol{\theta}) \\ & - \beta \times \ln P(\boldsymbol{D}_{W\mapsto A} \mid \boldsymbol{z}, \boldsymbol{\theta}) \end{aligned} \tag{8}$$

The labeled training set $\boldsymbol{D}_{W\mapsto A}$ may include alternative analyses for some of the words. Let $A(w_j) = \{a_{j1}, \ldots, a_{jk}\}$ be the set of known analyses for word w_j. Assuming the training samples are independent, and giving equal weight for each analysis, the likelihood of the labeled data would be

$$P(\boldsymbol{D}_{W\mapsto A} \mid \boldsymbol{\theta}) = \prod_{j=1}^{|\boldsymbol{D}_{W\mapsto A}|} \prod_{a_{jk}\in A(w_j)} \prod_{i=1}^{|a_{jk}|} P(M = m_{jki} \mid \boldsymbol{\theta}). \tag{9}$$

However, when the analyses of the words are fixed, the product over alternative analyses in A is problematic, because the model cannot select several of them at the same time. A sum over $A(w_j)$:s would avoid this problem, but then the logarithm of the likelihood function becomes nontrivial (i.e., logarithm of sum of products) and too slow to calculate during the training. Instead, we use the hidden variable $\boldsymbol{Z}$ to select only one analysis also for the labeled samples, but now with the restriction that $Z_j \in A(w_j)$. The likelihood function for $\boldsymbol{D}_{W\mapsto A}$ is then equivalent to Equation 2. Because the recursive algorithm search assumes that a string is segmented in the same way irrespective of its context, the labeled data can still get zero probabilities. In practice, zero probabilities in the labeled data likelihood are treated as very large, but not infinite, costs.

2.5 Segmenting new words

After training the model, a Viterbi-like algorithm can be applied to find the optimal segmentation of each word. As proposed by Virpioja and Kohonen (2009), also new morph types can be allowed by utilizing an approximate cost of adding them to the lexicon. As this enables reasonable results also when the training data is small, we use a similar technique. The cost is calculated from the decrease in the probabilities given in Equations 3 and 4 when a new morph is assumed to be in the lexicon.

3 Experiments

In the experiments, we compare six different variants of the Morfessor Baseline algorithm:

- **Unsupervised:** The classic, unsupervised Morfessor baseline.
- **Unsupervised + weighting:** A held-out set is used for adjusting the weight of the likelihood α. When $\alpha = 1$ the method is equivalent to the unsupervised baseline. The main effect of adjusting α is to control how many segments per word the algorithm prefers. Higher α leads to fewer and lower α to more segments per word.
- **Supervised:** The semi-supervised method trained with only the labeled data.
- **Supervised + weighting:** As above, but the weight of the likelihood β is optimized on the held-out set. The weight can only affect which segmentations are selected from the possible alternative segmentations in the labeled data.
- **Semi-supervised:** The semi-supervised method trained with both labeled and unlabeled data.
- **Semi-supervised + weighting:** As above, but the parameters α and β are optimized using the the held-out set.

All variations are evaluated using the linguistic gold standard evaluation of Morpho Challenge 2009. For supervised and semi-supervised methods, the amount of labeled data is varied between 100 and 10 000 words, whereas the held-out set has 500 gold standard analyzes. To obtain precision-recall curves, we calculated weighted F0.5 and F2 scores in addition to the normal F1 score. The parameters α and β were optimized also for those.

3.1 Data and evaluation

We used the English and Finnish data sets from Competition 1 of Morpho Challenge 2009 (Kurimo et al., 2009). Both are extracted from a three million sentence corpora. For English, there were 62 185 728 word tokens and 384 903 word types. For Finnish, there were 36 207 308 word tokens and 2 206 719 word types. The complexity of Finnish morphology is indicated by the almost ten times larger number of word types than in English, while the number of word tokens is smaller.

We applied also the evaluation method of the Morpho Challenge 2009: The results of the morphological segmentation were compared to a linguistic gold standard analysis. Precision measures whether the words that share morphemes in the proposed analysis have common morphemes also in the gold standard, and recall measures the opposite. The final score to optimize was F-measure, i.e, the harmonic mean of the precision and recall.[2] In addition to the unweighted F1 score, we have applied F2 and F0.5 scores, which give more weight to recall and precision, respectively.

Finnish gold standards are based on FINTWOL morphological analyzer from Lingsoft, Inc., that applies the two-level model by Koskenniemi (1983). English gold standards are from the CELEX English database. The final test sets are the same as in Morpho Challenge, based on 10 000 English word forms and 200 000 Finnish word forms. The test sets are divided into ten parts for calculating deviations and statistical significances. For parameter tuning, we applied a small held-out set containing 500 word forms that were not included in the test set.

For supervised and semi-supervised training, we created sets of five different sizes: 100, 300, 1 000, 3 000, and 10 000. They did not contain any of the word forms in the final test set, but were otherwise randomly selected from the words for

[2]Both the data sets and evaluation scripts are available from the Morpho Challenge 2009 web page: `http://www.cis.hut.fi/morphochallenge2009/`

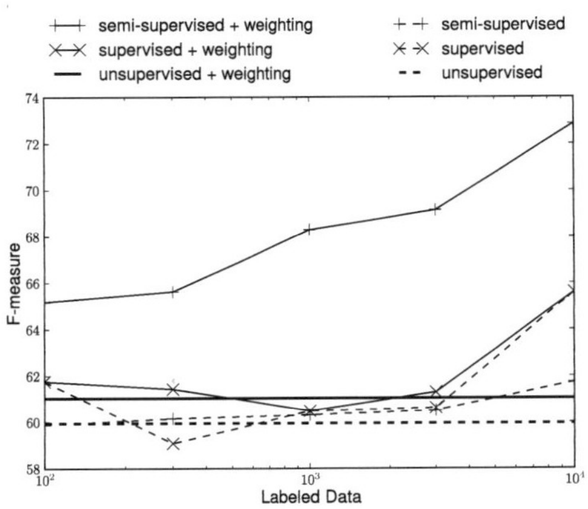

Figure 1: The F-measure for English as a function of the number of labeled training samples.

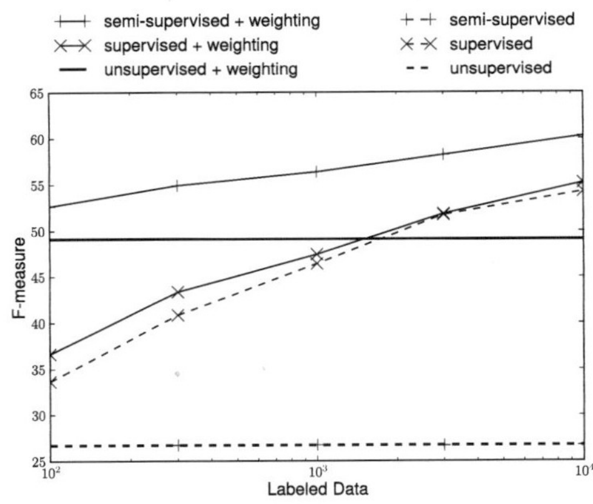

Figure 2: The F-measure for Finnish as a function of the number of labeled training samples. The *semi-supervised* and *unsupervised* lines overlap.

which the gold standard analyses were available. In order to use them for training Morfessor, the morpheme analyses were converted to segmentations using the Hutmegs package by Creutz and Lindén (2004).

3.2 Results

Figure 1 shows a comparison of the unsupervised, supervised and semi-supervised Morfessor Baseline for English. It can be seen that optimizing the likelihood weight α alone does not improve much over the unsupervised case, implying that the Morfessor Baseline is well suited for English morphology. Without weighting of the likelihood function, semi-supervised training improves the results somewhat, but it outperforms weighted unsupervised model only barely. With weighting, however, semi-supervised training improves the results significantly already for only 100 labeled training samples. For comparison, in Morpho Challenges (Kurimo et al., 2009), the unsupervised Morfessor Baseline and Morfessor Categories-MAP by Creutz and Lagus (2007) have achieved F-measures of 59.84% and 50.50%, respectively, and the all time best unsupervised result by a method that does not provide alternative analyses for words is 66.24%, obtained by Bernhard (2008).[3] This best unsupervised result is surpassed by the semi-supervised algorithm at 1000 labeled samples.

As shown in Figure 1, the supervised method obtains inconsistent scores for English with the smallest training data sizes. The supervised algorithm only knows the morphs in the training set, and therefore is crucially dependent on the Viterbi segmentation algorithm for analyzing new data. Thus, overfitting to some small data sets is not surprising. At 10 000 labeled training samples it clearly outperforms the unsupervised algorithm. The improvement obtained from tuning the weight β in the supervised case is small.

Figure 2 shows the corresponding results for Finnish. The optimization of the likelihood weight gives a large improvement to the F-measure already in the unsupervised case. This is mainly because the standard unsupervised Morfessor Baseline method does not, on average, segment words into as many segments as would be appropriate for Finnish. Without weighting, the semi-supervised method does not improve over the unsupervised one: The unlabeled training data is so much larger that the labeled data has no real effect.

For Finnish, the unsupervised Morfessor Baseline and Categories-MAP obtain F-measures of 26.75% and 44.61%, respectively (Kurimo et al., 2009). The all time best for an unsupervised method is 52.45% by Bernhard (2008). With optimized likelihood weights, the semi-supervised Morfessor Baseline achieves higher F-measures with only 100 labeled training samples. Furthermore, the largest improvement for the semi-supervised method is achieved already from 1000 labeled training samples. Unlike English, the supervised method is quite a lot worse than the unsupervised one for small training data. This is natural because of the more complex morphology

[3]Better results (68.71%) have been achieved by Monson et al. (2008), but as they were obtained by combining of two systems as alternative analyses, the comparison is not as meaningful.

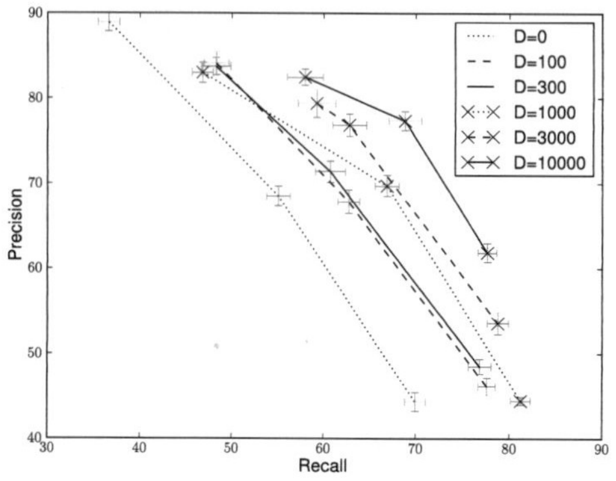

Figure 3: Precision-recall graph for English with varying amount of labeled training data. Parameters α and β have been optimized for three different measures: F0.5, F1 and F2 on the held-out set. Precision and recall values are from the final test set, error bars indicate one standard deviation.

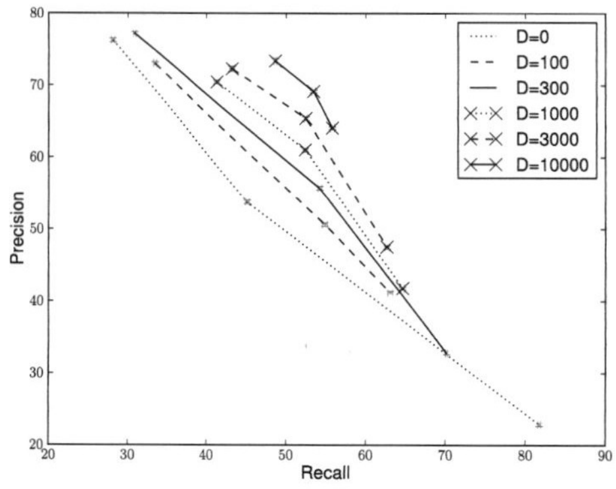

Figure 4: Precision-recall graph for Finnish with varying amount of labeled training data. Parameters α and β have been optimized for three different measures: F0.5, F1 and F2 on the held-out set. Precision and recall values are from the final test set, error bars indicate one standard deviation, which here is very small.

in Finnish; good results are not achieved just by knowing the few most common suffixes.

Figures 3 and 4 show precision-recall graphs of the performance of the semi-supervised method for English and Finnish. The parameters α and β have been optimized for three differently weighted F-measures (F0.5, F1, and F2) on the held-out set. The weight tells how much recall is emphasized; F1 is the symmetric F-measure that emphasizes precision and recall alike. The graphs show that the more there are labeled training data, the more constrained the model parameters are: With many labeled examples, the model cannot be forced to achieve high precision or recall only. The phenomenon is more evident in the Finnish data (Figure 3), where the same amount of words contains more information (morphemes) than in the English data. Table 1 shows the F0.5, F1 and F2 measures numerically.

Table 2 shows the values for the F1-optimal weights α and β that were chosen for different amounts of labeled data using the held-out set. As even the largest labeled sets are much smaller than the unlabeled training set, it is natural that $\beta \gg \alpha$. The small optimal α for Finnish explains why the difference between unsupervised unweighted and weighted versions in Figure 2 was so large. Generally, the more there is labeled data, the smaller β is needed. A possible increase in overall likelihood cost is compensated by a smaller α. Finnish with 100 labeled words is an exception; probably a very high β would end in overlearning of the small set words at the cost of overall performance.

4 Discussion

The method developed in this paper is a straightforward extension of Morfessor Baseline. In the semi-supervised setting, it should be possible to develop a generative model that would not require any discriminative reweighting, but could learn, e.g., the amount of segmentation from the labeled data. Moreover, it would be possible to learn the morpheme labels instead of just the segmentation into morphs, either within the current model or as a separate step after the segmentation. We made initial experiment with a trivial context-free labeling: A mapping between the segments and morpheme labels was extracted from the labeled training data. If some label did not have a corresponding segment, it was appended to the previous label. E.g., if the labels for "found" are "find_V +PAST", "found" was mapped to both labels. After segmentation, each segment in the test data was replaced by the most common label or label sequence whenever such was available. The results using training data with 1 000 and 10 000 labeled samples are shown in Table 3. Although precisions decrease somewhat, recalls improve considerably, and significant gains in F-measure are obtained. A more advanced, context-sensitive labeling should perform much better.

English			
labeled data	*F0.5*	*F1*	*F2*
0	69.16	61.05	62.70
100	73.23	65.18	68.30
300	72.98	65.63	68.81
1000	71.86	68.29	69.68
3000	74.34	69.13	72.01
10000	76.04	72.85	73.89
Finnish			
labeled data	*F0.5*	*F1*	*F2*
0	56.81	49.07	53.95
100	58.96	52.66	57.01
300	59.33	54.92	57.16
1000	61.75	56.38	58.24
3000	63.72	58.21	58.90
10000	66.58	60.26	57.24

Table 1: The F0.5, F1 and F2 measures for the *semi-supervised + weighting* method.

	English		**Finnish**	
labeled data	α	β	α	β
0	0.75	-	0.01	-
100	0.75	750	0.01	500
300	1	500	0.005	5000
1000	1	500	0.05	2500
3000	1.75	350	0.1	1000
10000	1.75	175	0.1	500

Table 2: The values for the weights α and β that the semisupervised algorithm chose for different amounts of labeled data when optimizing F1-measure.

The semi-supervised extension could easily be applied to the other versions and extensions of Morfessor, such as Morfessor Categories-MAP (Creutz and Lagus, 2007) and Allomorfessor (Virpioja and Kohonen, 2009). Especially the modeling of allomorphy might benefit from even small amounts of labeled data, because those allomorphs that are hardest to find (affixes, stems with irregular orthographic changes) are often more common than the easy cases, and thus likely to be found even from a small labeled data set.

Even without labeling, it will be interesting to see how well the semi-supervised morphology learning works in applications such as information retrieval. Compared to unsupervised learning, we obtained much higher recall for reasonably good levels of precision, which should be beneficial to most applications.

	Segmented	**Labeled**
English, $D = 1\,000$		
Precision	69.72%	69.30%
Recall	66.92%	72.21%
F-measure	68.29%	70.72%
English, $D = 10\,000$		
Precision	77.35%	77.07%
Recall	68.85%	77.78%
F-measure	72.86%	77.42%
Finnish, $D = 1\,000$		
Precision	61.03%	58.96%
Recall	52.38%	66.55%
F-measure	56.38%	62.53%
Finnish, $D = 10\,000$		
Precision	69.14%	66.90%
Recall	53.40%	74.08%
F-measure	60.26%	70.31%

Table 3: Results of a simple morph labeling after segmentation with semi-supervised Morfessor.

5 Conclusions

We have evaluated an extension of the Morfessor Baseline method to semi-supervised morphological segmentation. Even with our simple method, the scores improve far beyond the best unsupervised results. Moreover, already one hundred known segmentations give significant gain over the unsupervised method even with the optimized data likelihood weight.

Acknowledgments

This work was funded by Academy of Finland and Graduate School of Language Technology in Finland. We thank Mikko Kurimo and Tiina Lindh-Knuutila for comments on the manuscript, and Nokia foundation for financial support.

References

Delphine Bernhard. 2006. Unsupervised morphological segmentation based on segment predictability and word segments alignment. In *Proceedings of the PASCAL Challenge Workshop on Unsupervised segmentation of words into morphemes*, Venice, Italy. PASCAL European Network of Excellence.

Delphine Bernhard. 2008. Simple morpheme labelling in unsupervised morpheme analysis. In *Advances in Multilingual and Multimodal Information Retrieval, 8th Workshop of the CLEF*, volume 5152 of *Lecture Notes in Computer Science*, pages 873–880. Springer Berlin / Heidelberg.

Mathias Creutz and Krista Lagus. 2002. Unsupervised discovery of morphemes. In *Proceedings of the Workshop on Morphological and Phonological Learning of ACL'02*, pages 21–30, Philadelphia, Pennsylvania, USA.

Mathias Creutz and Krista Lagus. 2005. Unsupervised morpheme segmentation and morphology induction from text corpora using Morfessor 1.0. Technical Report A81, Publications in Computer and Information Science, Helsinki University of Technology.

Mathias Creutz and Krista Lagus. 2007. Unsupervised models for morpheme segmentation and morphology learning. *ACM Transactions on Speech and Language Processing*, 4(1), January.

Mathias Creutz and Krister Lindén. 2004. Morpheme segmentation gold standards for Finnish and English. Technical Report A77, Publications in Computer and Information Science, Helsinki University of Technology.

Mathias Creutz, Teemu Hirsimäki, Mikko Kurimo, Antti Puurula, Janne Pylkkönen, Vesa Siivola, Matti Varjokallio, Ebru Arisoy, Murat Saraçlar, and Andreas Stolcke. 2007. Morph-based speech recognition and modeling of out-of-vocabulary words across languages. *ACM Transactions on Speech and Language Processing*, 5(1):1–29.

Sajib Dasgupta and Vincent Ng. 2007. High-performance, language-independent morphological segmentation. In *the annual conference of the North American Chapter of the ACL (NAACL-HLT)*.

Arthur P. Dempster, Nan M. Laird, and Donald B. Rubin. 1977. Maximum likelihood from incomplete data via the em algorithm. *Journal of the Royal Statistical Society, Series B (Methodological)*, 39(1):1–38.

John Goldsmith. 2001. Unsupervised learning of the morphology of a natural language. *Computational Linguistics*, 27(2):153–189.

Kimmo Koskenniemi. 1983. *Two-level morphology: A general computational model for word-form recognition and production*. Ph.D. thesis, University of Helsinki.

Mikko Kurimo, Mathias Creutz, and Matti Varjokallio. 2008. Morpho Challenge evaluation using a linguistic Gold Standard. In *Advances in Multilingual and MultiModal Information Retrieval, 8th Workshop of the Cross-Language Evaluation Forum, CLEF 2007, Budapest, Hungary, September 19-21, 2007, Revised Selected Papers*, Lecture Notes in Computer Science , Vol. 5152, pages 864–873. Springer.

Mikko Kurimo, Sami Virpioja, Ville T. Turunen, Graeme W. Blackwood, and William Byrne. 2009. Overview and results of Morpho Challenge 2009. In *Working Notes for the CLEF 2009 Workshop*, Corfu, Greece, September.

Wei Li and Andrew McCallum. 2005. Semi-supervised sequence modeling with syntactic topic models. In *AAAI'05: Proceedings of the 20th national conference on Artificial intelligence*, pages 813–818. AAAI Press.

Christian Monson, Alon Lavie, Jaime Carbonell, and Lori Levin. 2004. Unsupervised induction of natural language morphology inflection classes. In *Proceedings of the Workshop of the ACL Special Interest Group in Computational Phonology (SIGPHON)*.

Christian Monson, Jaime Carbonell, Alon Lavie, and Lori Levin. 2008. ParaMor: Finding paradigms across morphology. In *Advances in Multilingual and MultiModal Information Retrieval, 8th Workshop of the Cross-Language Evaluation Forum, CLEF 2007, Budapest, Hungary, September 19-21, 2007, Revised Selected Papers*, Lecture Notes in Computer Science , Vol. 5152. Springer.

Hoifung Poon, Colin Cherry, and Kristina Toutanova. 2009. Unsupervised morphological segmentation with log-linear models. In *NAACL '09: Proceedings of Human Language Technologies: The 2009 Annual Conference of the North American Chapter of the Association for Computational Linguistics*, pages 209–217. Association for Computational Linguistics.

Jorma Rissanen. 1989. *Stochastic Complexity in Statistical Inquiry*, volume 15. World Scientific Series in Computer Science, Singapore.

Benjamin Snyder and Regina Barzilay. 2008a. Cross-lingual propagation for morphological analysis. In *AAAI'08: Proceedings of the 23rd national conference on Artificial intelligence*, pages 848–854. AAAI Press.

Benjamin Snyder and Regina Barzilay. 2008b. Unsupervised multilingual learning for morphological segmentation. In *Proceedings of ACL-08: HLT*, pages 737–745, Columbus, Ohio, June. Association for Computational Linguistics.

Sami Virpioja and Oskar Kohonen. 2009. Unsupervised morpheme analysis with Allomorfessor. In *Working notes for the CLEF 2009 Workshop*, Corfu, Greece.

Jia Xu, Jianfeng Gao, Kristina Toutanova, and Hermann Ney. 2008. Bayesian semi-supervised chinese word segmentation for statistical machine translation. In *COLING '08: Proceedings of the 22nd International Conference on Computational Linguistics*, pages 1017–1024, Morristown, NJ, USA. Association for Computational Linguistics.

Xiaojin Zhu. 2005. *Semi-supervised Learning with Graphs*. Ph.D. thesis, CMU. Chapter 11, Semi-supervised learning literature survey (updated online version).

Morpho Challenge competition 2005-2010: Evaluations and results

Mikko Kurimo, Sami Virpioja, Ville Turunen, Krista Lagus
Adaptive Informatics Research Centre
Aalto University, Espoo, Finland
Firstname.Lastname@tkk.fi

Abstract

Morpho Challenge is an annual evaluation campaign for unsupervised morpheme analysis. In morpheme analysis, words are segmented into smaller meaningful units. This is an essential part in processing complex word forms in many large-scale natural language processing applications, such as speech recognition, information retrieval, and machine translation. The discovery of morphemes is particularly important for morphologically rich languages where inflection, derivation and composition can produce a huge amount of different word forms. Morpho Challenge aims at language-independent unsupervised learning algorithms that can discover useful morpheme-like units from raw text material. In this paper we define the challenge, review proposed algorithms, evaluations and results so far, and point out the questions that are still open.

1 Introduction

Many large-scale natural language processing (NLP) applications, such as speech recognition, information retrieval and machine translation, require that complex word forms are analyzed into smaller, meaningful units. The discovery of these units called morphemes is particularly important for morphologically rich languages where the inflection, derivation and composition makes it impossible to even list all the word forms that are used. Various tools have been developed for morpheme analysis of word forms, but they are mostly based on language-specific rules that are not easily ported to other languages. Recently, the performance of tools based on language-independent unsupervised learning from raw text material has improved significantly and rivaled the language-specific tools in many applications.

The unsupervised algorithms proposed so far in Morpho Challenge typically first generate various alternative morphemes for each word and then select the best ones based on relevant criteria. The statistical letter successor variation (LSV) analysis (Harris, 1955) and its variations are quite commonly used as generation methods. LSV is based on the observation that the segment borders between the sub-word units often co-occur with the peaks of variation for the next letter. One popular selection approach is to minimize a cost function that balances between the size of the corpus when coded by the morphemes and the size of the morpheme codebook needed. Selection criteria that produce results resembling the linguistic morpheme segmentation include, for example, the Minimum Description Length (MDL) principle and maximum a posteriori (MAP) probability optimization (de Marcken, 1996; Creutz and Lagus, 2005).

The Morpho Challenge competition was launched in 2005 to encourage the machine learning people, linguists and specialists in NLP applications to study this field and come together to compare their best algorithms against each other. The organizers selected evaluation tasks, data and metric and performed all the evaluations. Thus, participation was made easy for people who were not specialists in the chosen NLP applications. Participation was open to everybody with no charge. The competition became popular right from the beginning and has gained new participants every year.

Although not all the authors of relevant morpheme analysis algorithms have yet submitted their algorithms for this evaluation campaign, more than 50 algorithms have already been evaluated. After the first five years of Morpho Challenge, a lot has been learned on the various possible ways to solve the problem and how the different methods work in various NLP tasks. How-

Proceedings of the 11th Meeting of the ACL-SIGMORPHON, ACL 2010, pages 87–95,
Uppsala, Sweden, 15 July 2010.

ever, there are still open questions such as: how to find meaning for the obtained unsupervised morphemes, how to disambiguate among the alternative analyses of one word, and how to use context in the analysis. Another recently emerged question that is the special topic in 2010 competition is how to utilize small amounts of labeled data and semi-supervised learning to further improve the analysis.

2 Definition of the challenge

2.1 Morphemes and their evaluation

Generally, the morphemes are defined as the smallest meaningful units of language. Rather than trying to directly specify which units are meaningful, the Morpho Challenge aims at finding units that would be useful for various practical NLP applications. The goal is to find automatic methods that can discover suitable units using unsupervised learning directly on raw text data. The methods should also not be restricted to certain languages or include many language and application dependent parameters that needed to be hand tuned for each task separately. The following three goals have been defined as the main scientific objectives for the challenge: (1) To learn of the phenomena underlying word construction in natural languages. (2) To discover approaches suitable for a wide range of languages. (3) To advance machine learning methodology.

The evaluation tasks, metrics and languages have been designed based on the scientific objectives of the challenge. It can not be directly verified how well an obtained analysis reflects the word construction in natural languages, but intuitively, the methods that split everything into letters or pre-specified letter n-grams, or leave the word forms unanalyzed, would not be very interesting solutions. An interesting thing that can be evaluated, however, is how close the obtained analysis is to the linguistic gold standard morphemes that can be obtained from CELEX or various language-dependent rule-based analyzers. The exact definition of the morphemes, tags, or features available in the gold standard to be utilized in the comparison should be decided and fixed for each language separately.

To verify that a proposed algorithm works in various languages would, ideally, require running the evaluations on a large number of languages that would be somehow representative of various important language families. However, the resources available for both computing and evaluating the analysis in various applications and languages are limited. The suggested and applicable compromise is to select morphologically rich languages where the morpheme analysis is most useful and those languages where interesting state-of-the-art evaluation tasks are available. By including German, Turkish, Finnish and Arabic, many interesting aspects of concatenative morphology have already been covered.

While the comparison against the linguistic gold standard morphemes is an interesting subgoal, the main interest in running the Morpho Challenge is to find out how useful the proposed morpheme analyses are for various practical NLP applications. Naturally, this is best evaluated by performing evaluations in several state-of-the-art application tasks. Due to the limitations of the resources, the applications have been selected based on the importance of the morpheme analysis for the application, on the availability of open state-of-the-art evaluation tasks, and on the effort needed to run the actual evaluations.

2.2 Unsupervised and semi-supervised learning

Unsupervised learning is the task of learning without labeled data. In the context of morphology discovery, it means learning without knowing where morpheme borders are, or which morphemes exist in which words. Unsupervised learning methods have many attractive features for morphological modeling, such as language-independence, independence of any particular linguistic theory, and easy portability to a new language.

Semi-supervised learning can be approached from two research directions, namely unsupervised and supervised learning. In an essentially unsupervised learning task there may exist some labeled (classified) data, or some known links between data items, which might be utilized by the (typically generative) learning algorithms. Turned around, an essentially supervised learning task, such as classification or prediction, may benefit also from unlabeled data which is typically more abundantly available.

In morphology modeling one might consider the former setup to be the case: the learning task is essentially that of unsupervised modeling, and morpheme labels can be thought of as known links between various inflected word forms.

Until 2010 the Morpho Challenge has been defined only as an unsupervised learning task. However, since small samples of morphologically labeled data can be provided already for quite many languages, also the semi-supervised learning task has become of interest.

Moreover, while there exists a fair amount of research and now even books on semi-supervised learning (Zhu, 2005; Abney, 2007; Zhu, 2010), it has not been as widely studied for structured classification problems like sequence segmentation and labeling (cf. e.g. (Jiao et al., 2006)). The semi-supervised learning challenge introduced for Morpho Challenge 2010 can thus be viewed as an opportunity to strengthen research in both morphology modeling as well as in semi-supervised learning for sequence segmentation and labeling in general.

3 Review of Morpho Challenge competitions so far

3.1 Evaluation tasks, metrics, and languages

The evaluation tasks and languages selected for Morpho Challenge evaluations are shown in Figure 1. The languages where evaluations have been prepared are Finnish (FIN), Turkish (TUR), English (ENG), German (GER), and Arabic (ARA). First the morphemes are compared to linguistic gold standards in direct morpheme segmentation (2005) and full morpheme analysis (since 2007). The practical NLP application based evaluations are automatic speech recognition (ASR), information retrieval (IR) and statistical machine translation (SMT). Morphemes obtained by semi-supervised learning can be evaluated in parallel with the unsupervised morphemes. For IR, evaluation has also been extended for full sentences, where the morpheme analysis can based on context. The various suggested and tested evaluations are defined in this section.

year	new languages	new tasks
2005	FIN, TUR, ENG	segmentation, ASR
2007	GER	full analysis, IR
2008	ARA	context IR
2009	-	SMT
2010	-	semi-supervised

Table 1: The evolution of the evaluations. The acronyms are explained in section 3.1.

3.1.1 Comparisons to linguistic gold standard

The first Morpho Challenge in 2005 (Kurimo et al., 2006) considered unsupervised segmentation of words into morphemes. The evaluation was based on comparing the segmentation boundaries given by the competitor's algorithm to the boundaries obtained from a gold standard analysis.

From 2007 onwards, the task was changed to full morpheme analysis, that is, the algorithm should not only locate the surface forms (i.e., word segments) of the morphemes, but find also which surface forms are realizations (allomorphs) of the same underlying morpheme. This generalizes the task for finding more meaningful units than just the realizations of morphemes that may be just individual letters or even empty strings. In applications this is useful when it is important to identify which units carry the same meaning even if they have different realizations in different words.

As an unsupervised algorithm cannot find the morpheme labels that would equal to the labels in the gold standard, the evaluation has to be based on what word forms share the same morphemes. The evaluation procedure samples a large number of word pairs, such that both words in the pair have at least one morpheme in common, from both the proposed analysis and the gold standard. The first version of the method was applied in 2007 (Kurimo et al., 2008) and 2008 (Kurimo et al., 2009a), and minor modifications were done in 2009 (Kurimo et al., 2009b). However, the organizers have reported the evaluation results of the 2007 and 2008 submissions also with the new version, thus allowing a direct comparison between them. A summary of these results for English, Finnish, German and Turkish for the best algorithms is presented in Table 2. The evaluations in 2008 and 2009 were also performed on Arabic, but these results and not comparable, because the database and the gold standard was changed between the years. The exact annual results for all participants as well as the details of the evaluation in each year can be reviewed in the annual evaluation reports (Kurimo et al., 2006; Kurimo et al., 2008; Kurimo et al., 2009a; Kurimo et al., 2009b).

Already the linguistic evaluation of Morpho Challenge 2005 applied some principles that have been used thereafter: (1) The evaluation is based on a subset of the word forms given as training data. This not only makes the evaluation procedure lighter, but also allows changing the set when

English			
Method	P	R	F
2009			
Allomorfessor	68.98	56.82	62.31
Monson PMU	55.68	62.33	58.82
Lignos	83.49	45.00	58.48
2008			
Monson P+M	69.59	65.57	67.52
Monson ParaMor	63.32	51.96	57.08
Zeman 1	67.13	46.67	55.06
2007			
Monson P+M	70.09	67.38	**68.71**
Bernhard 2	67.42	65.11	66.24
Bernhard 1	75.61	57.87	65.56

Finnish			
Method	P	R	F
2009			
Monson PMU	47.89	50.98	49.39
Monson PMM	51.75	45.42	48.38
Spiegler PROMODES C	41.20	48.22	44.44
2008			
Monson P+M	65.21	50.43	**56.87**
Monson ParaMor	49.97	37.64	42.93
Monson Morfessor	79.76	24.95	38.02
2007			
Bernhard 2	63.92	44.48	52.45
Bernhard 1	78.11	29.39	42.71
Bordag 5a	72.45	27.21	39.56

German			
Method	P	R	F
2009			
Monson PMU	52.53	60.27	56.14
Monson PMM	51.07	57.79	54.22
Monson PM	50.81	47.68	49.20
2008			
Monson P+M	64.06	61.52	**62.76**
Monson Morfessor	70.73	38.82	50.13
Monson ParaMor	56.98	42.10	48.42
2007			
Monson P+M	69.96	55.42	61.85
Bernhard 2	54.02	60.77	57.20
Bernhard 1	66.82	42.48	51.94

Turkish			
Method	P	R	F
2009			
Monson PMM	48.07	60.39	53.53
Monson PMU	47.25	60.01	52.88
Monson PM	49.54	54.77	52.02
2008			
Monson P+M	66.78	57.97	**62.07**
Monson ParaMor	57.35	45.75	50.90
Monson Morfessor	77.36	33.47	46.73
2007			
Bordag 5a	81.06	23.51	36.45
Bordag 5	81.19	23.44	36.38
Zeman	77.48	22.71	35.13

Table 2: The summary of the best three submitted methods for years 2009, 2008 and 2007 using the linguistic evaluation of Morpho Challenge 2009. The complete results tables by the organizers are available from `http://www.cis.hut.fi/morphochallenge2009/`. The three columns numbers are precision (P), recall (R), and F-measure (F). The best F-measure for each language is in boldface, and the best result that is not based on a direct combination of two other methods is underlined.

the old one is considered to be "overlearned". (2) The frequency of the word form plays no role in evaluation; rare and common forms are equally likely to be selected, and have equal weight to the score. (3) The evaluation score is balanced F-measure, the harmonic mean of precision and recall. Precision measures how many of the choices made by the algorithm are matched in gold standard; recall measures how many of the choices in the gold standard are matched in the proposed analysis. (4) If the linguistic gold standard has several alternative analysis for one word, for full precision, it is enough that one of the alternatives is equivalent to the proposed analysis. The same holds the other way around for recall.

All of the principles can be also criticized. For example, evaluation based on the full set would provide more trustworthy estimates, and common word forms are more significant in any practical application. However, the third and the fourth principle have problems that can be considered to be more serious.

Balanced F-measure favors methods that are able to get near-to-equal precision and recall. As many algorithms can be tuned to give either more or less morphemes per word than in the default case, this encourages using developments sets to optimize the respective parameters. The winning methods in Challenge 2009—Monson's ParaMor-Morfessor Union (PMU) and ParaMor-Morfessor

Mimic (PMM) (Monson et al., 2009), and Allomorfessor (Virpioja and Kohonen, 2009)—did this, more or less explicitly.[1] Moreover, it can be argued that the precision would be more important than recall in many applications, or, more generally, that the optimal balance between precision and recall is application dependent. We see two solutions for this: Either the optimization for F-measure should be allowed with a public development set, which means moving towards semi-supervised direction, or precision-recall curves should be compared, which means more complex evaluations.

The fourth principle causes problems, if the evaluated algorithms are allowed to have alternative analyses for each word. If several alternative analyses are provided, the obtained precision is about the average over the individual analyses, but the recall is based on the best of the alternatives. This property have been exploited in Challenges 2007 and 2008 by combining the results of two algorithms as alternative analyses. The method, Monson's ParaMor+Morfessor (P+M) holds still the best position measured in F-measures in all languages. Combining even better-performing methods in a similar manner would increase the scores further. To fix this problem, either the evaluation metric should require matching number of alternative analyses to get the full points, or the symmetry of the precision and recall measures has to be removed.

Excluding the methods that combine the analyses of two other methods as alternative ones, we see that the best F-measure (underlined in Table 2) is held by Monson's ParaMor-Morfessor Mimic from 2009 (Monson et al., 2009) in Turkish and Bernhard's method 2 from 2007 (Bernhard, 2006) in all the other three languages. This means that except for Turkish, there is no improvement in the results over the three years. Furthermore, both of the methods are based purely on segmentation, and so are all the other top methods presented in Table 2 except for Bordag's methods (Bordag, 2006) and Allomorfessor (Virpioja and Kohonen, 2009).

3.1.2 Speech recognition

A key factor in the success of large-vocabulary continuous speech recognition is the system's ability to limit the search space using a statistical language model. The language model provides the probability of different recognition hypothesis by using a model of the co-occurence of its words and morphemes. A properly smoothed n-gram is the most conventional model. The n-gram should consist of modeling units that are suitable for the language, typically words or morphemes.

In Morpho Challenge state-of-the-art large-vocabulary speech recognizers have been built for evaluations in Finnish and Turkish (Kurimo et al., 2006). The various morpheme analysis algorithms have been compared by measuring the recognition accuracy with different language models each trained and optimized based on units from one of the algorithms. The best results were quite near to each other, but Bernhard (Bernhard, 2006) and Morfessor Categories MAP were at the top for both languages.

3.1.3 Information retrieval

In the information retrieval task, the algorithms were tested by using the morpheme segmentations for text retrieval. To return all relevant documents, it is important to match the words in the queries to the words in the documents irrespective of which word forms are used. Typically, a stemming algorithm or a morphological analyzer is used to reduce the inflected forms to their stem or base form. The problem with these methods is that specific rules need to be crafted for each language. However, these approaches were also tested for comparison purposes. The IR experiments were carried out by replacing the words in the corpora and queries by the suggested morpheme segmentations. Test corpora, queries and relevance assessments were provided by Cross-Language Evaluation Forum (CLEF) (Agirre et al., 2008).

To test the effect of the morpheme segmentation, the number of other variables will have to be minimized, which poses some challenges. For example, the term weighting method will affect the results and different morpheme analyzers may perform optimally with different weighting approaches. TFIDF and Okapi BM25 term weighting methods have been tested. In the 2007 Challenge, it was noted that Okapi BM25 suffers greatly if the corpus contains a lot of frequent terms. These terms are often introduced when the algorithms segment suffixes from stems. To overcome this problem, a method for automatically generating stop lists of frequent terms was intro-

[1] Allomorfessor was trained with a pruned data to obtain a higher recall, whereas ParaMor-Morfessor is explicitly optimized for F-measure with a separate Hungarian data set.

duced. Any term that occurs more times in the corpus than a certain threshold is added to the stop list and excluded from indexing. The method is quite simple, but it treats all morpheme analysis methods equally as it does not require the algorithm to tag which morphemes are stems and which are suffixes. The generated stoplists are also reasonable sized and the results are robust with respect to the stop list cutoff parameter. With a stop list, Okapi BM25 clearly outperformed TFIDF ranking method for all algorithms. However, the problem of choosing the term weighting approach that treats all algorithms in an optimal way remains open.

Another challenge is analyzing the results as it is hard to achieve statistically significant results with the limited number of queries (50-60) that were available. In fact, in each language 11-17 of the best algorithms belonged to the "top group", that is, had no statistically different result to the top performer of the language. To improve the significance of the results, the number of queries should be increased. This is a known problem in the field of IR. However, it is important to test the methods in a real life application and if an algorithm gives good results across languages, there is evidence that it is doing something useful.

Some conclusions can be drawn from the results. The language specific reference methods (Porter stemming for English, two-layer morphological analysis for Finnish and German) give the best results, but the best unsupervised algorithms are almost at par and the differences are not significant. For German and Finnish, the best unsupervised methods can also beat in a statistically significant way the baseline of not doing any segmentation or stemming. The best algorithms that performed well across languages are ParaMor (Monson et al., 2008), Bernhard (Bernhard, 2006), Morfessor Baseline, and McNamee (McNamee, 2008).

Comparing the results to the linguistic evaluation (section 3.1.1), it seems that methods that perform well at the IR task tend to have good precision in the linguistic task, with exceptions. Thus, in the IR task it seems important not to oversegment words. One exception is the method (McNamee, 2008) which simply splits the words into equal length letter n-grams. The method gives surprisingly good results in the IR task, given the simplicity, but suffers from low precision in the linguistic task.

3.1.4 Machine translation

In phrase-based statistical machine translation process there are two stages where morpheme analysis and segmentation of the words into meaningful sub-word units is needed. The first stage is the alignment of the parallel sentences in the source and target language for training the translation model. The second one is training a statistical language model for the production of fluent sentences in a morphologically rich target language.

In the machine translation tasks used in the Morpho Challenge, the focus has so far been in the alignment problem. In the evaluation tasks introduced in 2009 the language-pairs were Finnish-English and German-English. To obtain state-of-the-art results, the evaluation consists of minimum Bayes risk (MBR) combination of two translation systems trained on the same data, one using words and the other morphemes as the basic modeling units (de Gispert et al., 2009). The various morpheme analysis algorithms are compared by measuring the translation performance for different two-model combinations where the word-based model is always the same, but the morpheme-based model is trained based on units from each of the algorithms in turns.

Because the machine translation evaluation has yet been tried only in 2009, it is difficult to draw conclusions about the results yet. However, the Morfessor Baseline algorithm seems to be particularly difficult to beat both in Finnish-German and German-English task. The differences between the best results are small, but the ranking in both tasks was the same: 1. Morfessor Baseline, 2. Allomorfessor, 3. The linguistic gold standard morphemes (Kurimo et al., 2009b).

3.2 Evaluated algorithms

This section attempts to describe very briefly some of the individual morpheme analysis algorithms that have been most successful in the evaluations.

Morfessor Baseline (Creutz and Lagus, 2002): This is a public baseline algorithm based on jointly minimizing the size of the morph codebook and the encoded size of the all the word forms using the minimum description length MDL cost function. The performance is above average for all evaluated tasks in most languages.

Allomorfessor (Kohonen et al., 2009; Virpioja and Kohonen, 2009): The development of this method was based on the observation that the

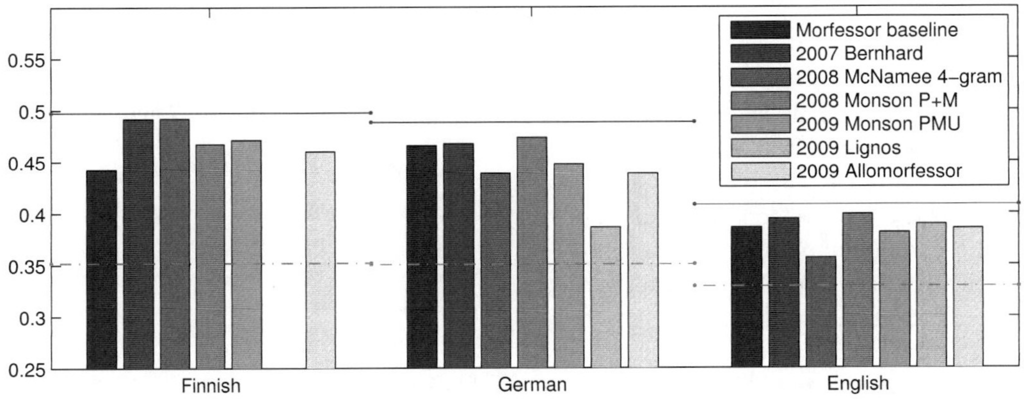

Figure 1: Mean Average Precision (MAP) values for some of the best algorithms over the years in the IR task. The upper horizontal line shows the "goal level" for each language, i.e. the performance of the best language specific reference method. The lower line shows the baseline reference of doing no stemming or analysis.

morph level surface forms of one morpheme are often very similar and the differences occur close to the morpheme boundary. Thus, the allomorphemes could be modeled by simple mutations. It has been implemented on top of the Morfessor Baseline using maximum a posteriori (MAP) optimization. This model slightly improves the performance in the linguistic evaluation in all languages (Kurimo et al., 2009b), but in IR and SMT there is no improvement yet.

Morfessor Categories MAP (Creutz and Lagus, 2005): In this method hidden Markov models are used to incorporate morphotactic categories for the Morfessor Baseline. The structure is optimized by MAP and yields slight improvements in the linguistic evaluation for most languages, but not for IR or SMT tasks.

Bernhard (Bernhard, 2006): This has been one of the best performing algorithms in Finnish, English and German linguistic evaluation and in IR (Kurimo et al., 2008). First a list of the most likely prefixes and suffixes is extracted and alternative segmentations are generated for the word forms. Then the best ones are selected based on cost functions that favour most frequent analysis and some basic morphotactics.

Bordag (Bordag, 2006): This method applies iterative LSV and clustering of morphs into morphemes. The performance in the linguistic evaluation is quite well for Turkish and decent for Finnish (Kurimo et al., 2008).

ParaMor (Monson et al., 2008): This method applies an unsupervised model for inflection rules and suffixation for the stems by building linguistically motivated paradigms. It has obtained one of the top performances for all languages when combined with the Morfessor Baseline (Kurimo et al., 2009a). Various combination methods have been tested: union, weighted probabilistic average and proposing both the analyses (Monson et al., 2009).

Lignos (Lignos et al., 2009): This method is based on the observation that the derivation of the inflected forms can be modeled as transformations. The best transformations can be found by optimizing the simplicity and frequency. This method performs much better in English than in the other languages (Kurimo et al., 2009b).

Promodes (Spiegler et al., 2009): This method presents a probabilistic generative model that applies LSV and combines multiple analysis using a committee. It seems to generate a large amount of short morphemes, which is difficult for many of the practical applications. However, it obtained the best performance for the linguistic evaluation in Arabic 2009 (Kurimo et al., 2009b), but did not survive as well in other languages, and particularly not in the IR application.

4 Open questions and challenges

Although more than 50 algorithms have already been tested in the Morpho Challenge evaluations and many lessons have been learned from the results and discussions, many challenges are still open and untouched. In fact, the attempts to solve the problem have perhaps produced even more open questions than there were in the beginning.

The main new and open challenges are described in this section.

What is the best analysis algorithm? Some of the suggested algorithms have produced good test results and some even in several tasks and languages, such as Bernhard (Bernhard, 2006), Monson ParaMor+Morfessor (Monson et al., 2008) and Allomorfessor (Virpioja and Kohonen, 2009). However, none of the methods perform really well in all the evaluation tasks and languages and their mutual performance differences are often rather small, even though the morphemes and the algorithmic principles are totally different. Thus, no dominant morpheme analysis algorithm have been found. Furthermore, reaching the performance level that rivals, or even sometimes dominates, the rule-based and language-dependent reference methods does not mean that the solutions are sufficient. Often the limited coverage or unsuitable level of details in the analysis for the task in the reference methods just indicates that they are not sufficient either and better solutions are needed. Another observation which complicates the finding and determination of the best algorithm is that in some tasks, such as statistical language models for speech recognition, very different algorithms can reach the same performance, because advanced modelling methods can compensate for unsuitable morpheme analysis.

What is the meaning of the morphemes? In some of the fundamental applications of morpheme analysis, such as text understanding, morpheme segmentation alone is only part of the solution. Even more important is to find the meaning for the obtained morphemes. The extension of the segmentation of words into smaller units to identification of the units that correspond to the same morpheme is a step taken to this direction, but the question of the meaning of the morpheme is still open. However, in the unsupervised way of learning, solutions to this may be so tightly tied to the applications that much more complex evaluations would be needed.

How to evaluate the alternative analyses? It is clear that when a word form is separated from the sentence context where it was used, the morpheme analysis easily becomes ambiguous. In the Morpho Challenge evaluations this has been taken into account by allowing multiple alternative analyses. However, in some evaluations, for example, in the measurement of the recall of the gold standard morphemes, this leads to unwanted results and may favour methods that always provide a large number of alternative analysis.

How to improve the analysis using context? A natural way to disambiguate the analysis involves taking the sentence context into account. Some of the Morpho Challenge evaluations, for example, the information retrieval, allow this option when the source texts and queries are given. However, this has not been widely tried yet by the participants, probably because of the increased computational complexity of the modelling task.

How to effectively apply semi-supervised learning? In semi-supervised learning, a small set of labeled data in the form of gold standard analysis for the word forms are provided. This data can be used for improving the unsupervised solutions based on unlabeled data in several ways: (1) The labeled data is used for tuning some learning parameters, followed by an unsupervised learning process for the unlabeled data. (2) The labeled morphemes are used as an ideal starting point to bootstrap the learning on the unlabeled words (self-training). (3) Using the EM algorithm for estimating a generative model, the unlabeled cases can be treated as missing data.

The best and most practical way of using the partly labeled data will be determined in future when the semi-supervised task has been evaluated in the future Morpho Challenge evaluations. For the first time this task will be evaluated in the ongoing Morpho Challenge 2010.

Acknowledgments

We are grateful to the University of Leipzig, University of Leeds, Computational Linguistics Group at University of Haifa, Stefan Bordag, Ebru Arisoy, Nizar Habash, Majdi Sawalha, Eric Atwell, and Mathias Creutz for making the data and gold standards in various languages available to the Challenge. This work was supported by the Academy of Finland in the project *Adaptive Informatics*, the graduate schools in Language Technology and Computational Methods of Information Technology, in part by the GALE program of the Defense Advanced Research Projects Agency, Contract No. HR0011-06-C-0022, and in part by the IST Programme of the European Community, under the FP7 project EMIME (213845) and PASCAL Network of Excellence.

References

Steven Abney. 2007. *Semisupervised Learning for Computational Linguistics*. Chapman and Hall/CRC.

Eneko Agirre, Giorgio M. Di Nunzio, Nicola Ferro, Thomas Mandl, and Carol Peters. 2008. CLEF 2008: Ad hoc track overview. In *Working Notes for the CLEF 2008 Workshop*.

Delphine Bernhard. 2006. Unsupervised morphological segmentation based on segment predictability and word segments alignment. In *Proc. PASCAL Challenge Workshop on Unsupervised segmentation of words into morphemes*, Venice, Italy. PASCAL European Network of Excellence.

Stefan Bordag. 2006. Two-step approach to unsupervised morpheme segmentation. In *Proc. of the PASCAL Challenge Workshop on Unsupervised segmentation of words into morphemes*, Venice, Italy. PASCAL European Network of Excellence.

Mathias Creutz and Krista Lagus. 2002. Unsupervised discovery of morphemes. In *Proc. SIGPHON/ACL'02*, pages 21–30.

Mathias Creutz and Krista Lagus. 2005. Inducing the morphological lexicon of a natural language from unannotated text. In *Proc. AKRR'05*, pages 106–113.

Adria de Gispert, Sami Virpioja, Mikko Kurimo, and William Byrne. 2009. Minimum bayes risk combination of translation hypothesis from alternative morphological decompositions. In *Proc. NAACL'09*, pages 73-76.

C. G. de Marcken. 1996. *Unsupervised Language Acquisition*. Ph.D. thesis, MIT.

Zellig S. Harris. 1955. From phoneme to morpheme. *Language*, 31(2):190–222. Reprinted 1970 in Papers in Structural and Transformational Linguistics, Reidel Publishing Company, Dordrecht, Holland.

Feng Jiao, Shaojun Wang, Chi-Hoon Lee, Russell Greiner, and Dale Schuurmans. 2006. Semi-supervised conditional random fields for improved sequence segmentation and labeling. In *Proc. ACL'06*, pages 209–216.

Oskar Kohonen, Sami Virpioja, and Mikaela Klami. 2009. Allomorfessor: Towards unsupervised morpheme analysis. In *Evaluating systems for Multilingual and MultiModal Information Access, 9th Workshop of the Cross-Language Evaluation Forum, CLEF 2008, Revised Selected Papers*, Lecture Notes in Computer Science , Vol. 5706. Springer.

Mikko Kurimo, Mathias Creutz, and Krista Lagus. 2006. Unsupervised segmentation of words into morphemes - challenge 2005, an introduction and evaluation report. In *Proc. PASCAL Challenge Workshop on Unsupervised segmentation of words into morphemes*, Venice, Italy. PASCAL European Network of Excellence.

Mikko Kurimo, Mathias Creutz, and Matti Varjokallio. 2008. Morpho Challenge evaluation using a linguistic Gold Standard. In *Advances in Multilingual and MultiModal Information Retrieval, 8th Workshop of the Cross-Language Evaluation Forum, CLEF 2007, Revised Selected Papers*, Lecture Notes in Computer Science , Vol. 5152, pages 864–873. Springer.

Mikko Kurimo, Ville Turunen, and Matti Varjokallio. 2009a. Overview of Morpho Challenge 2008. In *Evaluating systems for Multilingual and MultiModal Information Access, 9th Workshop of the Cross-Language Evaluation Forum, CLEF 2008, Revised Selected Papers*, Lecture Notes in Computer Science , Vol. 5706. Springer.

Mikko Kurimo, Sami Virpioja, Ville T. Turunen, Graeme W. Blackwood, and William Byrne. 2009b. Overview and results of Morpho Challenge 2009. In *Working Notes for the CLEF 2009 Workshop*, Corfu, Greece.

Constantine Lignos, Erwin Chan, Mitchell P. Marcus, and Charles Yang. 2009. A rule-based unsupervised morphology learning framework. In *Working Notes for the CLEF 2009 Workshop*, Corfu, Greece.

Paul McNamee. 2008. Retrieval experiments at morpho challenge 2008. In *Working Notes for the CLEF 2008 Workshop*, Aarhus, Denmark, September.

Christian Monson, Jaime Carbonell, Alon Lavie, and Lori Levin. 2008. ParaMor: Finding paradigms across morphology. In *Advances in Multilingual and MultiModal Information Retrieval, 8th Workshop of the Cross-Language Evaluation Forum, CLEF 2007, Revised Selected Papers*, Lecture Notes in Computer Science , Vol. 5152. Springer.

Christian Monson, Kristy Hollingshead, and Brian Roard. 2009. Probabilistic paraMor. In *Working Notes for the CLEF 2009 Workshop*, Corfu, Greece, September.

Sebastian Spiegler, Bruno Golenia, and Peter Flach. 2009. PROMODES: A probabilistic generative model for word decomposition. In *Working Notes for the CLEF 2009 Workshop*, Corfu, Greece, September.

Sami Virpioja and Oskar Kohonen. 2009. Unsupervised morpheme discovery with Allomorfessor. In *Working Notes for the CLEF 2009 Workshop*, Corfu, Greece, September.

Xiaojin Zhu. 2005. Semi-supervised learning literature survey. Technical Report 1530, Computer Sciences, University of Wisconsin-Madison.

Xiaojin Zhu. 2010. Semi-supervised learning. In *Encyclopedia of Machine Learning*. To appear.

Author Index